A NEW CONTINENT OF LIBERTY

A NEW CONTINENT of LIBERTY

EUNOMIA IN NATIVE AMERICAN
LITERATURE FROM OCCOM TO ERDRICH

GEOFF HAMILTON

University of Virginia Press · Charlottesville and London

University of Virginia Press
© 2019 by the Rector and Visitors of the University of Virginia
All rights reserved
Printed in the United States of America on acid-free paper

First published 2019

9 8 7 6 5 4 3 2 1

Library of Congress Cataloging-in-Publication Data

Names: Hamilton, Geoff, 1972– author.
Title: A new continent of liberty : Eunomia in Native American literature from Occom to Erdrich / Geoff Hamilton.
Description: Charlottesville : University of Virginia Press, 2019. | Includes bibliographical references and index.
Identifiers: LCCN 2018047473 | ISBN 9780813942445 (cloth : alk. paper) | ISBN 9780813942452 (pbk. : alk. paper) | ISBN 9780813942469 (ebook)
Subjects: LCSH: American literature—History and criticism. | American literature—Indian authors—History and criticism. | Autonomy in literature. | Natural law in literature. | Social structure in literature.
Classification: LCC PS153.I52 H35 2019 | DDC 810.9/897—dc23
LC record available at https://lccn.loc.gov/2018047473

For Henry Rafael

CONTENTS

	Acknowledgments	ix
	Introduction	1
ONE	*Eunomia* Regained and Lost: Thomas Jefferson and Samson Occom	17
TWO	Prospective Domination, Retrospective Liberation: Ralph Waldo Emerson and William Apess	43
THREE	Lighting Out, Circling In: Mark Twain and Sarah Winnemucca	69
FOUR	The Tent and the *Thipi* I: Ernest Hemingway and Zitkala-Ša	95
FIVE	The Tent and the *Thipi* II: Joseph Heller and N. Scott Momaday	121
SIX	*Eunomia* Lost and Regained: Don DeLillo, Louise Erdrich, and Gerald Vizenor	145
	Epilogue	179
	Notes	185
	Works Cited	195
	Index	203

ACKNOWLEDGMENTS

I am deeply grateful for the wise contributions to this book provided by a number of fellow scholars—among them Trevor Cook, Andre Furlani, Michael Gregg, and Brian Jones. Whatever is unwise here remains, of course, entirely my own fault. I would also like to thank the anonymous peer reviewers commissioned by the University of Virginia Press, who furnished extremely astute recommendations for improvement of this project's drafts.

A NEW CONTINENT OF LIBERTY

Introduction

The stories about the time following the creation are filled with metaphorical tales about transgressions in the so-called ecological compact. These myths, stories of creation, and stories of origin and of emergence are similar in the sense that they are told by Indigenous people all over the world and all describe compacts built on relationships established between humans and other living things.... Unless one understands his/her place in the whole, there is always a tendency to move beyond, to glorify, to self-aggrandize.
—Gregory Cajete (Tewa), *Native Science: Natural Laws of Interdependence*

LONG AGO, ACCORDING TO ONE version of the Haudenosaunee creation myth, a divine being named Sky Woman tumbled from the heavens and, with the assistance of various obliging creatures, established earthly life on the back of a turtle. Her daughter gave birth to twins, Teharonghyawago ("Skyholder") and Tawiskaron ("Flinty Rock"), whose oppositional struggles determined such things as the availability of animals, the agreeability of the weather, and the fertility of crops. From the twins came lessons, which humans ignored at their peril, on how to behave within a nexus of relational being. In this mythic worldview, communal life was embedded within a supernal order and organized according to a set of laws that sprang from the natural world and set the conditions for flourishing within it.

Archaic Greece provides a compelling analogue for this "ecological compact," this blending of human law with the natural and divine, in the goddess Eunomia ("Good Pasture/Rule/Law"), daughter of Themis (goddess of divine law) and a member of the Horae ("the Seasons"). According to this cosmology, human affairs were ultimately subject to

Eunomia's exercise of natural law: "[She] reveals all that is orderly and right, and often restrains the unjust. She makes rough things smooth, limits excess, reduces hubris, sterilizes the flowering of destruction, straightens crooked judgments, tames acts of pride, and ends sedition and the wrath of calamitous strife. Under her all things for humans are proper and rational" (Solon "Fragment 4" 88).[1] Such governance, like that of the Haudenosaunee's Skyholder, bound and nourished humans within the "rule" of the nonhuman environment, establishing the context in which any self, and any collection of selves, might thrive: a *eunomia*, the ideal fusion of the human and the natural.

These mythoi may provide, I suggest, an illuminating dialectical framework for understanding American literary history. Although the Haudenosaunee's well-known narrative (and its many tribal variants) may seem wholly alien to Euro-America's own mythopoeic beginnings, the traditions reflect an ironic—and neglected—correspondence: the early American republic, which nearly annihilated the Haudenosaunee, also imagined its social order according to a fusion of the natural and the human. In defining autonomy ("self-rule") at both the personal and collective level, the "one people" of the United States famously declared their right to "assume among the powers of the earth, the separate and equal station to which the Laws of Nature and of Nature's God entitle them" (Jefferson "Declaration" 19). The American Arcadia, Jefferson would go on to affirm, was morally and spiritually sustained by its eunomic dimensions: "Those who labour in the earth are the chosen people of God, if ever he had a chosen people, whose breasts he has made his peculiar deposit for substantial and genuine virtue" (*Notes* 170). Earthly power is, by these reckonings, grounded in, and fundamentally dependent upon, the divine order and potency of the earth itself.

The personal and collective selves defined within Native American and Euro-American traditions, along with the versions of autonomy they have aspired to, differ greatly, of course, and reveal remarkable changes over the past several hundred years. In a previous work, *The Life and Undeath of Autonomy in American Literature*, I charted the evolution of the concept of self-rule in Euro-American literature through a series of critical stages, from the Declaration to the contemporary moment. My selection of texts focused on male authors who, by and large, represented the experiences and aspirations of a historically empowered category of self—white men—who have had fullest access to the potential of self-rule. In the narrative trajectory I established, autonomy began its mythopoeic life cycle within a vital, eunomic blending of natural and human law in which the self was subordinated (as in the Native American mythos, though much less radically) to both the divine and a larger human community. From the late nineteenth century onward, I argued, the concept of autonomy declined amid eunomic dissolution, or *dysnomia,* to an eventual undeath, marked by the self's sterile relationship to both social and natural worlds as it effectively collapsed upon itself.

With *A New Continent of Liberty:* Eunomia *in Native American Literature from Occom to Erdrich,* I tell another story that runs alongside, and profoundly interacts with, that first one, but which reveals an intriguingly opposite narrative trajectory. Representative examples of Euro-American literature are employed here as a conceptual background, again with a focus on male authors who explore a privileged American selfhood and self-rule. These authors offer a means to delineate, with telling clarity, the decline of that autonomy amid increasingly extreme expressions of what the Greeks called *hybris,* or what Cajete describes as "a tendency to move beyond [holistic understanding], to glorify, to self-aggrandize" (38). The foreground of this study tracks several hundred years of autonomy's mythic revitalization in Native American texts, beginning with the writings of Samson Occom (Mohegan), and extending through a range of fiction and nonfiction works by William Apess (Pequot), Sarah Winnemucca (Northern Paiute), Zitkala-Ša (Yankton Dakota), N. Scott Momaday (Kiowa), Louise Erdrich (Anishinaabe), and Gerald Vizenor (Anishinaabe).[2] As I look closely at how these authors have sought to reclaim and redefine versions of autonomy, I sketch, against works by Euro-American authors from Thomas Jefferson to Don DeLillo, a movement of gradual, tragically belated, but resolute *ascent,* from often desperate early efforts, pitted against the historical realities of genocide and cultural destruction, to preserve any sense of self and community, toward expressions of a resurgent autonomy that affirm—in their emphasis on the *self* in self-rule as intimately linked and subject to a community of other selves as well as to divine presences permeating the natural world—new, Indigenous models of *eunomia*.

On the surface of it, such a dialectical approach would appear to run counter to a relatively recent trend in Native American literary criticism, which favors local, tribally specific interpretations of authors and works and seeks to avoid incorporating (and obscuring) a discrete body of literature within the familiar terms of the dominant culture. However, my aim is to complement rather than detract from this effort by doing justice to the distinctiveness of the texts explored here, drawing attention to some of their unique moral, religious, philosophical, and aesthetic assumptions. In deploying the concept of *eunomia*, along with two other terms drawn from classical literature—*themis* ("divine law") and *nomos* ("social law/rule/order," but originally "pasture")—I am not implying that Native American literature is simply a late re-iteration of a Western (or, in fact, *pre*-Western) idea; nor do I claim that the small selection of Native American authors engaged in this study represent a fixed, essential canon or that their concerns are somehow the only authentic ones among a wide and rapidly growing body of writing. Rather, my intent is to sketch the contours of a dialectical bridge between important elements of two literary histories, bringing their salient features into a productive dialogue of equals and thereby, as in any such dialogue, highlighting similarities and differences between them, sharpening our understanding of each through contrast, and searching for higher-order dialectical truth that may improve our understanding of both.[3] The value of such a bridge will become clear, I hope, as this study's various chapters explore eunomic dissolution and the increasingly extreme pathologies of self-rule in one tradition, alongside the vital reclamation of a eunomic autonomy in another.

Although some critics prefer the term *sovereignty* to *autonomy* in describing the concept of self-law, there are good reasons for preferring the latter. The concept of sovereignty is little more than seven hundred years old and denotes, as its Latin root (*super,* "above") implies, the relatively narrow sense of having supreme power or authority. Autonomy, in contrast, has a much older and richer history, as I briefly summarize in *The Life and Undeath of Autonomy*:

> [The] ancient Greek noun *autonomia* combines *auto-*, "self," with *-nomos*, whose root snakes down from our "custom," "convention," "rule," or "law" (*nomos*), to the critical archaic Greek gesture of *nemo*, which Homer frequently employed, in reference to food and drink, to mean "deal out, dispense, order, or assign." *Nemo* was, however, associated in other, more complex ways with the management of earthly sustenance; it can mean "to pasture or tend flocks" in a *nomos* (as "pasture"), "to feed upon or graze" (in the Greek "middle" sense of self-reference), "to have to oneself or possess," "to inhabit," and, metaphorically, "to consume (in a fire)" and "to spread (like an ulcer)." *Autonomia* thus presents a vivid semantic palette, imbuing the auto-nomy that figures so prominently in the American imaginary with root-shades of "self-pasture," "self-possession," "self-inhabitance," "self-consumption," and even, should the self itself become pasture, "self-destruction." (4)[4]

These senses take on fresh and evocative significance in the context of traditional Native American beliefs, which typically insist that any vital self is interwoven with the earth that sustains it and that a form of natural (divine) law properly governs autonomous life. Personal and collective struggles over *nomos* (as pasture)—and religio-philosophical differences over whether land itself can be possessed (and a people lawfully dispossessed from it)—have been and remain central, of course, to Native Americans' efforts at preserving and re-creating their autonomy. As Massasoit, the Great Sachem of the Wampanoag Confederacy, is reported to have said to the Pilgrim settlers he had once saved from starvation: "What is this you call property? It cannot be the earth, for the land is our mother, nourishing all her children, beasts, birds, fish and all men. The woods, the streams, everything on it belongs to everybody and is for the use of all. How can one man say it belongs only to him?" (qtd. in Magill 931). According to Indigenous traditions, autonomy involves intimate, shared connections to natural processes—a communal, divinely infused self-pasture. For those who have practiced such traditions, Euro-American autonomy has exemplified the menacing figural senses of *nemo,* amounting to a terminal self-inhabitance, an ulcerous, hypertrophic spread across the land, and the fiery consumption of all that would resist it.[5]

Sovereignty—to cite a further reason for avoiding the alternative term—is most commonly used by scholars in Indigenous Studies and other disciplines in a collective sense. Although my interest here extends to the representation of both personal and collective autonomy in Native American literature, my emphasis, I should note, ultimately falls on the former—that is, on self-rule as it has been imagined at the level of so-called individuals, not the larger groups of which they are a part. To put the point another way, I am primarily concerned with the relationship of individuals to groups, as in a particular literary character's efforts to rediscover and share in Indigenous traditions, rather than different groups' relationships with each other, as in a tribe's struggles to wrest a measure of autonomy from the federal government. This focus is intended to highlight remarkable and profound contrasts, evolving over several centuries, between Native American and Euro-American definitions of individual selfhood. Each chapter in this study aims to develop these contrasts and contribute to an illuminating overview of a larger, roughly chiastic pattern: as the ruling self gradually declines in one tradition amid a welter of pathologies and eunomic dissolution or *dysnomia,* it gains a remarkable vitality, and a revitalized understanding of *eunomia,* in another.

Distinctions between the personal and the collective are complicated, of course, not only by the fact that these concepts inevitably inform and overlap with one another, but by the characteristically plural and relational qualities of Native selfhood. That selfhood suggests, in fact, anything but a singular or isolate entity, and when properly defined it is inseparable and finally indistinguishable from a broad set of intrinsic, reciprocal relations with both the human and nonhuman. In his landmark essay on homing plots in twentieth-century Native American novels, William Bevis identifies a crucial divergence in definitions of Native American and Euro-American selfhood:

> These books suggest that "identity," for a Native American, is not a matter of finding "one's self," but of finding a "self" that is transper-

sonal and includes a society, a past, and a place. To be separated from that transpersonal time and space is to lose identity. These novels are important, not only because they depict Indian individuals coming home while white individuals leave but also because they suggest—variously and subtly and by degrees—a tribal rather than an individual definition of being. (585)

We may turn back to the Haudenosaunee's creation myth for a compelling model of this relational selfhood: in contrast to Jefferson's celebration of the yeoman farmer, whose independence is his great virtue and whose mandate it is to subdue the nonhuman presences on the territory he commands, it is the cooperative action of the world's interdependent beings that matters most here. Skyholder's virtue is his commitment to seeing himself as embedded within a network of relations, rather than, like his brother, Flinty Rock, an external actor upon them. His "behavior is participatory," as Lisa Brooks (Abenaki) explains in her reading of one version of the myth, and "the activity of participation is held in higher regard" than solitary "doing" (*Common* 110).

An intriguing paradox thus lies at the heart of this inquiry: the individual Native self is, finally, no individual at all, but rather a compound, fluid entity whose proper rule is interwoven with that of other presences in a natural (divine) order. Vine Deloria Jr. (Standing Rock Sioux) puts the point bluntly: "The concept of an individual alone in a tribal religious sense is ridiculous. The very complexity of tribal life and the interdependence of people on one another makes this concept improbable at best, a terrifying loss of identity at worst" (195). This, then, is the basic divergence that distinguishes traditional Native American notions of personal autonomy from those that have gradually become more pronounced in Euro-America: against the latter's emphasis on isolate selfhood, the preeminence of the human, and the regulative power of human law, Indigenous conceptions of self and rule favor a relational selfhood, the recognition of nonhuman agencies, and the ascendancy of a divine law unassimilable to the human.

In her novel *Ceremony*, Leslie Marmon Silko (Laguna Pueblo) provides a useful illustration of the essential terms of this divergence. As the novel's narrator explains, Pueblo traditions posit a multidimensional reality in which all selves are fundamentally bound to kinship networks and various divine presences intermingle with the human. These beliefs, Silko's narrator suggests, have been fractured by exposure to Euro-American religion and its emphasis on isolate selfhood: "Christianity separated the people from themselves; it tried to crush the single clan name, encouraging each person to stand alone, because Jesus Christ would save only the individual soul; Jesus Christ was not like the Mother who loved and cared for them as her children, as her family" (68). The spiritual healing of the novel's protagonist, Tayo, demands recognition of a relational selfhood set in opposition to Euro-America's individualist commitments:

> [Tayo wanted] to yell the things the white doctors had yelled at him—that he had to think only of himself, and not about the others, that he would never get well as long as he used words like "we" and "us." But he had known the answer all along, even while the white doctors were telling him he could get well and he was trying to believe them: medicine didn't work that way, because the world didn't work that way. His sickness was only part of something larger, and his cure would be found only in something great and inclusive of everything. (125–26)

That "everything," the teeming Indigenous *nomos* long assailed by Euro-American rule, radically embeds the human and nonhuman. Such embeddedness is a condition of selfhood or personhood, and it generates, as Thomas M. Norton-Smith (Shawnee) explains, a binding ethos: "[In] American Indian traditions an animate being is a *person* by virtue of its membership and participation in an actual network of social and moral relationships and practices with other persons, so moral agency is at the core of a Native conception of persons . . . . This means that one cannot be a person in isolation in Native traditions . . ." (90). Tayo's efforts to realize autonomy involve, in other words, a movement out of atomic self-possession and self-inhabitance toward a eunomic—and, in a critical sense, self-*less*—self-pasture.

The works considered in this study represent complex responses to historical realities which have led to the near extinction of Indigenous peoples in what is now the United States. The impact of, for instance, military incursions and treaty violations, or state-sponsored policies of removal and forced assimilation, form a crucial context for the story being told here. In the hope of placing particular literary works in a clarifying relation to that context, I have aimed to sketch, in each chapter, some of the relevant history that surrounds and enshadows them. However, my ultimate objective here is not, finally, to identify how specific works are grounded in unique historical and legal settings, nor in anatomizing how the two traditions juxtaposed here have influenced and interpreted each other, but rather to explore and illuminate a general pattern of conceptual change itself. That pattern—of decline in one tradition and ascendance in another—thus takes precedence over considerations of how, for instance, particular Euro-American authors have defined themselves against a Native other or how Native authors have responded to specific abuses and existential challenges. My overarching interest, in short, is in highlighting what, exactly, Euro-American literature lost in its conception of self-rule and what its Native American counterpart has preserved and re-created.

Each chapter begins with a relatively brief consideration of a representative characterization of autonomy in the work of a Euro-American author and then examines, at greater length, the work of one or more Native Americans published around the same time. My intent is, once again, to clarify features of two literary histories—particularly as they concern relationships between the self, its human and nonhuman community, and the divine—as I chart an inverse pattern in regard to notions of self-rule. Such a strategy should help elucidate key conceptual divergences within these histories at particular moments, bringing into dialogue, for instance, Ralph Waldo Emerson and William Apess on the question of whether and how the self can thrive when detached from ancestral relations. The book's chapters also seek to emphasize connections and developments across time, such as affinities between Samson Occom in the eighteenth century and Gerald Vizenor in the twentieth and twenty-first, when it comes to assumptions about the dynamic communality of eunomic life. The opening two chapters, focused on the late eighteenth to the early nineteenth century, first explore stirring endorsements of the self's powers in works by Euro-Americans (Jefferson, Emerson) before turning to Native Americans who seek the preservation of a viable Indigenous selfhood and its eunomic context in the face of cultural devastation (Occom, Apess). The next two chapters track representations of nomistic detachment signaling autonomy's decline in Euro-American fiction (Mark Twain, Ernest Hemingway) and then examine contrasting Native American fiction and nonfiction works exploring emerging possibilities for nomistic engagement and the augmentation of eunomic autonomy (Winnemucca, Zitkala-Ša). In the final two chapters I look first at Euro-American authors who diagnose intensifying autonomistic pathologies and the de facto termination (but lingering undeath) of seminal mythologies of the self (Joseph Heller, Don DeLillo), before proceeding to Native American authors (Momaday, Erdrich, Vizenor) whose notions of autonomy restore—or begin to restore—a version of *eunomia* which, for all its significant differences in time, place, and expression, is strikingly analogous to that of foundational Euro-American mythology.

Chapter 1 begins by exploring Thomas Jefferson's conception of autonomy in *Notes on the State of Virginia* (1785). In his articulation of American *eunomia*, the human *nomos* is nourished by the divine, the people's moral life and destiny framed by a benevolent natural order. Personal and collective self-pasture will lead, he affirms, to maximal human flourishing as the American flock essentially shepherds itself, avoiding the nomistic corruptions that blight an urbanized, monarchical Europe. Of particular interest here is Jefferson's faith in the self's powers to assume a commanding rule as it surveys and inventories its experience, subordinating the world within its gaze and exposing all traditional beliefs, at last, to skeptical critique. This endorsement of reduced collective governance and commitment to questioning nomistic conventions opens an imaginative path, I contend, to the more extreme notion of personal autonomy articulated by Emerson, as well as to autonomy's ultimate hubristic pathologies in twentieth- and twenty-first-century Euro-American literature.

From Jefferson I turn to a selection of texts by Samson Occom which record the devastating assaults upon Indigenous traditions occasioned by Euro-American expansion and which describe efforts to preserve some degree of collective Native identity and autonomy. Occom's texts clearly mark out a gulf between the eunomic self-pasture envisioned by Jefferson and its abject negation in the conditions of much Native American life in the Northeast. They also reveal, however, complex struggles to negotiate the endurance of Native traditions against the threat of total destruction. In contrast to Jefferson, Occom's Native conception of *eunomia* emphasizes the self's communal and historical embeddedness, its interdependence with, and relational responsibilities to, networks of human and nonhuman presences grounded in a specific locale. As I note, Occom hoped to promote unity among diverse tribes and ultimately to stake new claims to self-rule based on a blending of Indigenous and Western traditions. In 1785 his journal records how he joined with a group of Native Americans seeking to preserve a modicum of self-rule and "proceeded to form into a Body Politick," founding Brotherton, or "in Indian, Eeyamquittoowauconnuck" (308). The "Indian" name Occom cites is suggestive of the visionary reclamation involved in this effort at self-rule; it can be translated as "he does so like someone looking in a certain direction or a certain way" (qtd. in J. Brooks 25 n28). Occom's particular concerns for communality, a relational model of selfhood, and the centrality of place to identity will, as the study's remaining chapters demonstrate, be adapted by Native authors with increasing success over the next several centuries.

In chapter 2 I juxtapose Emerson's long essay *Nature* (1836) with two of Apess's autobiographical texts—"The Experience of the Missionary" (1833) and *A Son of the Forest* (1831)—and his *Eulogy on King Philip* (1836), a prophetic reappraisal of the Wampanoag chief Metacomet as well as the broader history of Euro-American and Native American relations. Emerson extends Jefferson's notions of autonomy, I suggest, by offering an even grander affirmation of the powers of the autonomous self as it communes with the divine through the natural world—amounting to a kind of self-deification—along with a much more pronounced emphasis on that self's nomistic detachment. At their most ecstatic heights, Emerson's descriptions of communion with the divine assume the falling away of all historical and communal ties and the cultivation of a resolutely (though not permanently or terminally) private self-pasture. Like Jefferson, his conviction is that the creative products of such radical self-shepherding might ultimately be shared with others and harmonized with a redeemed social order. Extending, too, Jefferson's endorsement of the self's technocratic mastery, Emerson goes so far as to license the complete subordination of the natural world as an appropriate extension of the self's power: "Nature is thoroughly mediate. It is made to serve. It receives the dominion of man as meekly as the ass on which the Savior rode" (*Nature* 21). Though decidedly innocent as it is sketched in the essay, this inclination toward material domination will gradually take on destructive characteristics in the Euro-American tradition.

Apess offers dramatically contrasting definitions of Indigenous selfhood and self-rule. In seeking to preserve a sense of Native identity and forge a stable and equitable place for Indigenous peoples within the nomistic order, his focus falls on the importance of *recovering* buried histories and of understanding the self as humbly intertwined with its ancestral and living kin, with "council fires ... and all the ancient customs of our fathers" ("Eulogy" 295). Autonomy is to be claimed not by breaking with the past but by strengthening historical continuities—not by separating the self from its *nomos*, but by subordinating it within a network of other presences, both human and nonhuman. Much more extensively and forcefully than Occom, Apess outlines a vision of how eunomic autonomy might yet be claimed. In doing so he anticipates the succeeding Native authors in this study, who will take up his efforts at preserving traditional worldviews and extend them into new, recreative visions of Indigenous self-rule.

Chapter 3 contrasts Twain's *Adventures of Huckleberry Finn* (1884) with Sarah Winnemucca's memoir and ethnohistory *Life among the Piutes: Their Wrongs and Claims* (1883), works which articulate, among other differences, roughly opposite attitudes toward nomistic detachment.[6] In Twain we arrive at an important transition point in Euro-American autonomy's trajectory, as Emerson's exuberant celebration of self-rule yields here to a more equivocal account of its contemporary potential. The self's separation from its *nomos* still holds, for Twain, an enduring appeal—charmingly rendered in Huck Finn's restless energies—but its productive possibilities are now markedly reduced and begin to suggest a drift into sterile isolation. The socially toxic potential of Euro-American self-rule is made clear, moreover, in a range of predatory characters thematically linked to Huck himself.

In contrast, Winnemucca's work invests Native American autonomy with even greater vitality, affirming augmented possibilities for Native Americans *within* the cultural mainstream, based on the recovery and celebration of Indigenous traditions threatened with extinction. Acting in the role of cultural mediator and shaman, Winnemucca argues for the value and viability of preserving those traditions while adapting to Euro-American culture. Her praise of kinship networks and a communal, cooperative form of autonomy—the basis for her understanding of Native identity—stand in stark contrast to Huck's distrust of family and preference for personal self-rule: "In the evening the head men... discuss everything, for the chiefs do not rule like tyrants; they discuss everything with their family, as a father would with his family" (52). Winnemucca's accounts of her own cultural mediations speak to the productive potential of nomistic integration and surpass Apess in imagining how an integrated life might actually be lived. In affirming the value of Paiute traditions in themselves and as instructive models for Euro-Americans, she also introduces a pronounced emphasis on the creative roles to be played by women in nomistic life.

With chapter 4 we reach a rough chiastic intersection of the imaginative trajectories explored thus far. Euro-American autonomy, represented here by several of Hemingway's Nick Adams stories from *In Our Time* (1925), reveals an obvious waning of much of its positive potential, whereas its Native American counterpart, illustrated by Zitkala-Ša's *Old Indian Legends* (1901) and *American Indian Stories* (1921), reflects an augmentation of possibilities for the dynamic *re-creation*, rather than merely tenuous defense, of versions of eunomic autonomy. Hemingway examines here, within a context of overt eunomic dissolution, a self-pasture much more limited in its access to a vital themistic order, and more vulnerable and troubled in its nomistic separation, than that represented by Twain. For his protagonist, interactions with his *nomos* are understood to be inevitably corruptive of self-rule; Nick would live, at least in spirit, outside the social order, rejecting communal life and its traditions. Definitively estranged from other selves—a status symbolized in the private tent he pitches in "Big Two-Hearted River"—he also evidences a specific pathology in relation to self-consciousness, as the autonomous self begins, in its uneasy isolation, to feed on itself.

Although Zitkala-Ša shares Hemingway's thematic concern for what might heal traumatized selves, she inverts her counterpart's basic assumptions by championing a Native autonomy informed by tradition and framed by a eunomic blending of social and natural orders. Eschewing the isolate autonomy epitomized by the private tent of Hemingway's Nick, she acclaims the virtues of a self-rule founded on the communality of the teepee. Committed to sharing a vision of "the possible earnestness of life as seen through the teepee door" (6), Zitkala-Ša thus surveys the remnants of a past nomistic world and affirms the imaginative basis for a present and future one. A major element in this imaginative enterprise is her retelling of narratives involving the spider spirit and trickster Iktomi, who exposes the perils of an atomic self-pasture for both Native and Euro-America. Like Winnemucca, Zitkala-Ša also insists on the fundamental role to be played by women in the reclamation of self-rule. She departs from each of the precursors examined in this study, however, in offering a much less conciliatory version of adaptation to the dominant culture and in creatively reconstituting Native selfhood and its vital possibilities in her contemporary moment. Where Occom, Apess, and Winnemucca carried out a largely preservative enterprise as they attempted, as it were, to keep alive the flame of traditional lifeways amid the storms of historical oppression, Zitkala-Ša offers bold, imaginative *re*kindlings of that flame.

In chapter 5 I examine two novels focused on protagonists who struggle to adapt to the pathological conditions of their nomistic worlds: Heller's *Something Happened* (1974) and Momaday's *House Made of Dawn* (1968). Heller's Bob Slocum, a superficially successful business executive, represents a barrenly isolate form of autonomy. In him we reach, I suggest, the terminus of Jefferson and Emerson's faith in the autonomous self's nomistic critique, for his version of such scrutiny becomes a parody of truth-seeking devoted to an ultimately static and self-serving orchestration of self-condemnation and self-gratification. With no hope of escaping a claustrophobic *nomos*, nor any significant connection to a redemptive divinity in the natural world, Slocum turns neurotically inward—as if elaborating the negative, self-consumptive potential encountered in Twain's Huck and Hemingway's Nick—and begins to disintegrate *as* a self.

Momaday's account of a newly vital, if still rather tentative, form of eunomic autonomy contrasts with Heller's descriptions of a terminally isolate self-rule. In *House Made of Dawn,* a wounded protagonist is ultimately able to reconnect with ancestral traditions as he communes with and begins to be healed by spiritual presences rooted in place. Rather than merely emphasizing the perverting influences of nomistic powers and the destructive consequences of a placeless self-pasture, Momaday affirms a model of community tied to specific geographies and framed by natural (divine) law. The novel's reimagination of both Euro-American and Native narratives finally offers, I contend, a bracing challenge to the dominant culture's morbidities, and a re-creation of Indigenous traditions swelling with eunomic potential.

Chapter 6 first discusses an endgame of Euro-American autonomy in Don DeLillo's *Cosmopolis* (2003). The novel's protagonist, Eric Packer, is a billionaire currency trader who grazes a synthetic "Nature" within his insulated, information-saturated limousine, achieving a terminal version of Emersonian transcendence and its claims to masterful vision as he seeks solitary communion with the divine. DeLillo cogently illustrates here the destructive figural senses of *nemo*: a ruthlessly competitive self-rule ultimately amounting to an ulcerous, blazingly consumptive self-inhabitance, alienated from and exploitive of both natural and social environments. Jefferson's and Emerson's conceptions of an abstract, boundless autonomy reach a bizarre climax in Packer's fantasy of disembodied self-rule as "quantum dust": "The idea was to live outside the given limits, in a chip, on a disk, as data, in whirl, in radiant spin, a consciousness saved from void" (DeLillo *Cosmopolis* 206).

From here I turn to Louise Erdrich's *The Plague of Doves* (2008), which presents a critique of Euro-American autonomy in many ways parallel to DeLillo's but also sets forth a vibrant Indigenous alternative. Elaborating assumptions about the proper conditions of self-rule articulated from Occom through Momaday, the novel affirms, above all, a fundamental ethical link between the self and a web of human and nonhuman presences. The self's subordination within an animate, unpredictable, ultimately benevolent natural order is, the novel implies, essential to a flourishing self-rule. Exceeding Momaday's heuristic sketch of a potentially resurgent autonomy for Native peoples, Erdrich ultimately presents here—while acknowledging the toxicity of long-standing and ongoing colonial abuse—a tenable context for the realization of eunomic life.

Finally, I consider Gerald Vizenor's *Chair of Tears* (2012), which exemplifies possibilities for Native autonomy within a harmonious blending of the human and the natural. Whereas Erdrich's emphasis falls on the complex communal relations of her protagonists, Vizenor focuses his on the extraordinary conceptual transformations enabled by Native self-rule. The novel's central figure, a trickster named Captain Shammer, represents an exuberant alternative to the mastering presumptions of Emersonian vision. His efforts to Indigenize his community—which draw from, but freely modernize, tribal traditions—encourage personal and collective exposure to mutability and chance and posit a *nomos* based on the unpredictable interplay of the human and non-human. Vizenor thus brings to imaginative fruition the centuries-long struggle of Native authors not merely to preserve or even adapt traditional notions of autonomy in the face of Euro-America's consumptive rule, but to vigorously and joyfully reconceive them. His work seeks nothing less, that is, than to chart a new "continent of liberty" (Vizenor *Chair* 112), rich in creative possibilities for a cooperative, relational selfhood—a distinctively Indigenous *eunomia*.

ONE

Eunomia Regained and Lost
Thomas Jefferson and Samson Occom

THE PERSPECTIVES ON autonomy held by the principal author of the Declaration and the first Native American to publish in English could not, on first appraisal, be more contrary. Thomas Jefferson, imagining the future of the new republic in the late eighteenth century, saw the personal and collective self-rule of Americans spreading gradually across the continent and beyond, a triumphant "empire of liberty."[1] Samson Occom, while vigorously and creatively struggling to preserve a measure of self-rule for Mohegans and other tribes in the Northeast, confronted a rapidly shrinking land base, widespread impoverishment, meagre political power, and the real possibility of cultural annihilation. Under such conditions, the legitimacy and futurity of a Native selfhood was mortally threatened.

Beyond these stark sociopolitical inequalities, key conceptual differences distinguish these figures' understandings of the ideal of self-rule and the contrasting traditions from which they flow. Jefferson's sense of a personal self is rooted in Enlightenment principles that posit certain endowments (such as the right to private property and freedom from arbitrary authority) as the self's incontestable possessions no matter what *nomos* might frame it. His own inflection of these ideas includes a faith in the extraordinary potential of the self's rule to leverage what it possesses into a commanding agency as it orders its experience and exposes traditional beliefs and bonds to rational critique. America itself, in Jefferson's vision, allowed for the salutary ranging of autonomous selves within the nation's collective autonomy: an abundance of what political theorists now often call negative liberty (the self's freedom from external constraints, such as governmental interference) would lead, in accordance with natural law, to positive liberty (the self's capacity to develop its highest potential in the context of social life).

Occom's Native conception of self-rule, discernible in his writings in spite of the historical forces that severely complicated its expression, reflects an opposing emphasis not on the powers to be claimed according to what the self alone possesses and rules but on the value of its communal and historical embeddedness. Autonomy is, in this view, inherently a matter of positive liberty, involving the self's (ultimately liberating) bonds with other selves and its relations within a specific natural environment. In his effort to preserve Indigenous notions of selfhood in the face of cataclysmic change, Occom affirms a reverence for ancestral practices and relational responsibilities to both human and nonhuman presences. The separatist community he helped found at Brotherton would, he hoped, preserve these distinctive characteristics in the exercise of Native self-rule.

In spite of all that sets these two figures apart, however, intriguing similarities stand out in their conceptions of autonomy. Though Occom often and justifiably voiced his displeasure at how Euro-American autonomy was actually being exercised, we may find in his own definitions of self-rule a compelling correspondence with Jefferson's. Both men suggest that human life flourishes only when harmonized with the divine order of the natural world. It is, as Jefferson wrote in the Declaration, the "Laws of Nature" (a version of Themis) and "Nature's God" (a version of the Greeks' Eunomia) that sanction and protect a people's autonomy (19). For Occom, Native autonomy, though distinguished from its colonial counterpart by (among other things) its emphasis on relational obligations and the *subordination* of the self to them, also requires the eunomic fusion of human and natural orders. The proper terms of self-rule are understood to originate in the themistic order of the nonhuman environment: on this "Boundless Continent," he reminds us, Indigenous peoples once flourished according to the "Natural Priviledges" bestowed by the "Most Great, The Good and The Supream ^Spirit above^" (149).[2]

My primary interest in the following chapters is in what happened to Euro-American and Native American conceptions of eunomic autonomy over the span of the nation's literary history. The trajectories of the respective traditions follow, I contend, a roughly chiastic pattern, with the former ultimately declining into a peculiar sterility and the latter increasing in vigor as we pass from representative works of the late eighteenth century to those in the early twenty-first. In this first chapter I set the stage for these unfolding stories, beginning with a consideration of Jefferson's *Notes on the State of Virginia* (1785), a work which enthusiastically (and in some ways imperiously) surveys his home state as well as the nation more generally. The assumptions we discover here about the self's command of its environment and its license to judge the nomistic order prefigure, I suggest, the development of pathologies charted in works by later Euro-American authors as autonomy is emptied of its productive potential. From here I turn to a selection of Occom's letters, sermons, legal petitions, and journal entries produced during roughly the same period. I hope to demonstrate that we encounter in these writings a prophetic struggle to preserve a Native version of eunomic autonomy against the hostile rule of settler culture—to keep its flame alive, that is, within a nomistic environment bent on extinguishing it. What I seek to describe here, above all, is the essence of that originary flame—kindled long before the arrival of the white man and perfectly independent of him—before moving on, in later chapters, to chart its effortful, improbable, and finally heroic re-creation.

Responding to a series of queries sent to him in 1780 by François Barbé-Marbois, the secretary of the French legation to the United States, Jefferson composed an ambitious account of his home state's geography, natural resources, history, politics, social customs, and economic structure, as well as a philosophical consideration of its ideals and long-term prospects. The document, astonishingly learned and eclectic in its commentary, turns from lengthy inventories of facts to impassioned reflections on topics ranging from religious liberty to the fate of slavery. Jefferson was motivated to write, in part, by the derisory claims of the French naturalist Georges-Louis Leclerc, Comte de Buffon, who had argued that the American biosphere was inferior to that of Europe. With *Notes on the State of Virginia*, Jefferson would provide a totalizing view of Virginia and indeed of the new republic as a whole—one that would ground the exceptional virtues of its nomistic world in the vivifying *themis* of its natural environment. Among his guiding assumptions, which elaborate Enlightenment principles in a New World setting, are a belief that the physical universe operates according to eternal (and ultimately benevolent) laws, that a moral sense is an integral part of human nature, that pastoral life is uniquely and invaluably stimulating, and that the American land itself harbors a sublime potency. These assumptions will, as we shall see, take on even grander proportions in Emerson before progressively deteriorating, along with and inseparable from the dysnomic deterioration in the Euro-American notion of autonomy, in the works of Twain, Hemingway, Heller, and DeLillo.

Jefferson's home state is, for him, exemplary of the American Arcadia, offering a eunomic fusion of the pastoral and political essential to the realization of human potential.[3] In a brief section of *Notes* devoted to an appraisal of manufacturing and trade, he begins by highlighting some of the critical differences between old and new worlds. European land is, he explains, "either cultivated, or locked up against the cultivator" (170), and a highly developed industrial sector has contributed there to an unwholesome concentration of labor and capital in the cities. In contrast, Virginia possesses "an immensity of land courting the industry of the husbandman" (170), making it possible for the majority of its population to reap the spiritual rewards available to farmers. His imagination seemingly inspired by these arguments—and unburdened, in a grotesque irony, by considerations of the forced industry of African American slaves—Jefferson then abruptly shifts from a practical to a passionate tone, celebrating, in one of his most famous proclamations, the themistic possibilities of blending natural and social orders: "Those who labour in the earth are the chosen people of God, if ever he had a chosen people, whose breasts he has made his peculiar deposit for substantial and genuine virtue. It is the focus in which he keeps alive that sacred fire, which otherwise might escape from the face of the earth" (170). In that fire, Eunomia is reborn in America.

Part of what inspired such an endorsement was Jefferson's experience in Europe of teeming slums and perilous factories. He associated cities with the worst kinds of decadence, for they denied citizens, he insisted, an essential spiritual sustenance only available through direct contact with the natural world. Cut off from that contact, personal and collective autonomy is subordinated to the withering vicissitudes of merely human networks: "Corruption of morals in the mass of cultivators is a phaenomenon of which no age nor nation has furnished an example. It is the mark set on those, who not looking up to heaven, to their own soil and industry, as does the husbandman, for their subsistance, depend for it on the casualties and caprice of customers. Dependance begets subservience and venality, suffocates the germ of virtue, and prepares fit tools for the designs of ambition" (170–71). Jefferson's wordplay here—the blessed husbandmen apparently look "up" to the heavenly soil—seemingly includes an allusion to the fate of Cain, a "tiller of the ground" (Gen. 4:2 *KJV*) who, marked by God after committing fratricide, "builded a city" (4:17) and begat a toolmaker in Tubalcain, "an instructer of every artificer in brass and iron" (4:20). As Jefferson goes on to recommend, however wistfully, the walling-off of the American economy, he offers vivid figurations of the pathologies—the marks of Cain—associated with urban, industrial spaces: "The mobs of great cities add just so much to the support of pure government, as sores do to the strength of the human body. It is the manners and spirit of a people which preserve a republic in vigour. A degeneracy in these is a canker which soon eats to the heart of its laws and constitution" (*Notes* 171). Autonomous life, for Jefferson, needs room to thrive—a healthy spacing of individual selves making possible genuine, salvific contact with the earth and its divine potencies.

Notes reflects Jefferson's scrupulous study of Virginia's ecosystems, and his long inventories of facts imply, notwithstanding his occasional qualifications about the limits of objective human knowledge, the self's power to assume a rational mastery over all it would survey. He opens the book with a detailed summation of the state's geographic coordinates, underscoring with this initial orientation lesson a technocratic concern for scientific precision and including a reminder of the superior dimensions of the state when compared to those of its former colonial master: "[Virginia's] boundaries include an area somewhat triangular, of 121,525 square miles, whereof 79,650 lie westward of the Alleghaney mountains, and 57,034 westward of the meridian of the mouth of the Great Kanhaway. This state is therefore one third larger than the islands of Great Britain and Ireland, which are reckoned at 88,357 square miles" (5). Jefferson's careful measurements of rainfall and temperature—"I have taken five years observations, to wit, from 1772 to 1777, made in Williamsburgh and its neighbourhood, have reduced them to an average for every month in the year, and stated those averages in the following table, adding an analytical view of the winds during the same period" (80)—offer further rebuttals of Buffon's claims about the inhospitableness of the American environment. With the assistance of contemporary mensurative technology—tools not yet imaginatively implicated in the destructive legacy of Tubalcain—Jefferson sets this world under the dominion of his comprehensive gaze and its cataloguing imperatives. The exhilarating possibilities of such unbounded surveillance and control find their champion in Emerson, and their terminal elegist in DeLillo, whose doomed surveyor, Eric Packer, seeks the world's comprehensive reduction to data in the digital age.

Jefferson's imagination of territorial dominion on a national scale is implied in another text, the Land Ordinance of 1784, on which he served as principal author shortly before the publication of *Notes*. The resolution, which calls for the parceling out of western lands into new American states, reflects a similar technocratic ordering of the land (and, of course, its prior inhabitants):

> Resolved, that so much of the territory ceded, or to be ceded by individual states, to the United States, as is already purchased, or shall be purchased, of the Indian inhabitants, and offered for sale by Congress, shall be divided into distinct states in the following manner, as nearly as such cessions will admit; that is to say, by parallels of latitude, so that each state shall comprehend from north to south two degrees of latitude, beginning to count from the completion of forty-five degrees north of the equator .... (n.p.)

Though the ordinance was a statement of intent rather than an immediately realizable decree—the actual territory identified by it would not fall securely under American control for decades—it reflects key elements of Jefferson's (and Euro-America's) conception of the nonhuman environment and human relations with it. Eric Hinderaker, summing up the sensibility apparent in the map depicting "the boundary lines of a new American empire," notes that "[where] earlier cartographers had labored for years to portray the complicated reality of the Ohio Valley's human and geographic forms, Jefferson's proposal swept away the region's complexities ... [the] plan divided the trans-Appalachian west into 16 states, separated by straight-line boundaries that reflected no appreciation of the region's geographical contours" (228). Land is, in the blunt terms articulated here, mere manipulable property, available for abstract delineation and distribution by those who claim to rule it.

Jefferson's warmer, more personal responses to American geography also suggest an assumption of extraordinary human agency—one that, by his reckoning in this early stage of national history, does not herald destructive possibilities for Euro-Americans themselves. Two oft-quoted passages indicate the terms of this empowered selfhood. The first involves a description of the confluence of the Potomac and Shenandoah rivers from a position "on a very high point of land" (*Notes* 21). A spectator may witness there, we are told, what is "perhaps one of the most stupendous scenes in nature":

> In the moment of their junction they rush together against the mountain, rend it asunder, and pass off to the sea. The first glance of this scene hurries our senses into the opinion, that this earth has been created in time, that the mountains were formed first, that the rivers began to flow afterwards, that in this place particularly they have been dammed up by the Blue ridge of mountains, and have formed an ocean which filled the whole valley; that continuing to rise they have at length broken over at this spot, and have torn the mountain down from its summit to its base. The piles of rock on each hand, but particularly on the Shenandoah, the evident marks of their disrupture and avulsion from their beds by the most powerful agents of nature, corroborate the impression. But the distant finishing which nature has given to the picture is of a very different character. It is a true contrast to the fore-ground. It is as placid and delightful, as that is wild and tremendous. For the mountain being cloven asunder, she presents to your eye, through the cleft, a small catch of smooth blue horizon, at an infinite distance in the plain country, inviting you, as it were, from the riot and tumult roaring around, to pass

through the breach and participate of the calm below. Here the eye ultimately composes itself; and that way too the road happens actually to lead. You cross the Patowmac above the junction, pass along its side through the base of the mountain for three miles, its terrible precipices hanging in fragments over you, and within about 20 miles reach Frederic town and the fine country round that. (*Notes* 21)

Drawing on Edmund Burke's categories of the sublime and beautiful, Jefferson presents fundamental aesthetic oppositions here, finally incorporating them within his own masterful vision. In identifying with the sublime spectacle and its resolution in beautiful, infinite tranquility, he constructs a narrative in which the land's long-term evolution, and all the terrific and sometimes terrifying power it evinces, culminate not simply in the road that leads, in the "calm below," to human civilization "and the fine country round that," but to his own authoritative, self-ruling spectatorship (the "eye" or "I" that "ultimately composes itself"). The visionary progress from mountain and river to road (and ultimately town) implies the basic terms of an exhilarating eunomic autonomy. Significantly, and in a prefiguration of Emerson's more explicit subordination of *nomos* to the self's visionary powers, the social world invoked as the resolution of his vision is kept at some distance in this description, its status as an extension of the natural, themistic order affirmed but its particulars left unmentioned. What stands out most vividly is Jefferson's emphasis on the self's commanding—and effectively extra-social—ability to integrate sublimity and beauty, the "wild and tremendous" with the "placid and delightful."

We find another illustration of such imaginative integration in Jefferson's description of the Natural Bridge, a celebrated geological formation located on land he had purchased about a decade before composing *Notes*. His opening description furnishes the scene's scientific coordinates, fixing the territory in place:

It is on the ascent of a hill, which seems to have been cloven through its length by some great convulsion. The fissure, just at the bridge, is, by some admeasurements, 270 feet deep, by others only 205. It is about 45 feet wide at the bottom, and 90 feet at the top; this of course determines the length of the bridge, and its height from the water. Its breadth in the middle, is about 60 feet, but more at the ends, and the thickness of the mass at the summit of the arch, about 40 feet. (26)

Moving away from this objective inventory to a subjective account of the Bridge's influence on him, Jefferson asserts, once again, the self's visionary power and imaginative control over the scene:

> Though the sides of this bridge are provided in some parts with a parapet of fixed rocks, yet few men have resolution to walk to them and look over into the abyss. You involuntarily fall on your hands and feet, creep to the parapet and peep over it. Looking down from this height about a minute, gave me a violent head ach. If the view from the top be painful and intolerable, that from below is delightful in an equal extreme. It is impossible for the emotions arising from the sublime, to be felt beyond what they are here: so beautiful an arch, so elevated, so light, and springing as it were up to heaven, the rapture of the spectator is really indescribable! (26)

Jefferson seemingly departs here from Burke, for whom the categories of the sublime and beautiful were mutually exclusive, as he resolves contraries in his aesthetic contemplation. The mastering self, notwithstanding the trouble of a headache, orchestrates the aesthetic triumph of beauty, elevation, and light in communion with a stimulating *themis*. Catherine L. Albanese, citing a point made by Garry Wills, notes a curious and important fact of that orchestration: in recalling the Natural Bridge from memory, Jefferson had mistaken some of the details of his experience and had actually described a view from above the formation (the sublime, terrifying perspective) as though it were available from below (the beautiful, delightful counterpart).[4] The mistake is telling: "It was an *American* sublime that he had experienced; and, in American sublime, rather than being terrified, one liked and enjoyed being on top. That Jefferson was the legal owner of the Natural Bridge as real estate only underlined the connection: American sublime hinted of empire and dominion" (Albanese 70). The self's domineering gaze is emancipatory for this ambitious seer, a requisite element of his imagined empire of liberty.

Within that empire, autonomous persons would vigorously exercise their rational powers, surveying nomistic convention with a critical eye. For a model of such self-rule operating collectively, Jefferson invokes—in what must strike us now as a remarkable irony—Native American political life.[5] Extending a discussion of what he takes to be humanity's innate moral sense, he turns his attention to the "little societies" of Indigenous peoples. These autonomous communities, he tells us, efficiently repel tyranny, for they "never submitted themselves to any laws, any coercive power, any shadow of government" (*Notes* 98):

> [The Virginia colony's tribes'] only controuls are their manners, and that moral sense of right and wrong, which, like the sense of tasting and feeling, in every man makes a part of his nature. An offence against these is punished by contempt, by exclusion from society, or, where the case is serious, as that of murder, by the individuals whom it concerns. Imperfect as this species of coercion may seem, crimes are very rare among them; insomuch that were it made a question, whether no law, as among the savage Americans, or too much law, as among the civilized Europeans, submits man to the greatest evil, one who has seen both conditions of existence would pronounce it to be the last: and that the sheep are happier of themselves, than under care of the wolves. It will be said, that great societies cannot exist without government. The savages therefore break them into small ones. (98–99)

Such "small" societies, leaning toward "no law," were close to Jefferson's ideal for America, and his pastoral metaphor highlights the basic assumption underlying his conception of autonomy: the wholesome, vivifying rightness of citizens shepherding themselves.

Jefferson underscores the importance of religious skepticism, in particular, as he summarizes Virginia's history of ecclesiastical persecution and its contemporary remnants. In presuming a monopoly on spiritual truth, he avers, bullying human authorities have often, in fact, obscured it. It is beneficial and just, therefore, that citizens question inherited revelation—"Reason and free inquiry are the only effectual agents against error" (*Notes* 165)—and reject human authorities when they inhibit citizens' eunomic "natural rights." This forceful endorsement of religious tolerance, which struck many of his contemporaries as outrageous, cast suspicion on nomistic authorities (who ought not to be viewed, necessarily, as aligned with *themis*) and minimized the significance of diverse or conflicting beliefs within a particular *nomos*: "The rights of conscience we never submitted, we could not submit. We are answerable for them to our God. The legitimate powers of government extend to such acts only as are injurious to others. But it does me no injury for my neighbour to say there are twenty gods, or no god. It neither picks my pocket nor breaks my leg" (165). Though Jefferson frames his argument in terms of the dissent of particular religious groups, he clearly also encourages the kind of personal freethinking that marked his own rigorous review of nomistic convention.

For Jefferson, such latitude in religious matters is finally beneficial to individuals and communities alike, since it denies the tyranny of arbitrary authorities and encourages the gradual identification and eradication of spiritual "errors." American selves, ranging freely in the "operations of the mind" (*Notes* 165), find ample nourishment in a natural progression from negative to positive liberty. Emerson, the Euro-American subject of the next chapter, will proffer an even stronger endorsement of nomistic detachment and the powers of selves who determine their own laws. From Twain's Huck Finn through Hemingway's Nick Adams and Heller's Bob Slocum, however, such detachment will come to seem increasingly problematic, the productive potential of autonomy replaced by a host of pathologies. With DeLillo's Eric Packer, we meet, at last, the dismal endpoint of Jefferson's ideal of autonomy. Committed to a hyper-rationalist critique devoid of concern for other selves and aided by technological prosthetics that grant, as never before, the imperial reduction of the "laws of Nature and of Nature's God" to manipulable data, Packer effectively merges with a reduced and unnourishing *themis* before finally collapsing as a self.

Samson Occom, a member of the Mohegan nation and reputed descendant of the Great Sachem Uncas, was born near New London, Connecticut, in 1723. Greatly impressed by the revivalism of the Great Awakening, he converted to Christianity as a teenager and was eventually ordained as a Presbyterian minister. Though his upbringing and social status are a world away from Jefferson's, his career rivals the latter's in its productivity and range of achievements: Occom became an influential minister and missionary, tribal councillor, teacher, hymnist, book binder, carpenter, lay physician, and international fund-raiser for a so-called Indian charity school, while also authoring the first two English-language books by a Native American and helping to found the separatist settlement known as Brotherton.

Much of Occom's writing is, on its face, dominated by his agonistic reaction to the seemingly overpowering environment of Euro-American aggression, within which he attempted to preserve the fragile elements of Indigenous autonomy. Relentless incursions by Euro-American settlers and deceptive legal (often extralegal) strategies enacted by their political representatives had progressively fractured the lifeways of Native peoples throughout the eighteenth century. Joanna Brooks summarizes the various solvents of Mohegan cultural cohesion during Occom's lifetime:

> The impacts of colonization on traditional subsistence and trade economies made Native individuals and families especially vulnerable to the pressure to sell lands for money. Land sales, in turn, contributed to the dissolution of the place-based kinship and intertribal networks that economically, culturally, spiritually, and politically sustained tribal communities. The increasing vulnerability of tribal governments to colonial manipulation further exacerbated the vulnerability of tribal territories and tribal members. These changes spiraled and reverberated through every dimension of Mohegan life. Limited access to traditional hunting and planting grounds changed the way Mohegans worked, worshiped, celebrated, dressed, and ate; hungry Mohegan people left their homes seeking employment as laborers, sailors, or domestic servants; dispersion threatened the continuity of Mohegan language, ritual, and traditional knowledge. (11–12)

Writing to a friend in 1784 in a mood of despair at such realities, Occom proffers a devastating assessment of northeastern Indigenous life in the context of the new nation's recent struggle for liberty from Great Britain. The contrast with Jefferson—who was, contemporaneously, able to celebrate the emerging possibilities of eunomic self-rule for white

Virginians and other Americans—could not be more glaring in this portrait of Indigenous dysnomia:

> [There] is ^the^ Most Deplorable ... and Most Glomy aspect upon the Indians in this boundless Continent ^as ever was known^, as for the Indians Scatred among the English, is it a gone Case with them, they have been decreasing ever Since the Europians began to Settle this Country, and this War has been as a besom of Distruction to Sweep them ^from^ the Face of the Earth, there are but very few remaining among the English, and ^these^ remaining yet in the Land of the living, are very Careless, it Seems according to their appearance, are given up to hardness of Heart and to reprobate Mind everything that lookd well and promising, ^amongst them^ is now witherd and Died; Schools among the Indians are all Ceased and there is not one Missionary amongst them all that I know of, This Family Contention of the English, has been & is the most undoing war to the poor Indians that ever happen among them it has Stript them of every thing, both their Temporal and Spiritual Injoyments—It Seems to me, at Times that there is nothing but Wo, Wo, Wo, Writen in every Turn of the Wheel of Gods Providence against us, I am afraid we are Devoted to Distruction and Misery—^and I am Discouragd.... (Occom 121)

Though his work speaks, as we shall see, to his role as the voice of a distinctively Native *eunomia*, Occom's primary audience in his public writings was, of course, Euro-Americans. In addressing such readers he had to contend with restrictive stereotypes—typically positing an inherent savagery in Native Americans or, in the sentimental inversion, a noble primitivism—which cast doubt on the legitimacy of a Native self and generally assumed the certainty of the disappearance of Indigenous peoples with the spread of Euro-American culture. Though Jefferson was certainly exposed to his own share of opprobrium and slander, a good deal of it provoked by the sometimes heretical ideas expressed in *Notes* about slavery and religious liberty, he had an exceptional platform from which to combat it and did not have to argue for his essential capacity as a rational being deserving of respect. Occom, conversely, remained vulnerable to those who would dismiss him as merely a "poor Indian" or worse. If, that is, Jefferson could trust the stability of his power to gaze on the world and construct his agency within it, Occom continually found himself bound within others' limiting vision.

Occom's autobiographical narrative of 1768 provides a telling illustration of those limitations and of how his own self-expression was complicated by them.[6] He begins by offering up these details about his early upbringing:

> I was Born a Heathen and Brought up ... In Heathenism till I was between 16 & 17 Years of age, at a Place Calld Mohegan in New London Connecticut, in New England,—my Parents Livd a wandering life, ... ^as^ did all the Indians at Mohegan; they Chiefly Depended upon Hunting Fishing & Fowling ... for their Living and had no Connections with the English, excepting to [Traffic] with thim ... in ^their^ Small Trifles,—and they Strictly maintain'd and follow'd their Heathenish Ways, Customs & Religion. (52)

Occom's seeming rejection of traditional Native lifeways—and its implication that the eunomic fire he might have preserved had effectively gone out—is striking. He goes on to document his upbringing, conversion to Christianity, tutelage under the Congregational minister and educator Eleazar Wheelock, and career as a schoolmaster, minister, and missionary before turning, rather startlingly, to a piercing complaint about the extent of his work and the injustice of his being denied fair compensation for it. Whereas "other Missionaries" were granted "180 pounds" annually, he received the same amount, he asserts, "for 12 years Service" (58). Occom then concludes by—just as startlingly—citing his Native identity as the source of this neglect: "I must Say, I believe it is because I am [a] poor Indian. I Can't help that God has made me So; I did not make my self So" (58). Though several scholars have discovered in these lines a deliberate and emancipatory effort to ironize the logic of racial hierarchies, the affirmation here of a legitimate Native selfhood remains, at best, ambiguous.[7] Writing in the colonizer's language and within a genre, the conversion narrative, which demands that he renounce his connections to a traditional Indigenous identity, Occom's self-assertions become contaminated by a sense of self-negation.

A more positive (though still obviously self-constricted) assertion of Native identity can be found in the sometimes blistering letter Occom wrote to Wheelock in 1771. The fund-raising tour Occom had carried out in Great Britain five years earlier was to benefit, he had been promised, a school devoted to the education of Natives as Christian missionaries. Wheelock abandoned that project, however, in favor of an institution (what became Dartmouth College) serving only whites. With caustic wit, Occom's letter points to the prejudices informing this betrayal: "I am very Jealous that instead of your Semenary Becoming alma Mater, she will be too alba mater to Suckle the Tawnees" (98). Acting as a representative abroad of Native America (and, by extension, the possibilities of Indigenous conversion), Occom was, he suggests, exploited as a kind of racial front:

> I verily thought once that your Institution was Intended Purely for the poor Indians with this thought I Cheerfully Ventur'd my Body & Soul, left my Country my poor young Family all my friends and Relations, to sail over the Boisterous Seas to England, to help forward your School, Hoping, that it may be a lasting Benefit to my poor Tawnee Brethren, With this View I went a Volunteer—I was quite Willing to become a Gazing Stock, Yea Even a Laughing Stock, in Strange Countries to Promote your Cause—We Loudly Proclaimed before Multitudes of People from Place to Place, that there was a most glorious Prospect of Spreading the gospel of the Lord Jesus to the furthest Savage Nations in the Wilderness, thro your Institution.... (99)

Occom's indictment of Wheelock, while highlighting his sense of victimization and outrage, also manages—with a directness and force missing from the autobiographical narrative—a canny ironizing of the dominant rhetoric of impoverished Native selfhood. Deploying and redeploying the "poor Indian" commonplace (along with related modifiers), he draws attention to its obvious inadequacy and invites its subversion: "We told them, that we were Beging for poor Miserable Indians,—as for my part I went, purely for the poor Indians, and I Should be as ready as ever to promote your School acording to my poor Abilities ^if^ I Coud be Convincd by ocular Demonstration, that your pure Intention is to help the poor helpless Indians, but as long as you have no Indians, I am full of Doubts" (99). The proverbial poor Indian becomes, by the end of this passage, no Indian at all as the cliché is emptied of its conventional significance. Occom prefigures here the full-blown ironic revisionism of Gerald Vizenor, who some two centuries later will take on the role of a sort of *reverse* missionary, offering pointed instruction to Euro-America about the continents of liberty preserved, and now robustly re-created, in Native traditions.

In his most famous text, "A Sermon Preached at the Execution of Moses Paul, an Indian" (1772), Occom goes further in publicly affirming the equality of Native selfhood. Paul, a Wampanoag, had been convicted of killing a white man, Moses Cook, after a drunken spree. Occom delivered a version of the extant text before a large audience of Euro-Americans, Native Americans, and African Americans, who were no doubt intrigued to hear a Native preacher's framing of a Native criminal's transgression. As Occom notes in his introduction to the published work, its origin in "an uncommon quarter . . . may induce people to read it, because it is from an Indian" (177). While condemning Paul for his crime, Occom is careful to point out what some Euro-Americans listening to him may not, in spite of Christian principle, have been ready to acknowledge—the universal humility and spiritual destiny of all human selves, including those of nonwhites: "This must be the unavoidable portion of all impenitent sinners, let them be who they will, great or small, honorable or ignoble, rich or poor, bond or free. Negroes, Indians, English, or of what nations soever; all that die in their sins must go to hell together, for the wages of sin is death" (185). In a remarkable section of the sermon in which he makes a direct appeal to the Native members of his audience—"I shall now address myself to the Indians, my brethren and kindred according to the flesh" (192)—Occom condemns the sin of drunkenness but also adds an incisive aside in which he implicates Euro-America in Paul's (and, by extension, all Native America's) fate: "And here I cannot but observe, we find in sacred writ, a wo denounced against men, who put their bottles to their neighbors mouth to make them drunk, that they may see their nakedness: And no doubt there are such develish men now in our days, as there were in the days of old" (193). Paul may be guilty, but there is guilt enough to go around, and this single condemned figure ought, Occom implies, to be understood in terms of wider cultural relations and the abuses they generate. The point made here anticipates the even sharper judgments made by William Apess, who will likewise take up conventional Euro-American literary genres and use them to dislodge and refashion inhibiting assumptions about Native identities.

It is in Occom's legal petitions, however, that we find the most compelling evidence of the kind of eunomic autonomy he sought to preserve within a ferociously hostile environment. Land, he affirms in these documents, is an essential part of personal and collective identity, a nonfungible wellspring of meaning. Occom's arguments frequently turn to the long-standing history of Native Americans as inhabitants of a specific region and invoke the earth's marvelous natural abundance before the arrival of Euro-American colonists. In a 1785 petition to the Connecticut Assembly on behalf of the Mohegan and Niantic tribes, he tellingly cites "our Natural Priviledges, which the King of Heaven gave to our Fathers and to their Children forever" (148). Reporting the tribe's response to being told that their fishing rights were being strictly regulated, he includes a sly allusion to the irony of tyranny being exerted by those who had recently freed themselves from it:

> When we received an answer or grant to our petition, we were all amazed and astonished beyond measure. What? Only half a sein [net] allowed to Monooyauhegunnewuck [Mohegan], from the best friends to the best friends? We are ready to conclude, that the meaning must be, that in time to come we must not have only one canoe, one bow, one hook and line, among two tribes, and we must have taxes imposed on us also . . . Whilst the King of England had authority over here they order no such things upon us. (148)

The tribes' ancient presence on the land ought to guarantee, Occom reasons, their enduring access to it. His ultimate appeal here, in seeking to defend traditional lifeways, is to an eternal order—nominally Christian, but rather ambiguous in its particulars. A restriction on access to fishing injures a timeless, eunomic pact entered into by a tightly bound community and ignores the primacy of divine law, *themis*, over a merely human *nomos*.

Two other petitions from 1785 offer vivid representations, however idealized, of the kind of world the Mohegans and others had lost. Writing to the United States Congress on behalf of the Brotherton tribe, Occom summarizes Native history from its origins, when both natural and human life flourished, to the miserable deprivations of the present. The "Most Great, The Good and The Supream ^Spirit above^" gave the tribes' ancestors "this Boundless Continent, and it was well furnishd, and Stored with all Necessaries of Life for them, and here they have livd and Spread over the Face of this Wilderness World, no man knows ^how or^ how long" (149). Occom goes on to describe the great fecundity of the precontact world before citing the injustices that have denied Native Americans access to it. With the loss of ancestral lands, the petition explains, traditional lifeways linked to the natural world came under fatal threat when land fell subject to Euro-American values: "[Our] Fathers knew not the Value of Lands, for they had not other use for it only to Hunt on and to gather the Natural Fruits of it; & they have Sold all their Country, along the Sea Shore, and all our Hunting, Fishing and Fowling is now gone, our Father thought to live always by hunting, but they were greatly under a mistake for now we find our selves Stript of all our Natural Priviledges" (149). In a petition addressed to the State of New York on behalf of the Montaukett tribe, Occom offers an extended—and intriguingly ambiguous—description of life before and after colonization. The "Great and good spirit above," he writes,

> Saw it good to give us this great Continent & he fill'd this Indian World, with veriety, and a Prodigious Number of four footed Beasts, Fowl without number and Fish of all kinds great and Small, fill'd our Seas, Rivers, Brooks, and Ponds every where,—And it was the Pleasure of him ... to keep us in Porverty, Only to live upon the Provisions he hath made already at our Hands—Thus we lived, till it pleased the great and good Governor of the World, to Send your Fathers into these goings down of the Sun, and found us Naked and very poor Destitute of every thing, that your Father injoyed, only this that we had good and a Large Country to live in, and well furnished

with Natural Provisions, and there was not a Letter known amongst them all in this Boundless Continent.—But youre Fore Fathers Came With all the Learning, Knowledge, and Understanding, that was Necessary for Mankind to make them Happy, and they knew the goodness of our Land, and they Soon began to Settle and Cultivate the land, Some they bought almost for nothing, and we suppose they took a great deal without Purchase. And our Fathers were very Ignorant and knew not the value of Land, and they Cared nothing about it, they Imagin'd, they Should allways live by Hunting Fishing and Fowling, and gathering Wild Fruits—But alas at this age of the World, we find and plainly see by Sad experience, that by our Fore Fathers Ignorance and Your Fathers great Knowledge, we are undone for this Life.... We fare now harder than our Fore Fathers—For all our Hunting, Fowling, and Fishing is now ^almost^ gone and our Wild Fruit is gone, What little there is left the English would Ingross or take all ^to^ themselves.... (151)

The Indian World described here is a perfectly eunomic space, at odds with the (apparently conciliatory, but suggestively ironic) characterization of precontact Native peoples as destitute and oblivious. No matter the discord in such statements, these petitions affirm the dependence of Native identities on links with specific locales and the ancestral traditions practiced there. If Jefferson could come to understand his powers of self-rule alone, in exhilarating contemplation of a geography he surveyed with a masterly eye, Native autonomy demands, Occom implies, the self's humble, literally grounded connections with a communal past.

Occom's Boundless Continent contains the imaginative seeds, I suggest, of what Vizenor restores in his own work as a eunomic continent of liberty. Lisa Brooks has cogently demonstrated the ways in which early Native American writing, including Occom's, was rooted in complex, geographically specific systems of social and material exchange. Euro-Americans who "entered into this Native space ... [confronted] a network of relations and waterways containing many different groups of people as well as animal, plant, and rock beings that was sustained through the constant transformative 'being' of its inhabitants" (*Common* 3). Native authors of this period posit a "cooperative, interdependent Native environment . . . reflected in the metaphor of the 'common pot'" (3)—a version of *eunomia* emphasizing collective responsibility. As Brooks explains, in tying this metaphor to the creation narrative of the Haudenosaunee and its implicit ethics: "The common pot is that which feeds and nourishes. . . . The pot is Sky Woman's body, the network of relations that must nourish and reproduce itself" (3–4). Human selves are, according to this conceptual ideal, firmly and humbly rooted within their communities and the themistic order which sets the terms of their flourishing. The kind of eunomic autonomy implied here differs from Jefferson's, most obviously, in its central concerns for communality, reciprocity, and the subordination of individual humans to the broader relations between both human and nonhuman presences in a particular locale. Fittingly, Occom's journal entries reflect, Brooks notes, a sense not of individual possession of the land one occupies but of being possessed, among one's network of kin, *by* it: "Often traveling with relations, Occom demonstrated a keen understanding of geographic and social ties. As he wrote on a return trip from Montauk, 'We all returned home again to Mohegan, to several places where we belonged'" (227).

One of Occom's late sermons, from 1787, further adumbrates his notions of an Indigenized *themis* and the terms of autonomous life as it might ideally be pursued.[8] The sermon is devoted to the theme of loving one's neighbor and underscores, in particular, how constant strife among competing political entities in the Northeast has betrayed Christian principles: "[We] Should have the Same Love to other Nations as we have to our Nation; and if this took place, there woud be an End of Wicked Wars and Blood Shed among the Nations, O How happy the Nations of the World live if they were all Neighbourly to one another but alas it is not so, Nations are pulling down one another, and Distroying each other" (201). As he identifies such hypocrisy, however, Occom pointedly declares—in an anticipation of such nineteenth-century authors as Apess and Sarah Winnemucca—that it is in "the Indian Heathen in this great Continent" that one finds an authentic model of Christian ideals:

[They] Discover this Noble Human Self Love, they are very Compassionate one to another, very Liberal among themselves, and also to Strangers, When there is Scarsity of Food amongst them, they ^will^ yet Divide what little they have if there is but a mouth full a Piece, and When any of kills any Creature, they will equally divide it amongst them all and when they have Plenty especially in what they got in Hunting & Fishing,—and when anyone is destitute of a Blanket, he that has two, will freely give him one, and they are very kind to one another in Sickness, and they Weep with them that Weep— This I take to be a Human Love or Being Neighbourly, according to our Text. (203–4)

Later in the sermon, Occom draws a sharp contrast between religious hypocrites and such "natural" practitioners of brotherly love: "The Savage Indians, as they are so calld, are very kind to one another, and they are kind to Strangers;—But I find amongst those who are Calld Christians, Void of Natural affection, according to their Conduct in the World" (206). As in other passages, terms of contempt and entrenched binaries are arrestingly recast. Occom thus enacts—in ways that each of the succeeding Native authors in this study will profitably elaborate—an extraordinary recuperation of Indigenous identities through subversive redefinition.

Recent scholarship has profitably focused attention on the complex adaptations of Indigenous and Christian faith implied in Occom's writings.[9] Drew Lopenzina notes the wider syncretic tendencies of Indigenous religiosity in this period—"The Christian faith was not seen by all Natives as existing in opposition to their own prior belief systems, but rather as something that might be incorporated into, or worked in tandem with, existing cosmologies" (*Red* 247)—and, in assessing the above sermon's larger ambitions, aptly concludes that the Presbyterian minister "finds, in the traditional practices of Natives, an antidote to the self-destructive tendencies of Western civilization" (249). Those tendencies, as Occom defines them, are directly associated with the self's aggressive presumption to atomic rule, its effort to possess, as if elaborating the dark potential lurking in Jeffersonian autonomy, whatever it can for itself alone. Though Occom's sermon may seem, rather oddly, to deploy suspect notions of the noble savage—echoing Jefferson in his praise of Virginia tribes whose "only controuls are their manners, and that moral sense of right and wrong, which, like the sense of tasting and feeling, in every man makes a part of his nature" (*Notes* 98)—it also delineates, more profoundly, the essential characteristics of the Indigenous *themis* he wishes to preserve against the most toxic expressions of Euro-American self-rule.

In Occom's vision of proper moral conduct, Native ideals—above all, a respect for reciprocal exchange and communal welfare—are harmonized with Christianity to inform the themistic world he presents to his congregation. His illustrations of neighborliness and reciprocity (and their failure) repeatedly invoke acts of commercial exploitation that his Native audience would recognize as having been especially corrosive not just to the material well-being of communities but to their relational dynamics themselves. "[A] true Neighbour," he insists, "is ready to feed the hungry as he is willing to be fed when hungry himself, and he is just as willing to Sell to his Neighbour that is needy as he woud desire to have things sold to him when he Needs Some of his Neighbours things" (199). False neighbors, scheming to enrich themselves as they reject collective obligations, selfishly pledge to "do just as [they] please": "this is the Language of the Practice of all oppressors, over reachers, Defrauders, Extortioners with holders of Corn and other Necessaries that they have to Sell, from their Necessitous fellow men, them that keep their Commodities horded up and will not ^Sell^ at present in hopes of Selling, much more in a few Days" (201–2). Selfishness licenses brutal abuses of economic power, he explains, and incites the consumption, in grotesque disregard for communal welfare, of all that would stand in its way: "[These] Men will Buy up evry Necessary of Life in the Town or State, even of the Whole World, were it in their Power especially in the Time of great Want and Distress, and When they have Horded up What they can then they will set an Extravagant Price upon their Commodities at once" (202–3). This critique of capitalist exploitation exceeds that offered by Jefferson in emphasizing not merely the "subservience and venality" (*Notes* 171) that befall those who engage in trade rather than agriculture, but the devastating communal impact, amounting to an existential threat, of predatory commercial practices.

As a further suggestive illustration of the kind of eunomic autonomy Occom hoped to preserve, we may turn back to one of the earlier texts in the archive: a list he compiled, during the mid-1750s, of therapeutic "Herbs & Roots" used in Native medicine. Written in English along with a smattering of Algonquian words, Occom itemizes here dozens of plants and the illnesses they might treat:

> Elder Root & Sweet farm Root take a hand full of each, Put them in hot water, after it is taken of the Fire till it is Cold[,] good for collick.——1
> Sweet Farm Root & Swamp burey bark but most of the Farm, Soked in 2 Qts of water good for Poison.—2
> Elder bark that green Pounded & Mixt with Netes foot oil good for Burn—3.
> ... Burr Dock Leaf, Pounded & Mixt with fat—good for swelling.—4
> Swamp Shoemake Sap good for Warts.—5.
> Pecquauwoss, Some Quantity of Root, Boild in a gallon of water and take the water, and take a little bag—6. (44–45)

Jefferson's catalogue of Virginian plant life in *Notes* provides an intriguing contrast. His characteristic attitude, as noted above, was to emphasize the potential agency of the individual self in its encounter (and identification) with the divine powers of the natural world. Though he sometimes expressed doubt about the interpretive power of systems of classification—on some topics, he concedes, "Nature has hidden from us her modus agendi" (49)—his abstract, objective accounting reflects his trust, consonant with Enlightenment convention, in the efficacy and propriety of attempts to order the world's teeming diversity according to some objective standard. Listing a series of plants according to both their popular names and their "universal" Linnaean classifications, he efficiently subsumes them, according to four divisions, within the human order: "1. Medicinal, 2. Esculent, 3. Ornamental, or 4. Useful for fabrication" (39). The taxonomy Jefferson furnishes implies its own centrality in understanding the links between different plants, along with its essential portability as a guide accessible to anyone who comprehends the classificatory system itself. In other words, the Comte de

Buffon, sitting in his Parisian study and having never visited the New World, could be conceived as that guide's ideal reader.

Occom's list reveals an opposing emphasis, grounded in Mohegan traditions, on the self's subordination to a network of presences invested with reciprocal obligations. It derives, as Kelly Wisecup has demonstrated, from Indigenous assumptions about the spiritual dimension of plants and the significance of their particular relationships with the community members who harvest them:

> [Both] plants and medical practitioners were indebted to nonhuman forces for their power over disease, and practitioners had to appeal to these nonhuman entities to use herbs and cure diseases effectively. As a consequence, medical practitioners did not so much discover, extract, and classify the virtues of herbs as serve as mediators between plants and nonhuman forces, on the one hand, and plants and patients, on the other. (545)

The balance struck here between human and nonhuman agents—quite unlike Jefferson's tilt toward mastery over what he surveys in *Notes*—is key. We may locate in Occom's list, in fact, an early literary illustration of William Bevis's profound observation, framed in relation to the homing plots of twentieth-century Native American novels, that "Native American nature is urban": "The connotation to us of 'urban,' suggesting a dense complex of human variety, is closer to Native American 'nature' than is our word 'natural.' The woods, birds, animals and humans are all 'downtown,' meaning at the center of action and power, in complex and unpredictable and various relationships" (601). Rather than Jefferson's solitary surveyor, Occom posits a communal participant. Moreover, for Occom and other Natives, the notion of transferring knowledge far beyond the communities where it was generated would have been suspect: "Plants and medical practitioners alike were located in a series of networks outside of which their virtues and knowledge, respectively, lacked power or efficacy" (Wisecup 545). Meaning and identity—as each of the succeeding Native authors in the study will also suggest—flow from place and its interdependent relations.

The reciprocal and embedded emphases of Indigenous medicine, its acknowledgment of the ways in which nonhuman presences possess a spiritual dimension intertwined with place and community, imply a eunomic understanding of humanity's role within the natural order. In traditional Native cosmologies, Gregory Cajete explains, "perceptions of the cycles of nature, behavior of animals, growth of plants, and interdependence of all things in nature determined culture, that is, ethics, morals, religious expression, politics, and economics" (52). If Jefferson's own eunomic vision affirms the dominating agency of humans in measuring and claiming the nonhuman as de facto property, the Native vision seemingly reflected in Occom's text sponsors more humble, integrated relations of the self with what environs it. The political implications of these assumptions are profound and help mark out the most significant differences between Jefferson's and Occom's conceptions of self-rule:

> In the inclusive view of natural democracy, humans are related and interdependent with plants, animals, stones, water, clouds, and everything else. Thus, it becomes in every sense abnormal to view the world as dead matter, private property, commodities, or commercial resources. The manifestations and roots of the Native sense of democracy run much deeper than the modern American political version of democracy today in that all of nature, not only humans, has rights. This is the essential 'cosmological clash' between the foundations of Native culture and those of modern society. (Cajete 52)

It was, we may imagine, this "clash" that Occom tried to mediate as he practiced traditional medicine as a Christian minister.

By the early 1770s, Occom had determined that a separatist community was the best hope for Native autonomy in New England and, along with other tribal leaders, helped arrange the voluntary relocation of members of multiple tribes to Oneida territory in New York. In a journal entry dated November 7, 1785, he records that "we proceeded to form in^to^ a Body Politick—We Named our Town by the Name of Brotherton, in Indian Eeyawquittoowauconnuck" (308). The "Indian" name Occom cites suggests the kind of visionary reclamation involved in this effort at self-rule: it can be translated, according to the linguist Stephanie Fielding, as "he does so like someone looking in a certain direction or a certain way" (qtd. in J. Brooks 25 n28). Though the community was Christian and its organization at least superficially modeled on Euro-American towns, it sought to protect distinctively Indigenous traditions. Occom's recording of a 1778 tribal council provides insight into the town's emphasis on communal responsibilities:

> In the evening, the Tribe met together, to Consult about the Disposal of the Rent money, and as it has been agreed Unanimously heretofore once and again, that we Shall look upon one another as one Family, and Will Call or look upon no one as a Stranger, but Will take one another as pure and True Mohegans; and so at this Time, we unanimously ^agreed^ that the Money does belong to the Whole Tribe, and it shall be dispos'd of acordingly for the Benefit of the Whole. (147)

An emphasis on shared responsibility for land was fundamental to this effort at self-rule. As Reginald Dyck explains in his economic analysis of Occom's blending of Christian principles of neighborliness with Indigenous notions of communal responsibility: "Although the structures established to govern individual and communal land use and distribution were not traditional per se, they did help sustain the traditional value of mutuality. Their intent was not to re-create the past Indian world . . . but rather to maintain Native practices and Christian principles as they adapted to continually changing realities" (19). Brotherton survived after Occom's death in 1792, though in the 1830s it finally succumbed to government pressure and was relocated to Wisconsin. Lopenzina sums up the corrosive social factors leading to that outcome: "The community vision with which Brothertown was initiated gave way to the self-interest of a few, which, alongside the forces of colonization always waiting in the wings, was enough to eventually erode the power base that had hoped to keep the land under a common Native title" (*Red* 319).

In the trajectory I have begun to sketch in this study, Occom's writings represent early, prophetic attempts to preserve the fragile elements of an Indigenous mode of eunomic autonomy. The following chapters explore how later Native authors borrow his strategies and craft new ones, extending his largely defensive enterprise into increasingly bold and vital affirmations of self-rule within the broader nomistic order.

TWO

Prospective Domination, Retrospective Liberation
Ralph Waldo Emerson and William Apess

MOVING FROM JEFFERSON'S *Notes on the State of Virginia* (1785) to Emerson's *Nature* (1836) we find two remarkable developments in the Euro-American imagination of personal self-rule: the first, an enormous augmentation of the potential power of the autonomous self as it communes with the divine through the natural world; and the second, an increasing emphasis on that self's detachment from the social order (and thus a critical separation of *themis* from *nomos*). The exuberant rhetoric of the essay posits, in fact, an effectively deified self, licensed and indeed obligated to stand apart from its community, and from history, as it cultivates the extraordinary range of its personal autonomy. Believing, with Jefferson, in the inherent goodness of human self-shepherding, Emerson affirms here that such distancing will in fact serve the collective good.

William Apess's works, published between 1829 and 1836, take a strikingly different view of autonomy at both the personal and collective levels. Writing during a period of intense public debate about Indian removal, he confronts dire and escalating threats to the very existence of America's Indigenous peoples. Apess's arguments elaborate, and add significant force and depth to, many of those voiced by Occom, as he offers sustained critiques of a history of settler aggression that has resulted in the steady loss of Native lands and lifeways. Euro-American ideology is a particular target of his polemics: ingrained prejudices have had devastating consequences for nonwhites, he asserts, and presumptions about the racial and cultural inferiority of Natives themselves and the inevitability of their extinction represent major barriers to Native self-rule. Much as Sarah Winnemucca will do later in the century, Apess robustly affirms his *pride* in a Native identity, turning to the past not merely as something imperiled or lost, abused and forsaken—as is often the case in Occom's shocked responses to Euro-American abuses—but recoverable, redemptive, and ultimately transfigurative, a potential foundation for an authentic and inalienable Indigenous futurity. Among Apess's presiding aims, then, is to imagine how Native peoples might command respect as they are integrated, on their own terms, into the Euro-American *nomos*. He thus presents a remarkable inversion of Emerson's essential prescription: not a liberating removal of the private self from the American social order, but an *inclusion* of Indigenous selfhood within it, in ways that would both affirm its equality and retain its distinctive character.

This chapter begins with a sketch of some of the major assumptions and implications of Emerson's definition of personal autonomy in *Nature*—above all, his championing of a break from tradition and nomistic authority, his promise of the immense power to be cultivated in the self's privacy, and his endorsement of a thoroughgoing manipulation of the natural world as the proper extension of claims to that power. In later Euro-American authors, as subsequent chapters will demonstrate, this surging optimism about a eunomic self-rule declines as various pathologies emerge in the self's detachment from its *nomos* and, at last, its technocratic mastery of the environment. Turning from Emerson to Apess, I explore a much humbler definition of selfhood, one which underscores, in its efforts to preserve a vision of eunomic autonomy, the subordination of humans to a Christian *themis* associated with Indigenous traditions and which seeks communal solidarity and stronger connections with the past. Apess's work anticipates, I suggest, key emphases in the remaining Native authors of this study, who similarly negotiate the recovery of distinctive beliefs and practices, and who are able to imagine, with growing confidence, a more vibrant place for Native peoples—*as* Natives—within the broader social order.

Emerson's own nomistic world, he declares in *Nature*, has set its gaze unproductively on the past and its claims; what its members need is "an original relation to the universe," "a poetry and philosophy of insight and not of tradition," "a religion by revelation" (3). The essay, in elaborating its metaphor of visionary renewal, argues for a turn toward the themistic potencies of the natural world and *away* from the desiccated, merely human authority of the nomistic one: "Embosomed for a season in nature, whose floods of life stream around and through us, and invite us, by the powers they supply, to action proportioned by nature, why should we grope among the dry bones of the past, or put the living generation into masquerade out of its faded wardrobe?" (3). Tapping these natural resources, individual selves and the nation itself may assume, in defiance of the tyranny of historical precedent, a rule consonant with the insights of direct experience: "Let us demand our own works and laws and worship" (3).

Among the ideas for which Emerson is rightly known is his tremendous optimism about the self's ability to go inward, in solitary communion with *themis,* and fulfil such demands. Human vision, he assures us, is essentially unlimited in its transformative powers: the "eye [and, of course, the "I"] is the best composer," and there is "no object so foul that intense light will not make beautiful" (9). Exceeding Jefferson in the universal human endowments he posits, Emerson affirms that "every rational creature has all nature for his dowry and estate" and would justly "[take] up the world into himself" (11). What holds one back from developing this potential is timidity (in bowing to nomistic convention) and indolence (in declining requisite exertions), a finally voluntary slavishness.

The most famous passage in *Nature* dramatically illustrates the kinds of power Emerson imagines the self might wield. During a solitary walk, he relates, he has suddenly assumed divine vision: "Standing on the bare ground,—my head bathed by the blithe air, and uplifted into infinite space,—all mean egotism vanishes. I become a transparent eye-ball; I am nothing; I see all; the currents of the Universal Being circulate through me; I am part or particle of God" (6). At once nothing and everything, a deific self absorbs the world within its gaze. Not just embodiment dissolves here, and hence all contact with sensuous experience beyond vision, but also communal connections (and the reciprocal gaze of any other human self): "The name of the nearest friend sounds then foreign and accidental: to be brothers, to be acquaintances,—master or servant, is then a trifle and a disturbance. I am the lover of uncontained and immortal beauty. In the wilderness, I find something more dear and connate than in streets or villages" (6). With this discovery, nomistic convention becomes *only* convention, shallow and extraneous next to the natal profundities and infinite possibilities of the themistic order. Jefferson's masterful view of natural scenes in *Notes*, in which he identifies with the potency of the natural world but still remains separate from it, is trumped here by the self's boundless vision. Such *auto-nomia* perfects the most positive senses of the Greek verb *nemo*, reflecting an infinitely nourishing self-pasture, self-possession, self-inhabitance. At the same time, *themis* itself, in light of the ascendance of an effectively deified self, undergoes a curious conceptual diminution. No longer firmly and finally set apart from that self, an autonomous law of its own, it becomes, in effect, synonymous with it.

In the paragraph immediately succeeding the "transparent eye-ball" passage, Emerson notes his discovery of "an occult relation between man and vegetable" which assures him that "I am not alone and unacknowledged. They nod to me, and I to them" (6). The striking image seems to affirm, however playfully and ambiguously, a reciprocal selfhood in the nonhuman. Emerson overwhelms this suggestion, however, with heady blasts of anthropocentrism in the rest of the essay. In our communion with the divine, natural processes are defined in relation to their human-directed instrumentality:

> Nature, in its ministry to man, is not only the material, but is also the process and the result. All the parts incessantly work into each other's hands for the profit of man. The wind sows the seed; the sun evaporates the sea; the wind blows the vapor to the field; the ice, on the other side of the planet, condenses the rain on this; the rain feeds the plant; the plant feeds the animal; and thus endless circulation of the divine charity nourish man. (7–8)

Having apprehended the dynamics of this divine order, one is authorized, Emerson asserts, to manipulate the environment through which it is expressed. At his most extreme, he defines the natural world as a sort of obliging workshop or playground for its human master:

> Nature is thoroughly mediate. It is made to serve. It receives the dominion of man as meekly as the ass on which the Savior rode. It offers all its kingdoms to man as the raw material which he may mold into what is useful. Man is never weary of working it up.... One after another, his victorious thought comes up with and reduces all things, until the world becomes, at last, only a realized will,—the double of the man. (21)

The fantastically potent self imagined here converts its comprehensive seeing into doing as it pursues an effectively boundless rule.

What the self might ultimately see in its private revelations, according to Emerson's version of Neoplatonic idealism, is the ontological primacy of mental or spiritual phenomena. One looks through or beyond the natural world, that is, to apprehend (and channel) themistic power. In certain effusive passages, Emerson's idealism leads him to emphasize the utter *subordination* of the natural world to the human as mere medium for *themis* and the self's blending with it. Though revelations may be prompted by sylvan journeys, they in fact leave the natural world behind, like all other materiality, as a gateway to the divine. "The best moments of life," we are told, "are these delicious awakenings of the higher powers, and the reverential withdrawing of nature before its God" (25). At moments Emerson even expresses—in seeming contradiction of the thrust of his argument—a kind of contempt for the natural world as mere physicality: "Thus even in physics, the material is degraded before the spiritual. The astronomer, the geometer, rely on their irrefragable analysis, and disdain the results of observation. The sublime remark of Euler on his law of arches, 'This will be found contrary to all experience, yet is true;' had already transferred nature into the mind, and left matter like an outcast corpse" (29). Material nature, we are to understand, is not where genuine *life* may be discovered.

Emerson's endorsements of specular power are, for the most part, themselves rather speculative, leaving readers to fill in details about how, exactly, a visionary might behave in the world. He does, however, offer an extended and robust description of certain practical applications of human inventiveness, providing a much wider and warmer reception to the human adoption of technology than Jefferson in *Notes*.

Our manipulation of the world, Emerson suggests, rightly incorporates tools which increase the range of our powers and the expression of new forms of creativity:

> The useful arts are reproductions or new combinations by the wit of man, of the same natural benefactors. He no longer waits for favoring gales, but by means of steam, he realizes the fable of Aeolus's bag, and carries the two and thirty winds in the boiler of his boat. To diminish friction, he paves the road with iron bars, and, mounting a coach with a ship-load of men, animals, and merchandise behind him, he darts through the country, from town to town, like an eagle or a swallow through the air. By the aggregate of these aids, how is the face of the world changed, from the era of Noah to that of Napoleon! The private poor man hath cities, ships, canals, bridges, built for him. He goes to the post-office, and the human race run on his errands; to the book-shop, and the human race read and write of all that happens, for him; to the court-house, and nations repair his wrongs. He sets his house upon the road, and the human race go forth every morning, and shovel out the snow, and cut a path for him. (8)

This (seemingly sincere) celebration of a sort of technological sublime omits concerns—such as those raised by Jefferson—about the growth of urban, industrial environments that might threaten human access to the natural world. For Emerson in this period, as Leo Marx explains, "new inventions are evidence of man's power to impose his will upon the world. A youthful admirer of Bacon and Franklin, he qualifies but never repudiates the progressive idea of history. He is confident that the advance of science will be followed by a comparable improvement in political morality" (230). The self may, accordingly, be simply improved by its tools, which innocently extend the range of its vision. What this extension means when much more potent prosthetics are available is the subject of this study's last chapter: in DeLillo's techno-visionary Eric Packer, whose final contempt for the physical world sees him wishing for his own transformation into "quantum dust" (206), Emerson's "useful arts" lose their status as "natural benefactors" and become vehicles for a terminal self-consumption.

Conceptual revolutions seem to interest Emerson most, but he concludes his essay by turning it over to his "poet," who offers a soaring affirmation of practical—though nonspecific—applications of visionary power. No matter one's prior nomistic status, Nature's boundless resources lie waiting for development. "Build, therefore, your own world," we are instructed by this prophetic voice, for "[a]s fast as you conform your life to the pure idea in your mind, that will unfold its great proportions. A correspondent revolution in things will attend the influx of the spirit" (*Nature* 39). The inspired self, sparking "a revolution in things," will "[draw] beautiful faces, warm hearts, wise discourse, and heroic acts, around its way, until evil is no more seen" (39). Having "retained the spirit of infancy even into the era of manhood" (6), that self can now gaze at the world with infinite innocence. More than simply an invigorating return to childlike purity, however, the transformative act imagined here involves an emergence of the self, finally, out of nothing but itself. Self-inhabited and self-possessed, the autonomous become masters of their American pasture.

The masterful acts of individual selves will, Emerson assumes, ultimately contribute to a revitalized *nomos*. It is the stability and universality of the divine that guarantees the cohesiveness of a community of autonomous seers. Though his emphasis in the essay falls on the exhilarating possibilities of privacy, Emerson affirms that the wisdom gained in revelatory moments can and ought to be translated into actions involving, and ultimately benefiting, the nomistic world it is licensed, at least imaginatively, to leave behind. Transcendence offers, at last, a shared and binding insight into "the moral law [that] lies at the centre of nature and radiates to the circumference" (21). This benignant *themis* secures the wholeness and wholesomeness of the *nomos* eunomically aligned with it, no matter the solitary orientation of its members. Individual selves, grazing alone, still share a common, mutually sustaining pasture and will finally return to each other from their private pathways.

Emerson's vision of *eunomia*—a nourishing fusion of the political and pastoral just as idyllic as Jefferson's—will gradually yield, in later Euro-American authors considered in this study, to an emphasis on the dysnomic potential in nomistic detachment and solitary claims to *themis*. Lacking the utter, intoxicating authority Emerson had invested in personal autonomy, Twain's Huck Finn and Hemingway's Nick Adams must, in their solitude, negotiate its emerging shadows, while Heller's Bob Slocum is effectively consumed by a private darkness. Moreover, as DeLillo will make most clear, the enormous privilege of gazing without being gazed at (in the manner of a transparent eyeball) leaves blind spots, in particular when it comes to the damage—personal, social, and environmental—wrought by such autonomy as it is extended into actual worlds. DeLillo's Packer represents a seeming endpoint of this destructive self-rule and its spectacular abuses: his attempts at panoptic mastery, along with his ahistorical and asocial commitments, decisively shed their positive potential as the desire for a revelatory oneness with everything transitions into an unlimited, unconditioned mandate for brutal domination. No longer will a boundless autonomy seem innocent as "the world becomes, at last, only a realized will,—the double of the man" (21).

William Apess was born to a mixed-race Pequot family in Colrain, Massachusetts, in 1798. His childhood was marked by harrowing deprivations and abuse, including a nearly deadly beating, when he was four, by his grandmother. Removed from her home, Apess was then placed with a series of white families as an indentured servant. He ran away to join the military in his early teens, serving in the War of 1812 on the Canadian front. Like Occom, as a young adult Apess gradually developed profound commitments to both Christianity and political activism on behalf of Native peoples, eventually becoming a prominent Methodist minister, missionary, intertribal representative, orator, and author. Among the most notable of his political achievements was his decisive role in the so-called Mashpee Revolt: acting as a spokesman for the Mashpee Wampanoag, who sought to resist the encroachments of Euro-American settlers and mistreatment by religious overseers, he successfully petitioned the state government for a significant augmentation of their collective autonomy. Apess published five nonfiction books during a brief but remarkably productive literary career. My discussion here, in exploring the notions of eunomic self-rule that emerge in his work, focuses on two of his autobiographical texts—"The Experience of the Missionary" (1833) and *A Son of the Forest* (1831)—along with his *Eulogy on King Philip: As Pronounced at the Odeon, in Federal Street, Boston* (1836), a radical reconsideration not just of a major Indigenous leader in the early colonial era, but of the overall history of Euro-American and Native American relations.[1]

Euro-America, as Apess knew well, imagined no future for his people. The Pequot War (1636–38) set his ancestors against the combined forces of English colonists and several Native American allies, and the Pequots' resounding defeat seemed, to their conquerors, a guarantee of their imminent extinction. The majority of surviving tribal members were taken captive, sold into slavery, or dispersed in small numbers across the regions surrounding their original homelands, a fate celebrated by the Puritan John Mason as a righteous triumph of civilization over savagery: "God's hand from heaven was so manifested . . . so that the name of the Pequots (as of Amalech) is blotted out from under heaven, there being not one that is, or (at least) dare call himself a Pequot" (qtd. in Hauptman 76). In spite of the hegemonic culture's vigorous and sustained efforts to fulfill such aspirations, Apess, two centuries after the war, committed himself to securing the tribe's continuity. Against willful blindness, his writing insists on making visible the enduring presence of Native peoples in New England, the outrageous omissions in accounts of their history, and the ongoing injustices which plague them. Where Emerson seeks a break with history to free the self, Apess would heal historical fractures in the service of both personal and collective liberation. As we shall see, his writings, while typically emphasizing the importance of moving marginalized peoples toward an equal political status, also suggest the distinctive features of a Native identity he wished to preserve and develop within the larger *nomos*.

In "An Indian's Looking-Glass for the White Man," a polemical essay devoted to highlighting the hypocrisy of white Christians, Apess sums up the contemporary status of reservations in the Northeast, reporting that "with but few exceptions, we shall find them as follows: [inhabited by] the most mean, abject, miserable race of beings in the world—a complete place of prodigality and prostitution" (155). Such conditions are, he maintains, the result of centuries of outrageous exploitation (rather than inherent deficiencies in Native character), and ameliorating them must involve the frank exposure of that history. Emerson, defining the terms of a forward-looking Euro-American autonomy, ridicules a "retrospective" orientation as "[groping] among the dry bones of the past" (*Nature* 3), but for Apess—as for Winnemucca, Zitkala-Ša, Momaday, Erdrich, and Vizenor—such a turn, properly undertaken, is an exercise in the resuscitation of a potentially invigorating ancestry. Retrospection is exactly the means to a living future, for it promises the rediscovery and reclamation of distinctive elements of a Native identity and is *itself* one of those traditional elements. And where Emerson emphasizes immediate opportunities for the solitary cultivation of personal autonomy—and through it, the broader vitalization of the American *nomos*—Apess highlights and condemns systemic obstacles which prohibit Natives' full inclusion in the social order. As Philip F. Gura writes, Apess "strove to understand himself as a member of an indigenous nation within the United States of America, and so to claim for himself, his tribe, and Native Peoples in general a place in the new nation" (xvi). Apess's conceptual challenge is, in short, to affirm the legitimacy and legacy of a Native selfhood and thus establish the imaginative foundations for a resurgent self-rule.

We may recall here, as a sort of foil to the assumptions that guide Apess's arguments, some of the context for Emerson's hyperbolic descriptions of personal autonomy. Solitude is necessary for its development, we are told in *Nature*, and to secure it "a man needs to retire as much from his chamber as from society. . . . [If] a man would be alone, let him look at the stars. The rays that come from those heavenly worlds will separate between him and what he touches" (5). A productive nomistic detachment is easily accessible, we are to assume, for those who claim themistic powers by shifting their gaze from human institutions to the heavens. Striking erasures, of course, lie behind Emerson's accounts of innocent spectatorship. Though he may find that "[i]n the woods is perpetual youth" (6), a stimulus to creation that easily and appropriately sheds the past, the "bare ground" (6) he occupies has been made safe for men like himself to wander over by a specific (and hardly innocent) history. There would, that is, be no opportunity for his transparent eyeballing without the prior removal of Native peoples.

Emerson had some familiarity with that history, having read Lemuel Shattuck's *A History of the Town of Concord* (1835) and having reflected, in other writings, on the transition from what the Massachusetts tribe had named Musketaquid (both a river and town) to what he knew as the town of Concord, his adopted home. As Shattuck writes:

> When the English settlements first commenced in New England, that part of its territory, which lies south of New Hampshire, was inhabited by five principal nations of Indians:—the Pequots, who lived in Connecticut; the Narragansets, in Rhode Island; the Pawkunnawkuts, or Womponoags, east of the Narragansets and to the north as far as Charles river; the Massachusetts, north of Charles river and west of Massachusetts Bay; and the Pawtuckets, north of the Massachusetts.... At the commencement of the seventeenth century, [these nations] were able to bring into the field more than 18,000 warriors; but about the year 1612, they were visited with a pestilential disease, whose horrible ravages reduced their number to about 1800. Some of their villages were entirely depopulated. This great mortality was viewed by the first Pilgrims, as the accomplishment of one of the purposes of Divine Providence, by making room for the settlement of civilized man, and by preparing a peaceful asylum for the persecuted Christians of the old world. In what soever the event may be viewed, it no doubt greatly facilitated the settlements, and rendered them less hazardous.... [The Massachusetts tribe] was once powerful. Before the great sickness already mentioned, it could number 3000 warriors. That calamity, and the small-pox, which prevailed among them with great mortality in 1633, reduced it to nearly one tenth of that number. The Musketaquid Indians suffered in common with the brethren of their tribe elsewhere. When first visited by the English, their number was comparatively very small. (1–3)

This history is elided in *Nature*, but briefly acknowledged and then imaginatively dismissed in several of Emerson's poems. "Concord Hymn" and "Musketaquid," T. S. McMillin notes, offer paeans to progress as "the poet remembers the Musketaquid only so that it might be left behind; that ancient waterway is itself only a relic, a thing of the past to be surpassed and eventually transcended" (34). Natural and human history, here as elsewhere in Emerson's writing, are "thoroughly mediate" and "made to serve"; one recovers such histories in order to commune with the themistic potencies they might ultimately reveal.

For Apess, the preservation of Native selfhood demands, as a starting point, the rejection of such assumptions. In "The Experience of the Missionary," an autobiographical conversion narrative, he cites the importance of connecting past and present not only to fostering an understanding of the ongoing ramifications of historical injustice but to establishing the conditions of a communal identity. He opens the work by noting the representative quality of his life—his story is not that of an individual, at last, but of a people—along with the inextricable links between living Natives and their ancestors: "It is not my intention to descend to particulars in this pamphlet, any farther than to notice the origin of my life for the purpose of giving the youth a transient view between their condition and mine; or those poor children of the forest, who have had taken from them their once delightful plains and homes of their peaceful habitations; their fathers and mothers torn from their dwellings, and they left to mourn, and drop a tear, and die, over the ruins of their ancient sires" (119). Euro-America's power to gaze freely and selectively has, Apess contends, perniciously (and opportunistically) occluded Native Americans. He thus insists that Native peoples and their histories be seen, and that their *ways* of seeing—the transient views that would link the living and the dead—be fostered, too. The solitary autonomy endorsed by Emerson is, by this estimation, at the very least a luxury unavailable to Natives, who face, in daily life, a "tide of degradation" (119) from their oppressors. Under such conditions, one cannot, that is, simply retire from one's chambers or one's society in order to claim an autonomous life. Cultivating self-rule must involve a frank engagement with the deeply entrenched social structures obstructing such mobility, along with a recovery and affirmation of one's *own* social structures.

Apess's account of his spiritual conversion, in adopting standard expressions of Christian humility, develops this departure from Emerson's emphasis on solitary self-aggrandizement in ways consonant with a Native worldview. Communion with the divine demands here, as it would for any orthodox Methodist, a radical subordination of the self and collaboration with a community of the like-minded. The deepest, most transformative revelations emerge, seemingly, not out of private experiences but rather collective, humbling encounters with the themistic order:

> But when I acknowledged myself a sinner before the people and confessed what a sinner I had been, then the light of God's countenance broke into my soul, and I felt as if I were on the wings of angels and ready to leave this world. I united with the Methodists, and was baptized by immersion, and strove to walk with them in the way to heaven, and can say that I spent many happy hours with them in the worship of God. (132)

According to the conventional religious terms deployed in the narrative—which broadly align with the communal emphases Apess locates in his own Indigenous heritage—only by walking *with* others, in meek devotion to a tradition of authoritative beliefs, does one find one's way to the divine. Committed to Christianity, Apess nevertheless continues to affirm his pride in the particular identity he has been granted from above: "[Although] the white man finds so much fault because God has made us thus, yet if I have any vanity about it, I choose to remain as I am, and praise my Maker while I live that an Indian he has made" (130).

A Son of the Forest, Apess's extended spiritual autobiography, elaborates many of the themes broached in "The Experience of the Missionary." A central demand articulated here is for the inclusion in the broader social order of those he has served as an itinerant minister: "Look, brethren, at the natives of the forest—they come, notwithstanding you call them '*savage*,' from the 'east and from the west, the north and the south,' and will occupy seats in the kingdom of heaven before you" (51). Divine law recognizes the spiritual equality of nonwhites, Apess reminds us, and the American *nomos* must be reformed to acknowledge it. Key to that reform, he asserts, is the recovery of a hauntingly relevant history. A searing anecdote from his early life illustrates the kind of links between past and present he seeks. After being abandoned by his parents, Apess was taken in by his grandparents, who were impoverished and "wedded to the beastly vice of intemperance" (5). The periodic abuse and neglect he suffered came to a climax when he was a young child: his grandmother, returning home intoxicated after being "out among the whites," asked him if he "hated" her (5–6). Not knowing what the word meant, and wanting to please her, he answered that he did, inciting her to strike him with a club: "[She] continued asking me the same question, and I as often answered her in the same way, whereupon she continued beating me, by which means one of my arms was broken in three different places. I was then only four years of age and consequently could not take care of or defend myself—and I was equally unable to seek safety in flight" (6). We are made painfully aware here of the crushing influence of social and historical determinants, of the ramifying consequences of internalized self-hatred and its passage through generations. Rather than the innocent and inviolate child of Emerson's *Nature*, on whom adults might model their spiritual renovation, we encounter a figure of utter vulnerability, whose mere survival may seem astounding.

Even more audaciously than Occom, who similarly points out in his execution sermon that the crime committed by Moses Paul is framed by a history of whites' promotion of alcohol among Native communities, Apess reminds his audience of the broader context in which "cruel and unnatural conduct" (6) takes place. Individual pathologies radiate from systemic abuse: "I attribute it in a great measure to the whites, inasmuch as they introduced among my countrymen that bane of comfort and happiness, ardent spirits—seduced them into a love of it and, when under its unhappy influence, wronged them out of their lawful possessions—that land, where reposed the ashes of their sires" (7). Apess's invocation of the removal of Native peoples from their ancestral territory also highlights the significance of land itself, and the ancestral ties cultivated there, to the preservation of Native identity. The contrast with Emerson's antihistoricism is, once more, remarkably stark: if Euro-Americans were promised that "[i]n the woods, is perpetual youth" (*Nature* 6), a timeless reinvigoration and shedding of burdens, Native Americans in the Northeast, forced to adapt to social marginalization after having *lost* much of their wooded territory, have been compelled to bear the weight of past and ongoing dispossessions.

For Apess, a major challenge to Native autonomy lies simply in claiming and defining the legitimacy of Native selfhood. Seizing control of one's history and self-representation become essential tasks in the pursuit of self-rule, and a guiding strategy for Apess in *A Son of the Forest* is to identify and ironize the ways in which Indigenous identities have been disfigured. In noting the debilitating effects of having one's names chosen by (hostile) others, he deploys, for instance, an ironic revisionism that recalls Occom in his letter to Wheelock and prefigures Vizenor's creative recasting, centuries later, of inherited linguistic manacles:

> I thought it disgraceful to be called an Indian; it was considered as a slur upon an oppressed and scattered nation, and I have often been led to inquire where the whites received this word, which they so often threw as an opprobrious epithet at the sons of the forest. I could not find it in the Bible, and therefore concluded, that it was a word imported for the special purpose of degrading us. At other times I thought it was derived from the term *in-gen-uity.* (10)

Apess goes on to make a further claim, identifying Native Americans as one of the Ten Lost Tribes of Israel, with a skin tone ostensibly similar to that of Semitic peoples: "But the proper term which ought to be applied to our nation, to distinguish it from the rest of the human family, is that of '*Natives*'—and I humbly conceive that the natives of this country are the only people under heaven who have a just title to the name, inasmuch as we are the only people who retain the original complexion of our father Adam" (10). In this reorientation of the national mythos, Native Americans assume an ancient, authoritative history, along with a compelling claim to a sacred place within the American pasture.[2]

In another telling anecdote from his later childhood, Apess relates an occasion when, while out gathering berries in the woods, he came across a group of women whose skin was "as *dark* as that of the natives" (10; italics in original). Having identified with the attitudes of the white family that had taken him in, the young Apess fled from the women in terror: "[So] completely was I weaned from the interests and affections of my brethren that a mere threat of being sent away among the Indians into the dreary woods had a much better effect in making me obedient to the commands of my superiors than any corporal punishment that they ever inflicted" (10). Characteristically, he connects his response to a series of misrepresentations and a suppressed history:

> [The] great fear I entertained of my brethren, was occasioned by the many stories I had heard of their cruelty towards the whites—how they were in the habit of killing and scalping men, women and children. But the whites did not tell me that they were in a great majority of instances the aggressors—that they had imbrued their hands in the life blood of my brethren, driven them from their once peaceful and happy homes—that they introduced among them the fatal and exterminating diseases of civilized life. If the whites had told me how cruel they had been to the 'poor Indian,' I should have apprehended as much harm from them. (11)

As Apess recalls his racial indoctrination as a youth, he deftly undermines authoritative accounts of Euro-American and Native American relations, exposing the partiality of the historical and contemporary gaze in which his selfhood has been contained.

It is rewarding to return again to Emerson's fantasy of visual mastery in *Nature*, for it shares something with the oppressive forms of observation identified by Apess. As Richard Poirier points out:

> Obviously, the eyeball as a possessor is an imaginative analogue to the great American enterprise of the period. To a man of the early nineteenth century in America, possessing landscape was necessarily more than a romantic commonplace of descriptive-reflective poetry. Possession was also a national goal entrusted to enterprising men who faced an opportunity for profit unique in history. (64)

Indian removal, which reached its height during the decade in which both *Nature* and *A Son of the Forest* were published, was one such ambition, and it reflected the possessive hallucinations of thousands of enterprising men who presumed to see all while voiding inconvenient presences, imagining themselves onto bare ground as they imagined Indigenous peoples out of it. Such *auto-nomia* reflects the negative senses of the Greek verb *nemo* as consumption and ulcerous spread, a predatory self-rule absorbing all in its wake.[3]

As he anatomizes the implications of such autonomy, Apess underscores his concern for appropriate "retrospection," noting the past and ongoing injustices that have contributed to widespread oppression. Much of Euro-America, he maintains, has been willfully blind to the fate of its Indigenous population: "No doubt there are many good people in the United States, who would not trample upon the rights of the poor, but there are many others who are willing to roll in their coaches upon the tears and blood of the poor and unoffending natives—those who are ready at all times to *speculate* on the Indians, and defraud them out of their rightful possessions" (31; emphasis added). Apess's wordplay thus connects, as ever, an oppressive ideology with the concrete results of its extension into the world—specifically here, economic exploitation that finds its alibi in the rejection of the racial other's equality. The sight lines of settler culture's aggressive representatives have been, we are told, malignantly venal and selective: "It has been considered as a trifling thing for the whites to make war on the Indians for the purpose of driving them from their country, and taking possession thereof. This was, in their estimation, all right, as it helped to extend the territory, and enriched some individuals" (31). Euro-American visions of national expansion and individual profit have, by this reckoning, sponsored a narrowly personal and racially exclusive self-rule. Native presences have, in the Emersonian vocabulary, been "made to serve," to receive "the dominion of [the white] man as meekly as the ass on which the Savior rode" (*Nature* 21).

Beyond merely critiquing the pathologies flowing from Euro-American autonomy, Apess also provides in his autobiography, if briefly, resonant affirmations of the distinctive features of Native selfhood and eunomic autonomy as he understood them. The most extraordinary of these comes in his account of his travels after being discharged from the military. After drifting through a number of short-term jobs, his employment and spiritual health marred by his alcoholism, he was able to interact with a community of Tyendinaga Mohawk in the Bay of Quinte region. The encounter seems to have furnished him with a potent sense of belonging. Having been alienated from Pequot culture as a child, Apess nevertheless recovers here, through the example of a beleaguered but resilient tribal people, a profound connection to Indigenous traditions: "My brethren were all around me," he explains, "and it therefore seemed like home" (32). He goes on to describe, in terms strikingly contrary to Emerson's, a revelatory experience in the natural world:

> On the very top of a high mountain in the neighborhood there was a large pond of water, to which there was no visible outlet—this pond was unfathomable. It was very surprising to me that so great a body of water should be found so far above the common level of the earth. There was also in the neighborhood a rock that had the appearance of being hollowed out by the hand of a skilled artificer; through this rock wound a narrow stream of water: It had a most beautiful and romantic appearance, and I could not but admire the wisdom of God in the order, regularity, and beauty of creation; I then turned my eyes to the forest, and it seemed alive with its sons and daughters. There appeared to be the utmost order and regularity in their encampment. (32–33)

This moment does not imply an ecstatic transcendence of communal relations but instead grounds the self, eunomically, within a shared natural order. The themistic potencies discovered here remain receptive to, but finally separate from, their observer, for the wisdom of God is not, as in Emerson's revelatory moment, subsumed into the self. There is admiration for divine creation in Apess's description but no self-exalting, masterful channeling of *themis*. On a subsequent trip into the woods, he reports that "all nature seemed to smile and rejoice in the freshness and beauty of spring" (35), sponsoring an efflorescence of human activities: "My brethren appeared very cheerful on account of [springtime's] return and enjoyed themselves in hunting, fishing, basket making, etc." (35). Instead of Emerson's anti-nomistic, separatist preference—"In the wilderness, I find something more dear and connate than in streets or villages" (*Nature* 6)—we find the solitary self imaginatively enfolded into a social world both human and nonhuman. Its gaze takes in others as living kin, whose own eyes, we may assume, must be acknowledged.

While empowering, Apess's experience at the Bay of Quinte is also humbling, bringing him to a recognition of fundamental connections and responsibilities. Appropriately, he ends this chapter of his autobiography by turning once again to a communal perspective, framing his personal revelation within broader concerns for the collective he represents. The eunomic autonomy Apess has glimpsed is, he knows, delicate and imperiled. "Oh what a pity," he notes, "that this state of things should change. How much better would it be if the whites would act like a civilized people and, instead of giving my brethren of the woods 'rum!' in exchange for their furs, give them food and clothing for themselves and children" (33). Again in contrast to Emerson, Apess's focus here is not abstract but falls on specific interventions in the nomistic world suggested by his revelatory experience. As Lisa Brooks argues, this section of the autobiography signifies Apess's discovery of "an obligatory reciprocity to the forest that gave him birth and to its sons and daughters, who he now fully recognized as his relations" (*Common* 174). Drew Lopenzina ventures that, having drawn close, for the first time in his life, to "brethren" who still practiced traditional lifeways, Apess began to develop a compelling sense of positive Native identity, one which represents an "undercurrent of spiritual power flowing in hidden opposition to the surface waters of expressed Christian faith" (*Through* 127) and which implies the at least conceptual viability of a fusion of natural and human orders: "Once one has situated the account within its proper spiritual geography, the passage can only be seen as equating the order of God's creation with the order and harmony of Native ceremony" (*Through* 129). In the woods, we might say, Apess found not perpetual *youth*—a solitary Emersonian revivification eschewing hoary traditions—but tribal community and ancestral continuity, eunomic linkages with the past that might be extended into a redemptive future.

Eulogy on King Philip projects Apess's previously developed themes, and his prophetic vision of what might be recovered in Native traditions, onto a wider historical context. The work's immediate subject is the life and cultural significance of the Wampanoag leader Metacomet, whom the British had dubbed King Philip. Apess also provides here a revisionist account of the region's Puritan origins and a forceful argument for the inclusion of Natives within the American *nomos*. As he reimagines Euro-American and Native American relations through the lens of what came to be known as King Philip's War (1675–78), he overturns conventional narratives of historical conquest and deems Philip not the feared leader of Indigenous resistance, whose defeat was necessary for the triumph of civilization and the ultimate emergence of the nation, but rather, in an astonishing assertion, "the greatest man that ever lived upon the American shores" (290). Describing that greatness and its legacy, Apess offers a eunomic vision of Indigenous traditions through which, we are to understand, contemporary Native America, incorporating consonant elements of Christianity, might seek a vital resurgence.

Unlike Emerson, who would transcend evil through enthusiastic acts of the imagination, Apess would, as one part of his conceptual project, bring the reality of past and present evils to wider attention, challenging the convenient occlusions of cultural memory. *Eulogy* includes frequent reminders, therefore, of the violence involved—and typically forgotten—in forging the colonial world. We are told, for instance, of mass murders occurring before King Philip's War—"In 1619 a number of Indians went on board of a ship, by order of their chief, and the whites set upon them and murdered them without mercy" (282–83)—and after it:

> Upon the banks of [the] Ohio, a party of two hundred white warriors, in 1757 or about that time, came across a settlement of Christian Indians and falsely accused them of being warriors, to which they denied, but all to no purpose; they were determined to massacre them all. They, the Indians, then asked liberty to prepare for the fatal hour. The white savages then gave them one hour, as the historian said. They then prayed together; and in tears and cries, upon their knees, begged pardon of each other, of all they had done, after which they informed the white savages that they were now ready. One white man then begun with a mallet and knocked them down and continued his work until he had killed fifteen, with his own hand; then, saying it ached, he gave his commission to another. And thus they continued till they had massacred nearly ninety men, women, and children, all these innocent of any crime. (309)

In light of such testimony, Euro-America, implicated in genocidal outrages which made possible its political ascendance, loses its moral authority in chronicling its own and Natives' past. The nation's development has depended, Apess insists, on "white savagery," and a just renovation of the contemporary social order must take account of that ugly history.

As he unsettles and exposes the historical record, Apess points to stark divergences between the kind of rule practiced by Euro-Americans and Native Americans. In a particularly trenchant passage, he implores his (no doubt largely white) readership to overcome a conditioned blindness and see past depredations—and their ongoing dysnomic impact—more fully:

> Our groves and hunting grounds are gone, our dead are dug up, our council fires are put out, and a foundation was laid in the first Legislature to enslave our people, by taking from them all rights, which has been strictly adhered to ever since. Look at the disgraceful laws, disfranchising us as citizens. Look at the treaties made by Congress, all broken. Look at the deep rooted plans laid, when a territory becomes a state, that after so many years the laws shall be extended over the Indians that live within their boundaries. (306)

Two centuries of blinkered Euro-American *auto-nomia* are characterized in terms that further illustrate the destructive senses of the Greek verb *nemo* as fiery consumption or ulcerous spread. As Apess writes, "A fire, a canker, [was] created by the Pilgrims from across the Atlantic, to burn and destroy my poor unfortunate brethren, and it cannot be denied" (306).[4] According to this revisionist history, early settlers consumed all that stood before them, advancing across the continent in caustic self-pasture. Present-day New England remains afflicted, moreover, by a cancerous rule: "And will the sons of the Pilgrims aid in putting out the fire and destroying the canker that will ruin all that their fathers left behind them to destroy?" (306). Any honest attempt to grapple with the nation's history and to secure the autonomy of Native America must begin with an acknowledgment of ongoing injustices rooted, for Apess, in Euro-America's denial of Native selfhood and commitment to its own unfettered autonomy.

Against this mode of self-rule Apess posits a wholesome, redemptive alternative, itself obscured by the jingoism of "official" history but nevertheless preserved by remnant Native peoples. However idealistically, he positions Natives as consistently upholding an inherently peaceful ethos:

> Now, while we sum up this subject, does it not appear that the cause of all wars from beginning to end was and is for the want of good usage? That the whites have always been the aggressors, and the wars, cruelties, and bloodshed is a job of their own seeking, and not the Indians? Did you ever know of Indians hurting those who was kind to them? No. We have a thousand witnesses to the contrary. (307)

As in his autobiographical narratives, Apess condemns the hypocrisy of white Christians from the seventeenth century down to the contemporary moment and finds in the actual behavior of Native Americans an authentic expression of the faith's ideals of compassion and neighborliness. Invoking one of the most celebrated statements attributed to a representative of Native culture—quoted by Jefferson in *Notes* and no doubt familiar to much of the audience listening to or reading *Eulogy*—he drives home the contrast:

> The speech of Logan, the white man's friend, is no doubt fresh in your memory, that he intended to live and die the friend of the white man; that he always fed them and gave them the best his cabin afforded; and he appealed to them if they had not been well used; to which they never denied. After which they murdered all of his family in cool blood, which roused his passions to be revenged upon the whites. This circumstance is but one in a thousand. (309)

It is, again, the partiality of Euro-American vision, its willful blindness, which has only seen, and remembered, the decontextualized revenge of its antagonists. A broader vision of the nation's history would reveal compelling virtues in Native peoples absent in their oppressors.

The cultural negotiations taking place in Apess's critiques are complex and to some extent parallel those carried out by Occom. Like his predecessor, though in a much more sustained and trenchant form, Apess affirms his own Christianity while pointing out the failure of whites to fulfill the faith's ideals. In a remarkable passage quite distinct from Occom's occasional jibes at particular Christian representatives, however, he goes so far as to suggest that, in light of the atrocities committed by Christians, "every man of color" ought to consider "the 22nd of December [the purported date of the Pilgrims' landing] and the 4th of July" as "days of mourning and not of joy" (286) and "fast and pray to the great Spirit, the Indian's God, who deals out mercy to his red children, and not destruction" (286). This prophetic proposal is not repeated or elaborated in *Eulogy*, but it illustrates, startlingly, the kind of radical unsettlement Apess seeks, as well, perhaps, as his (understandably guarded) endorsement of distinctively Native traditions. In her personal essay "The Great Spirit" (first published in 1902 as "Why I Am a Pagan"), Zitkala-Ša will launch a similar criticism of Christian abuses and explicitly offer a benevolent alternative in her Native paganism. The final three Native authors of this study—Momaday, Erdrich, and Vizenor—will go even further in charting the specific features of "the Indian's God," a discrete Indigenous *themis* fully informing the life of a people and their eunomic autonomy.

Apess's treatment of Philip reflects another attitude he seeks to highlight as common to Indigenous peoples and to the identities he would preserve—an emphasis not on single figures but on collective wholes. Though the great leader is lauded for his exceptional virtues, *Eulogy* insists that his importance lies, finally, in what he epitomizes about Native culture more generally and what his example might provoke in terms of contemporary reforms affecting entire communities. As David L. Moore argues in his examination of the vision that emerges in *Eulogy*, Apess's reclamation of Philip "is communal, not personal or individualistic. His rhetorical logic has a directly social sense" (131). The opening of the work makes this orientation clear, as Apess declares that, far from simply seeking to lionize one man, his primary intent is to narrate the specific virtues of a people, to "bring before you beings made by the God of Nature, and in whose hearts and heads he has planted sympathies that shall live forever in the memory of the world, whose brilliant talents shone in the display of natural things, so that the most cultivated, whose powers shown with equal luster, were not able to prepare mantles to cover the burning elements of an uncivilized world" (277). On the foundation, that is, of Philip's "purer virtues" and "noble traits" (277), larger and stronger assertions of collective Native pride and autonomy might be built.

In imagining a speech Philip might make concerning the losses faced by Native Americans, Apess singles out the value of specific traditions:

> Brothers, you see this vast country before us, which the Great Spirit gave to our fathers and us; you see the buffalo and deer that now are our support. Brothers, you see these little ones, our wives and children, who are looking to us for food and raiment; and you now see the foe before you, that they have grown insolent and bold; that all our ancient customs are disregarded; the treaties made by our fathers and us are broken, and all of us insulted; our council fires disregarded, and all the ancient customs of our fathers; our brothers murdered before our eyes, and their spirits cry to us for revenge. Brothers, these people from the unknown world will cut down our groves, spoil our hunting and planting grounds, and drive us and our children from the graves of our fathers, and our council fires, and enslave our women and children. (295)

Native life is intimately linked, here and elsewhere, with the natural order, as Apess underscores the importance of communality and historical continuity, of "council fires ... and all the ancient customs of our fathers."

Apess's repeated associations of Natives with the nonhuman environment clearly emphasize a crucial element in his definition of an Indigenous *themis*. European colonizers, he suggests, came "into a country where nature shone in beauty, spreading her wings over the vast continent, sheltering beneath her shades those natural sons of an Almighty Being" (279). Though Euro-America's ulcerous autonomy has wrongly assumed that the eradication of Native America is part of a divine plan, themistic authority in fact sponsors, Apess insists, a more benevolent vision of personal and collective self-rule. That vision—of a profound neighborliness enshrined in Christian ideals but actually evidenced in Indigenous lifeways—is revealed through the natural order itself: "If such theologians would only study the works of nature more, they would understand the purposes of good better than they do: that the favor of the Almighty was good and holy, and all his nobler works were made to adorn his image, by being his grateful servants and admiring each other as angels, and not, as they say, to drive and devour each other" (287). Apess's accounts of Philip, "the hero of the wilderness" (277), posit an extraordinary, eunomic blending of the human with the divine order of the natural world as the primordial foundation of Indigenous life. Where George Washington was "assisted by all the knowledge that art and science could give," Philip, as a representative of Native peoples, "was naked as to any of these things, possessing only what nature, his mother, had bestowed upon him" (297). He achieved his greatness, finally, as a "son of nature, with nature's talents alone" (305). We encounter here, in other words, a sketch of Indigenous *eunomia* as it has existed and as it might, in spite of Euro-American efforts to extinguish it, be preserved in future generations. Apess thus limns the essential foundations of eunomic autonomy as it has been modeled in Indigenous peoples: a self-rule informed and licensed by the natural order environing human communities.

Fierce public debates about Indian removal form an important political backdrop to *Eulogy*, which invokes the Cherokee several times. We might turn now to Emerson's own remarks about the subject as a way of further clarifying Apess's position and his connection to later authors engaged in this study. Two years after the publication of *Nature*, Emerson protested what came to be known as the Trail of Tears in a public letter to President Martin Van Buren. The Cherokee Nation, he argued, had been cheated, the will of the American people ignored, and a false acquiescence to removal written into law. Though Emerson was clearly sympathetic to the plight of the Cherokee and ashamed of what removal policies suggested about his nation, his understanding of Indigenous peoples did not posit their cultural equality in relation to Euro-Americans. As he suggests early in his letter, what recommends the Cherokee, in particular, are their efforts to throw off "primitive" habits and surrender to assimilation:

> Even in our distant State some good rumor of their worth and civility has arrived. We have learned with joy their improvement in the social arts. We have read their newspapers. We have seen some of them in our schools and colleges. In common with the great body of the American people, we have witnessed with sympathy the painful labors of these red men to redeem their own race from the doom of

eternal inferiority, and to borrow and domesticate in the tribe the arts and customs of the Caucasian race. ("Letter" 49–50)

Emerson's assumptions do not suggest an autonomous future for Native Americans, who are given the option of languishing in inferiority or blending invisibly into the dominant *nomos*.[5]

As Apess's writings indicate, and as Vizenor's notion of survivance will ultimately suggest, there exists for Indigenous peoples a third, redemptive possibility in which they would reject their positioning at the inferior end of a presumed cultural binary and, in the cultivation of a eunomic autonomy, mediate Euro-American culture according to their own traditions. In the remaining Native authors considered in this study, the redemptive possibilities of those mediations—developing and finally fulfilling Apess's commitment to historical, communal interconnectedness—will continue their ascendance.

THREE

Lighting Out, Circling In
Mark Twain and Sarah Winnemucca

MARK TWAIN'S *Adventures of Huckleberry Finn* (1884) illustrates a critical inflection point in the trajectory of Euro-American autonomy we have been tracking. From Emerson's exaltation of self-rule we transition here to a more equivocal account of its contemporary potential. Though Twain affirms the enduring appeal of the self's separation from its *nomos,* he challenges Jefferson's and Emerson's faith in its productive possibilities: an essentially private communion with *themis* still remains rewarding, but prospects for the self's wholesome distancing from other selves, given a sprawling dysnomia and a themistic order now understood as ambiguously benevolent, have dimmed significantly. Huck Finn's efforts to transcend the constraints of his nomistic world are, at last, rather limited and precarious. Significant shadows emerge, moreover, around the expression of autonomy, as a range of predatory figures, thematically linked to Huck himself, indicate the destructive potential of the self's license to reject its nomistic inheritance. Twain charts here, I suggest, incipient forms of an isolate, pathological self-rule whose development will be explored, with mounting pessimism, by Hemingway, Heller, and DeLillo.

In Sarah Winnemucca's *Life among the Piutes: Their Wrongs and Claims* (1883), the trajectory of Native American autonomy continues its ascent, acquiring new vigor in its affirmation of possibilities for nourishing collaboration between Native selves and the broader nomistic world. Winnemucca's endorsement of a cooperative, communal form of autonomy stands in stark contrast to Huck's distrust of family and troubled preference for personal detachment. She presents here, with a keen sense of outrage at past and ongoing abuses but more optimistically and with less Christian alloy than Apess before her, a case for increased Native *engagement* with and inclusion within the Euro-American social order. Acting in the role of mediator for the Paiutes, Winnemucca appeals to the value and viability of maintaining a distinctively Indigenous selfhood—founded on eunomic principles—while negotiating assimilation. In vivid descriptions of her own bicultural status and efforts to secure autonomy for her people, she models the kinds of adaptation she seeks, in ways significantly more detailed, inclusive, and sanguine in their imagination of how nomistic integration might actually be lived than those offered by Apess in his own autobiographical writing. Natives may, Winnemucca affirms, plausibly assume an equal place among whites, and reciprocal relations may be maintained between genders as well as races. If, in Huck, the concept of Euro-American autonomy begins to be reduced to something like a tragic (boyish) fantasy, alluring but doomed, Winnemucca both exposes the destructive consequences of that fantasy and offers a promising alternative—one grounded in Paiute traditions and incorporating women's critical participation in nomistic life. In doing so she sets the stage, as the following chapter seeks to demonstrate, for Zitkala-Ša's unprecedented affirmations of Indigenous autonomy.

The notions of self-rule Twain explores through Huck Finn, though deployed in adolescent homespun, have a good deal in common with those of Jefferson and Emerson. For Huck, the natural world is a locus of themistic potency and authority, and he finds confirmation there of his instinct for nomistic detachment as he exposes mere convention to skeptical inquiry. Withdrawing to the woods, he broods on the apparent inefficacy of ritual prayer, finally concluding that its potential has been misrepresented to him and "there ain't nothing in it" (Twain 19). Critically, in Huck's sylvan retreat the selflessness counseled (if not always practiced) by his female guardians also appears decidedly suspect:

> [The Widow Douglas] said the thing a body could get by praying for it was "spiritual gifts." This was too many for me, but she told me what she meant—I must help other people, and do everything I could for other people, and look out for them all the time, and never think about myself. This was including Miss Watson, as I took it.

> I went out in the woods and turned it over in my mind a long time, but I couldn't see no advantage about it—except for the other people; so at last I reckoned I wouldn't worry about it any more, but just let it go. (19)

An Emersonian at least in this sense of trusting himself and his direct experience, Huck is disposed to let a good deal of inherited authority fall away. Like the ideal seer described in *Nature,* his gaze—when he can fully claim it—is radically prospective, and, notwithstanding his vulnerability to Tom Sawyer's book-sourced fantasies, he consistently enjoys "an original relation to the universe" (*Nature* 3). As Huck tells us in his rejection of the biblical Moses, whose associations with *collective* autonomy and scriptural authority make him an especially good foil, he "don't take no stock in dead people" (Twain 10). Living presences and the exigencies of survival are compelling realities, and Huck would confront them without mediation. His declarations of independence, memorably charming in their expression, clearly suggest a potential to build, as Emerson's poet had counseled, his own world out of his visionary experiences and communion with nature (*Nature* 39). This unschooled boy sees, we are to assume, more rightly than the *nomos* he has been born into, and his moral discoveries illuminate some of its grotesque faults.

And yet, Twain's novel also emphasizes its protagonist's weakness in translating these discoveries into positive action, his obvious and tragic inadequacy in helping to bring about, as an ideal Emersonian, a "correspondent revolution in things" (*Nature* 39). Where Emerson, in a burst of hyperbolic hopefulness, allows his prophetic poet to imagine that an inspirited self might "[draw] beautiful faces, warm hearts, wise discourse, and heroic acts, around its way, until evil is no more seen" (39), Twain invests his work with a bracing pessimism about the self's powers to change the world in which it must live. In spite of its appeal, Huck's instinct for liberty does not, in fact, herald much in the way of creative potential. Personal autonomy, as he seeks it, is largely a matter of so-called negative liberty, a freedom *from* what would inhibit him. Though he has ample reason to want to flee human authorities, having known the tyranny of his father, Pap, as well as that of the Widow

Douglas and Miss Watson, his commitment to movement—"All I wanted was to go somewhere; all I wanted was a change; I warn't particular" (Twain 10)—suggests a strong and definitive element of *mere* restlessness, a finally aimless evasion of constraining influences. Abducted and confined by Pap, he remains grateful simply for being freed from other tyrannies: "It was kind of lazy and jolly, laying off comfortable all day, smoking and fishing, and no books nor study.... It was pretty good times up in the woods there, take it all around" (34). Submission to the routines and restrictions of his nomistic world makes Huck "feel all cramped up" (10) and eager for exilic relief. He finds it, for a time, on the raft with Jim, as he tells us in one of the novel's most famous passages: "We said there warn't no home like a raft, after all. Other places do seem so cramped up and smothery, but a raft don't. You feel mighty free and easy and comfortable on a raft" (128). What the novel also insists upon, of course, is that such freedom, however esteemed, is only tenuously seized. The human order inevitably lays its claim to the raft, periodically separating its occupants from one another and depositing new tyrants, such as the King and Duke—fitting representatives of false authorities—into its fragile space.

Huck's efforts to shepherd himself often imply, in fact, an equivocal potential. Having escaped his father, who "said he was boss of his son" (31), he attempts to claim ownership of at least one part of Jackson's Island, ruling it on his own terms. Huck finds himself there, however, struggling to fight off a crippling feeling of isolation: "[The] next day I went exploring around down through the island. I was boss of it; it all belonged to me, so to say, and I wanted to know all about it; but mainly I wanted to put in the time" (49–50). Huck cannot feel at home in this natural environment, cannot assume anything approaching Jefferson's or Emerson's sense of mastery. He is left both fearing and desiring discovery, a predicament illustrated by his momentary retreat to the safety of a tree: "Well, I couldn't stay up there forever; so at last I got down, but I kept in the thick woods and on the lookout all the time" (50). Mere endurance becomes Huck's goal as he registers the insufficiency of an extreme (and seemingly permanent) detachment from his nomistic world. In these woods he does not finally discover, like his counterpart in *Nature*, a rejuvenating release from the social order but rather an onerous immersion in terminal, "lonesome" separation (49). The promise of self-rule falters in the absence of a viable pathway for the self's return, on empowered terms, to nomistic engagement.

Unlike his companion Jim, who has a focused and urgent purposiveness as a fugitive—the telos of familial reunion in a specific destination—there is no place, at last, Huck is going. His agency is constrained, as T. S. Eliot long ago pointed out, even at the site of his seeming emancipation from the nomistic world:

> But the river with its strong, swift current is the dictator to the raft or to the steamboat. It is a treacherous and capricious dictator.... [We] are continually reminded of the power and terror of Nature, and the isolation and feebleness of Man.... [Huck] must come from nowhere and be bound for nowhere. His is not the independence of the typical or symbolic "American Pioneer," but the independence of the vagabond. (24)

The "river god," as Eliot dubs it, pushes the raft's occupants where it will; if Jefferson or Emerson might channel themistic power in and for themselves, Twain's protagonist is, we are often reminded, humbly channeled *by* it.

Though in fact highly sociable through much of the novel, and capable of temporarily adapting himself to any number of domestic arrangements, Huck remains both attracted to the prospect of solitude and haunted by its morbid implications. Contrary to his claim about Moses, he does indeed, in one sense, take a great deal of stock in dead people—or rather in a variety of spectral forms which threaten him whenever he is alone. Repeatedly, if ambiguously, he expresses a yearning to join them:

> Then I set down in a chair by the window and tried to think of something cheerful, but it warn't no use. I felt so lonesome I most wished I was dead. The stars were shining, and the leaves rustled in the woods ever so mournful; and I heard an owl, away off, who-whooing about somebody that was dead, and a whippowill and a dog crying about somebody that was going to die; and the wind was trying to whisper something to me, and I couldn't make out what it was, and so it made

the cold shivers run over me. Then away out in the woods I heard that kind of a sound that a ghost makes when it wants to tell about something that's on its mind and can't make itself understood, and so can't rest easy in its grave, and has to go about that way every night grieving. I got so down-hearted and scared I did wish I had some company. (Twain 11)

J. Hillis Miller provocatively and aptly concludes that Huck has "so complete an openness to inhuman nature and to the presences of the dead within nature that it is as if Huck were already dead" (102). The two essential alternatives available to Twain's protagonist are, finally, self-corrosive: "If Huck chooses for silence and solitude, the book allows the reader no illusion about what these mean. They mean loss of language and a kinship with the dead. In solitude one becomes a kind of walking dead man, mute spectator of life. This, however, is preferable to the intolerable falsehood of existence within society" (103). Neither nomistic engagement nor disengagement might, finally, nourish such a self; every pasture, finally, is death-haunted. The bare themistic order implied here—though obviously leavened by the novel's comic dimensions and the ample distractions provided by Huck's spirited social interactions—anticipates that encountered, in increasingly grim permutations, by Hemingway's Nick, Heller's Slocum, and DeLillo's Packer, who discover, within dysnomic contexts, the strict limits or outright impossibility of pastoral relief and rejuvenation. In Huck, we might say, Twain limns the early stages of Euro-American autonomy's drift into desolate self-inhabitance, self-consumption, and finally self-destruction.

Nomistic detachment could, for Jefferson and Emerson, lead to beneficent communal results as autonomous selves share with others—heroically, when necessary—the wisdom they gain privately. Twain offers pointed indications, however, of the predominantly evasive nature of Huck's detachment and highlights the enormous obstacles he faces in any attempt to act on his privately gained wisdom. At his weakest moments, Huck expresses a miserable acquiescence to the corruption that envelops him. Reflecting on the exploitative practices of the King and Duke, for instance, he reveals a strong inclination to avoid, wherever possible, interference in others' affairs (a decidedly limp and morally dubious version of *laissez-faire*):

> But I never said nothing, never let on; kept it to myself; it's the best way; then you don't have no quarrels, and don't get into no trouble. If they wanted us to call them kings and dukes, I hadn't no objections, 'long as it would keep peace in the family; and it warn't no use to tell Jim, so I didn't tell him. If I never learnt nothing else out of pap, I learnt that the best way to get along with his kind of people is to let them have their own way. (Twain 137)

Given his experiences with Pap and his adoptive caretakers, family itself is, for Huck, heavily suspect, and his inclination to bury his moral qualms in order to survive within this malevolent version of it suggests, as ever, the value he places on personally eluding tyranny, rather than—as in the Emersonian ideal—attempting to resist and transform it.

Twain seems particularly concerned with drawing attention to the frailty of human goodness—qualifying a faith, that is, in what Jefferson called "that moral sense of right and wrong, which, like the sense of tasting and feeling, in every man makes a part of his nature" (*Notes* 98), and what Emerson posited as "the moral law [that] lies at the centre of nature and radiates to the circumference" (*Nature* 21). By the novel's end, Huck remains something of an ambivalent abolitionist, and he continues to accept slavery as essentially legitimate and to condemn himself, at least in some measure, for heeding the inner voice that would recognize his friend's humanity. In spite of what he learns from his relationship with Jim, he continues to feel that what is nomistically sanctioned—slavery itself—is divinely sanctioned, too:

> The more I studied about this, the more my conscience went to grinding me, and the more wicked and low-down and ornery I got to feeling. And at last, when it hit me all of a sudden that here was the plain hand of Providence slapping me in the face and letting me know my wickedness was being watched all the time from up there in heaven, whilst I was stealing a poor old woman's nigger that hadn't ever done me no harm, and now was showing me that there's One that's always on the lookout, and ain't agoing to allow no such

miserable doings to go only so fur and no further, I most dropped in my tracks I was so scared. (Twain 226)

When, in what is often identified as the novel's moral climax, Huck decides to accept the consequences of protecting Jim—"All right, then, I'll *go* to hell" (228)—he naively acknowledges the themistic force of his *nomos*, from which he has not been able to detach himself. He may defy convention but does not finally condemn its legitimacy. How easily Huck may be drawn in by corrupt authority is made clear in the novel's much-derided final chapters, where he accedes, in a seeming betrayal of all his "moral sense" has revealed, to what Tom calls "the best fun he ever had in his life" (262), the extended torture of Jim at the Phelps' plantation.

Though the compassion Huck shows for Jim during his most resolute moments suggests, without doubt, a redemptive potential in the self, in other passages feelings themselves—what might bind a community's members together—come to seem rather volatile and suspect. The point is made with comic gusto in Twain's send-up of the sentimental genre during Huck's visit to the Grangerfords. Huck's description of Emmeline, a deceased teenager obsessed with morbid paintings and poetry, exposes that genre as a kind of monstrous farce, a peculiarly mechanized deployment of overblown emotional clichés. "She didn't ever have to stop to think," Huck remarks of Emmeline's poetic powers. "She warn't particular; she could write about anything you choose to give her to write about just so it was sadful" (115–16). We are invited to laugh at Huck for his naive admiration but also to credit him, in other parts of the novel, for his own, authentic version of sentimental response. On the raft with Jim, he hears and is deeply moved by his companion's description of the wrong he committed against his daughter. *This* sort of sentimentalism has an ennobling potential, and it ultimately leads to Huck's moral revelation concerning Jim's humanity and decision not to betray his friend by returning him to slavery. Crucially, however, that revelation takes place in the temporarily sheltered, effectively a-nomistic conditions of raft life, apart from the corrupting influences of the broader nomistic world. On the shore, we are to understand, sentimentalism takes on fallen, conventionalized forms—

not just in ridiculous works of "art" but in related expressions of misplaced emotion, as in the murderous feud carried on by Emmeline's relatives against the Shepherdsons, their (equally vicious and irrational) neighbors. What remains dubious in Twain's novel, seemingly, is what Jefferson and Emerson robustly affirmed: the potential for translating private emotional experiences into genuine, positive, reformative expression within a community of other selves. The barriers to such translations are pronounced for Hemingway's Nick, in whom a fragile sentimentalism seemingly has little social outlet, and close to absolute for Heller's Slocum and DeLillo's Packer, whose feelings are, at last, essentially solipsistic.

Huck's ultimate plan to "light out for the Territory" (307) further underscores the equivocal terms of his autonomy. He has, of course, made similar attempts before: in the novel's second paragraph he relates that he "lit out" from the Widow Douglas's after he "couldn't stand it [or her] no longer" but was then enticed to return by Tom Sawyer: "[He] hunted me up and said he was going to start a band of robbers, and I might join if I would go back to the widow and be respectable. So I went back" (9). Tom also eyes the frontier, proposing that the three of them "slide out of here, one of these nights, and get an outfit, and go for howling adventures amongst the Injuns, over in the Territory, for a couple of weeks or two" (307). Asserting at least a *desire* to detach himself from such entanglements, Huck tells us that he intends to make the trip "ahead of the rest" (307). As Roy Harvey Pearce explains, Twain slyly alludes here

> to the Boomer movement that was a prime factor in the taking over of Indian lands, 'sivilizing' the Territory, and creating another American state.... With the curious prescience that Mark Twain gives him, [Huck] knows that in antebellum days (as Mark Twain surely knew in the summer of 1883), even in the Territory, he will be only one step ahead of the rest: Boomers, Dukes and Dauphins, Aunt Sallies, Colonel Sherburns, and Wilkses—civilizers all. (93, 95)

Some of the ironic dimensions of Euro-American autonomy are illustrated in that mass movement: seeking liberation in the very place it is being denied Native Americans, restless pioneers move, herdlike, into "empty" lands, where they reproduce a version of the old nomistic order. Huck, we are to assume, will soon be joined by them.[1]

Twain's novel had already suggested the suspect quality of autonomy, of course, in a series of characters who share Huck's love of negative liberty but not his moral ballast. Pap and Tom flout social norms as they victimize others, pursuing versions of a predatory self-rule. Most conspicuous among the narrative's dark doubles, though, are the King and Duke, whose ambitions insistently echo Huck's. As the Duke claims in spinning his false lineage: "'My great grandfather, eldest son of the Duke of Bridgewater, fled to this country about the end of the last century, to breathe the pure air of freedom" (Twain 134). The con men share with Huck a commitment to mobility—the Duke, planning his escape from the Wilkses' with their fortune, declares that he, too, is "for knocking off and lighting out" (190)—though in them it is paired with a practical need to avoid nomistic avengers. The nation's own commitment to negative liberty has, the novel makes obvious, historically not been translated into *positive* liberty—the freedom to develop one's potential—for the enslaved. Though he is writing decades after abolition, Twain represents versions of personal and collective self-rule that do not lead, inexorably, to human flourishing but in fact seem to make possible all manner of outrageous exploitations. He pessimistically emphasizes here the uncertain potential of Euro-American autonomy; self-shepherding, in spite of Jefferson's and Emerson's hopes, does not necessarily deliver individuals or communities into wholesome territory.

With the isolated representatives of Euro-American autonomy to come in Hemingway, Heller, and DeLillo, we find the innocence in the voice of Twain's protagonist (reflecting a goodness that survives in him no matter the coercions of his *nomos*) gradually drained away. What Huck discerns as the hostile elements of *themis*—nagging shadows on his ambitions for self-rule—will take on much darker shades, shifting autonomy, at last, into a mode of outright self-destruction.

In the opening paragraph of *Life among the Piutes: Their Wrongs and Claims,* Sarah Winnemucca relates that the "first white people" arrived in Northern Paiute territory "like a lion, yes, like a roaring lion, and have continued so ever since" (5).² She then turns to her grandfather Truckee's enthusiastic welcome of the settlers: "When the news [of the arrival] was brought to my grandfather, he asked what they looked like? When told that they had hair on their faces, and were white, he jumped up and clasped his hands together, and cried aloud,–'My white brothers,—my long-looked for white brothers have come at last!'" (5). Truckee's receptivity derives, we learn, from a traditional creation story. In the world's beginning there existed "a happy family" (6) composed of light- and dark-skinned children, but conflict among them caused their separation across an ocean for many generations. An eventual reunion was also prophesied: "the nation that sprung from the white children will some time send some one to meet us and heal all the old trouble" (7). The text goes on to document, in its account of a vulnerable people struggling to survive the presence of a "roaring lion," all manner of new troubles between light and dark peoples.

Winnemucca's invocation of her grandfather's initial optimism does not simply function, however, as an ironic departure point for the narrative. It gestures, rather, toward an enduring belief shared (and cleverly adapted) by her family members in the decades after first contact: that intercultural cooperation is possible and desirable and that the future of the Paiutes depends on it. Where Twain seems to eulogize the Euro-American self's waning possibilities for autonomy and terminal aspirations in solitary flight, Winnemucca affirms the potential of its Native counterpart in a staunchly optimistic and communal engagement with the nomistic world. For her, a benevolent themistic power might still sponsor a revitalized *nomos:* "When I think of my past life, and the bitter trials I have endured, I can scarcely believe I live, and yet I do; and, with the help of Him who notes the sparrow's fall, I mean to fight for my down-trodden race while life lasts" (6).

Born "near 1844" (5) in what is now Nevada, Winnemucca recalls being deeply afraid in her youth of early white settlers (those who, like Huck, had lit out for her people's territory) before gradually coming to embrace her role as a cultural mediator. As a teenager she went with her younger sister to live with a white family and acquired there a literacy in English as well as a deep understanding of Euro-American culture.³ Rejoining her family, Winnemucca participated in stage productions that dramatized the plight of Native Americans and highlighted her ostensibly "royal" status. Her charismatic performances gradually transformed her into a minor celebrity—a "Paiute Princess," as she was billed in advertisements. By adulthood, Winnemucca was fluent in a number of Native dialects as well as Spanish and English. She eventually worked for the US Army as a guide and translator and negotiated key diplomatic agreements between the Paiutes, other western tribes, and government overseers. In 1870 she first gained prominence as a writer, penning a letter to the superintendent of Indian Affairs for Nevada in which she outlined ongoing abuses by reservation agents; reprinted in *Harper's* magazine, the work helped bring her and the Paiutes themselves to national attention. Over the next two decades Winnemucca became an influential voice for Native American civil rights, delivering hundreds of lectures on both coasts, meeting with high-ranking government officials to discuss official policies (including a brief visit with President Rutherford B. Hayes), and cooperating with Euro-American reformers to raise awareness—and improve the actual conditions—of Native life. She founded the Peabody Indian School in 1885, a relatively short-lived but prescient model of Native pedagogy and self-rule. The bilingual institution, devoted to preserving traditional lifeways, kept its students in their homeland and in their families' care, offering an alternative to assimilationist boarding schools.

Winnemucca's public lectures became the basis for *Life among the Piutes,* a work that combines autobiography, ethnography, regional history, and cultural manifesto. Its eight chapters document the specifics of tribal customs and values, initial relations between the Paiutes and Euro-American settlers, key events such as the Bannock War of 1878, and Winnemucca's own complex role in furthering her tribe's endurance. Like Apess, one of her central goals as an author was to expose an obscured history so that contemporary dysnomic realities, and the plausibility of wholesome alternatives to them, might be fully understood. Winnemucca carefully documents, therefore, from the rare literary perspective of a Native woman, a traumatic record of settler incursions, massacres of innocents, sexual predation, intertribal strife, the steady loss of ancestral lands and lifeways, continual threats of starvation, and the sundry exploitations of reservation agents—as well as an extraordinary resilience on the part of Indigenous peoples in their efforts to survive.

Significantly, in constructing this narrative Winnemucca's emphasis falls not where Twain places it in Huck, on the fate of a single self, but on that of an entire people. The specifics of her personal response to the world—her private fears and desires—are largely set aside here as she tells a life story meant to direct attention toward the Paiutes and other Indigenous peoples. As Arnold Krupat aptly remarks, in a seminal discussion of the "synecdochic self" evidenced in Native American autobiographical writing, the "very title [*Life among the Piutes: Their Wrongs and Claims*] proclaims [Winnemucca's] individual life as comprehensible foremost in relation to the collective experience of her tribe" (229). The self we encounter here is, in other words, a part that cannot be understood separately from a larger whole, its individuality intimately and irrevocably bound up with, and finally subordinated to, the interests of a large community (and, as we shall see, that community's themistic worldview). Such communality is reflected, Winnemucca contends, in traditional Paiute political life, where power is diffused and the wide participation of tribal members encouraged: "The chief's tent is the largest tent, and it is the council-tent, where every one goes who wants advice. In the evenings the head men go there to discuss everything, for the chiefs do not rule like tyrants; they discuss everything with their people, as a father would in his family" (52). For the Paiutes, potent social bonds define one's identity, and a separation from them does not promise, as it does for Huck, an alluring freedom: "They would rather all die at once than be parted" (54).

Winnemucca's second chapter, "Domestic and Social Moralities," sets forth the values of her people and affirms, finally, the legitimacy of Native civilization. Where Twain insistently points to the destructive, ludicrous quality of social conventions and the failings of various parental role models from within Euro-America, Winnemucca carefully explains here how a sophisticated set of rituals productively guides the young into adulthood and helps preserve collective ideals. "Our children," she explains, "are very carefully taught to be good" (45). The close focus Winnemucca maintains on the routine conditions of Native life distinguishes her work from Apess's: where *Eulogy on King Philip*, for instance, attempts to define the lineaments of a beleaguered but persisting cultural tradition by exploring the representative qualities of a grand historical figure, *Life among the Piutes* turns its attention to the communal and quotidian, providing a detailed, compelling portrait of a living culture. That culture might, for Winnemucca, take its place alongside Euro-America's—in fact, she makes an explicit case, sometimes in highly idealistic terms, for the superiority of the Paiutes, contrasting their generosity and neighborliness with Euro-American rapacity, cruelty, and self-seeking. Her people practice their own version of Christian principles, she avers, and—as Occom and Apess had suggested—seem more genuinely aligned in their actual behavior with the ideals of Christianity: "But the whites have not waited to find out how good the Indians were, and what ideas they had of God, just like those of Jesus, who called him Father, just as my people do, and told men to do to others as they would be done by, just as my people teach their children to do" (51). Deftly countering racist assumptions about Native women in particular, Winnemucca describes the elaborate forms of courtship that lead to marriage and the extraordinary devotion typically cultivated between all family members. Modesty, loyalty, and a conservative regard for order and the endurance of traditions are, she insists, core elements of the Paiutes' ethical code.

That code is fundamentally informed and nourished by *themis,* and the Paiutes' shamanic "doctors" and "doctresses" play a special role in maintaining it as they "communicate with the holy spirits from heaven" (15). In writing *Life among the Piutes,* Winnemucca acts, I suggest, as a Paiute shaman herself, diagnosing nomistic ills responsible for personal and collective pathologies and prescribing the formation of new, therapeutic circles that would include both Euro-America and Native America. Anthropologist Harold Olafson, summarizing his research into the traditions of Northern Paiute culture in the 1960s, explains how shamans pursue holistic cures extending to "the moral-ethical components of negligent behaviors" (19). The reintegration of a community's alienated members to "the social world" is the shaman's ultimate goal:

This network of moral-mystical interdependence among people, with the pact between shaman and spirit at the center, probably did much to define the limits of Northern Paiute society. It is in the area of "wrong" behaviors that White doctors are found lacking. They are unable to go beyond physical manifestations of sickness and injury to their moral roots (e.g. to witchcraft). For this reason, Northern Paiute shamans do not have a residue of "diffuse health aberrations" which plague the Western practitioner with his fixation on the diseased organ and inability to diagnose in terms of the social milieu of the patient as a whole person. (19–20)

We may look ahead here, in considering the significance of this inclusive, relational view of selfhood and the treatment of its pathologies, to Momaday's representation of the healing processes undertaken by his protagonist Abel in *House Made of Dawn*. Encountering his own set of shamanic figures, and rejecting Western cures oblivious to the "moral roots" of his illness, Abel will, at last, begin to reintegrate himself with Indigenous cultural traditions and their connection to a vital *themis*. Winnemucca's patients include not only her own people, whose lifeways have been critically disrupted by settler culture, but pathological Euro-Americans, too. In her shamanic role, she will assess the broader context in which illnesses emerge for both cultures.

The radical negative liberty available to many Euro-American men in the frontier region—what Huck dreams of—has, Winnemucca makes clear, fostered highly corrosive forms of personal and collective autonomy. Corrupt government agents such as Major William V. Rinehart, whose authority over the Malheur Reservation has essentially gone unchecked, seek to dominate (and effectively annihilate) Indigenous populations through aggressive military action and by siphoning off essential resources.[4] Like a more socially respectable and powerful version of Twain's King and Duke, Rinehart is indifferent to the welfare of the vulnerable and devotes himself to profiting from those he can exploit. He becomes Winnemucca's epitome of a sickly leader, one who utterly betrays communal responsibilities in advancing his own interests—practicing, we might say, an autonomy which assumes an atomistic self and a rule reflecting the Greek verb *nemo* in its sense of ulcerous, consumptive spread. Winnemucca does maintain a faith in the potential of white leaders to work honestly for the good of Indigenous peoples—and commends one of them, Sam Parrish, for his virtuous behavior—but suggests that Paiute traditions best model what healthy leadership (and followership) looks like. The tribe's chiefs, she notes, eschew personal profit as they commit themselves to familial obligations: "They work with their people, and they are always poor for the following reason. It is the custom with my people to be very hospitable. When people visit them in their tents, they always set before them the best food they have, and if there is not enough for themselves they go without" (54). For Winnemucca, such practices epitomize a nourishing reciprocal self-pasture and the sacred circularity of communal relations.

Another pathology, also associated with the negative liberty afforded Euro-American men, is located in the sexual violence directed at Native girls and women. Winnemucca punctuates *Life among the Piutes* with numerous descriptions of abduction and rape, including assaults on her own family members: "The men whom my grandpa called his brothers would come into our camp and ask my mother to give our sister to them. They would come in at night, and we would all scream and cry; but that would not stop them" (34). For the Paiutes, such abuses have produced essentially lethal forms of nomistic illness: "My people have been so unhappy for a long time they wish now to *disincrease,* instead of multiply. The mothers are afraid to have more children, for fear they shall have daughters, who are not safe even in their mother's presence" (48). Under these conditions, the Paiutes' positive liberty is evacuated, as self-protective measures become, in effect, self-terminating.

In spite of such grim realities, Paiute traditions might, Winnemucca suggests once again, offer a curative balance to the predatory forms of masculinity that have plagued the Southwest. Augmenting a significant blankness in the writings of Occom and Apess, she highlights the salvific agency of women in Indigenous people's pursuit of autonomy. Though a gender hierarchy is seemingly enforced by the Paiutes, the tribe's political proceedings—which also rely on the sacred figure of the circle and its reciprocal relations—emphasize inclusiveness and grant women significant authority:

[If] the women are interested they can share in the talks. If there is not room enough inside, they all go out of doors, and make a great circle. The men are in the inner circle, for there would be too much smoke for the women inside. The men never talk without smoking first. The women sit behind them in another circle, and if the children wish to hear, they can be there too. The women know as much as the men do, and their advice is often asked. We have a republic as well as you. The council-tent is our Congress, and anybody can speak who has anything to say, women and all. They are always interested in what their husbands are doing and thinking about. And they take some part even in the wars. They are always near at hand when fighting is going on, ready to snatch their husbands up and carry them off if wounded or killed. (52–53)

We may recall here the first chapter of Twain's novel and Huck's spirited resistance to his female caretakers as the enforcers of a stifling nomistic code: "The Widow Douglas she took me for her son, and allowed she would sivilize me; but it was rough living in the house all the time, considering how dismal regular and decent the widow was in all her ways; and so when I couldn't stand it no longer I lit out. I got into my old rags and my sugar-hogshead again, and was free and satisfied" (Twain 9). Though he is harassed by his father and other male oppressors, Huck's yearning for self-rule seems particularly focused on an evasion of feminine authority and the domestic life it sponsors. In contrast, Winnemucca endorses a turn toward that authority as part of a broader healing process relevant to both Euro-America and Native America. "If women could go into your Congress," she contends, "I think justice would soon be done to the Indians" (53).

A crucial part of what women can offer, Winnemucca implies, is a sensitivity to feelings typically obscured and neglected in Euro-America's hypermasculinist operations. She often borrows, with obvious sincerity, the conventions of sentimental literature in order to make her moral pleas, and thus reverses the skepticism Twain deploys in his representation of the ridiculous Emmeline Grangerford. As Cheryl Walker explains:

> [One] can see the way Winnemucca's argument is positioned within the context of the 'culture of sentiment' that had nourished Elizabeth Peabody and Mary Peabody Mann [her East Coast patrons] for half a century. . . . Sarah's connection to them and the book she produced under their auspices represent the ongoing influence of sentimental reform ideology, its emphasis upon compassion and sacrifice in the face of an increasingly selfish and materialistic society. (149–50)

Winnemucca seeks out strong emotional responses in her readers and sometimes includes direct addresses meant to stir feelings of outrage and pity:

> Dear reader, I must tell a little more about my poor people, and what we suffer at the hands of our white brothers. Since the war of 1860 there have been one hundred and three (103) of my people murdered, and our reservations taken from us; and yet we, who are called blood-seeking savages, are keeping our promises to the government. Oh, my dear good Christian people, how long are you going to stand by and see us suffer at your hands?" (89)

Having identified the Paiutes as at least potentially ideal Christians, she leverages her readers' sense of religious responsibility to those who ought to be regarded, she insists, as spiritual peers:

> [Your] carbines rise upon the bleak shore, and your so-called civilization sweeps inland from the ocean wave; but, oh, my God! leaving its pathway marked by crimson lines of blood; and strewed by the bones of two races, the inheritor and the invader; and I am crying out to you for justice,—yes, pleading for the far-off plains of the West, for the dusky mourner, whose tears of love are pleading for her husband, or for their children, who are sent far away from them. (207)

The feelings which confirm familial bonds are, Winnemucca implies, a resource that might be trusted. Drawing on them, Euro-American definitions of the family must be expanded to include Native Americans.

We may turn for comparison again to Twain's novel, which proffers in Jim a man who, very much in harmony with Winnemucca, maintains profound commitments to familial life. Huck's suspicion of family, and mercurial relations with social life more generally, starkly contrast with his friend's utter dedication to kin. Jim's selfhood is, in other words, inextricably enmeshed with others in a way that seems affiliated with Paiute values but quite distinct from those of Huck, who has to learn to expand his own tight circle of moral concern. Jim's scathing judgment of his friend after being tricked aboard the raft, delivered with compelling authority, speaks precisely to the communal ethos that has been violated: "Dat truck dah is *trash;* en trash is what people is dat puts dirt on de head er dey fren's en makes 'em ashamed" (Twain 98). Hearing this, Huck seems to come to a profound moral realization—"It was fifteen minutes before I could work myself up to go and humble myself to a nigger; but I done it, and I warn't ever sorry for it afterwards, neither. I didn't do him no more mean tricks, and I wouldn't done that one if I'd a knowed it would make him feel that way" (98)—though he *will*, of course, ultimately play more tricks on Jim at the novel's end. Jim's defense of friendship and family act, in any case, as a revelatory indictment not just of Huck but of a culture's extension of sentiment more broadly. Like Winnemucca, Twain points out, in a protagonist otherwise to be admired for his social independence, the fatal limits of Euro-America's definition of communal obligations.

Although she does not linger over them, Winnemucca includes her own emotional responses in the narrative—she has been reduced to tears, we are told, because of her experiences in defending herself and her people—along with those of others who provide models, in effect, for responsive readers. Characteristically, she locates this potential to be moved not only in women but in men who have seen abuses perpetrated, too:

> While I was in Vancouver, Mr. Chapman, the interpreter, was sent over to Yakima to see if he could help my people. . . . He came back and told me my people were really starving. He said he never saw people in the condition they were in. He said he went into their tents to see if they had anything hidden away. He did not find anything; but he said he did it because Father Wilbur told him the people had plenty to eat. Sometimes they went four or five days without having a

thing to eat, nor had they any clothes. Poor man! the tears ran down his cheeks as he told me, and of course I cried. (243)

Winnemucca's implicit faith is that such emotions roused in readers encouraged to identify with the Paiutes and their plight may form the basis of redemptive political action. What is under siege in Twain's novel, and seemingly barred from wider social expression—an empathetic realization of the other's humanity—is affirmed here as a universal endowment which happens to be vitally developed in Paiute culture and which might be grafted onto Euro-American and Native relations. Sentiment might thus help further her shamanic enterprise, the formation of curative circles binding ostensible opposites. As Walker concludes, in describing Winnemucca's understanding of selfhood and communality: "Sarah's vision of the nation is not atomistic but familial. The community must be held together by loyalty and reciprocity; if necessary individuals must be prepared to sacrifice their own well-being for the good of others" (162). For Winnemucca there exists, that is, a nomistic world capable of redemptive emotional response, within which an improved moral life might be founded.

In a further illustration of her commitment to balance and reciprocity in regard to gender, Winnemucca also includes a number of scenes which describe her enacting a dynamic, physical intrepidity typically associated with male protagonists. Dramatic renderings of climactic scenes turn *Life among the Piutes,* at times, into a sort of western adventure story starring a female heroine (though one, as ever, whose *personal* virtues are carefully rendered as representative of her people, rather than simply individual excellence). During the Bannock War, for instance, Winnemucca takes on roles traditionally assigned, in both Euro-American and Native culture, to men, effecting a blending of gender roles and augmenting the imaginative possibilities conventionally ascribed to women. The Bannock tribe (originally affiliated with the Northern Paiute) entered into open conflict with the US military in 1878 and temporarily held Winnemucca's father and other family members hostage. Allying herself with the government soldiers against the Bannock (as well as some Paiutes) in the hope of resolving the conflict with as few casualties as possible, Winnemucca risked her own life in combat: "Yes, I went for the government when the officers could not get an Indian man or a white man to go for love or money. I, only an Indian woman, went and saved my father and his people" (164).

In acting as a translator and guide during the war, Winnemucca demonstrates a comprehensive knowledge of her home territory and its inhabitants and proves at least as capable a tracker as any man. Her narrative confirms her authority among the government agents themselves, who frequently defer to her knowledge: "Now, Sarah, you know this country better than we do, and you know what to do, and if we say go this way or that way you would blame us if anything should happen, and another thing we have come with you and are at your command. Whatever you say we will follow you" (156). In a climactic scene highlighting her intelligence, bravery, and usefulness as a bicultural interpreter, Winnemucca educates white soldiers about the significance of stone figures placed by Bannock warriors to fool those following them:

> Then General Howard called me and I went up to him. All the officers were there together. He said, "Sarah, what have you got to say now? The Indians seem to be there."
>
> "I have the same thing to say as before. I see nothing but rocks put there to deceive you."
>
> The officers took out their field-glasses and looked up and said, "Sarah, it surely looks like people there."
>
> I said, "Well, I can't say any more. Do as you think best."
>
> One of them gave me a field-glass and told me to look. I said, "I will show you that there are no Indians there. I will go up there."
>
> So I started to go, when General Howard called me back and said, "I don't want you to get killed. I will send the troops up."
>
> They found everything just as I had told them.
>
> How they did laugh that evening when we camped for the night. It is a way by which we Indians do deceive the white people by piling rocks on each other and putting round ones on the top to make them look like men. In this way we get time to get away from our enemy. (171)

Such scenes confirm—with a directness that has, admittedly, caused concern among some readers about the extent of her assimilation—

Winnemucca's faith in the possibilities of bicultural cooperation, even when it aligns her against other Native peoples.

Later scenes add further dimensions to Winnemucca's self-representation as a woman fully capable of taking on the role of warrior. She has, she makes clear, been more than willing to act violently when necessary. Isolated with her sister and pursued by hostile men bent, seemingly, on assault, she declares her willingness to defend herself: "[We] must," she declares, "die fighting" (229). On another occasion, Winnemucca strikes back against a man attempting to rape her: "I jumped up with fright and gave him such a blow right in the face. I said, 'Go away, or I will cut you to pieces, you mean man!' He ran out of the house, and Mr. Anderson got up and lighted a candle. There was blood on the side of the bed, and on my hands and the floor" (231). Blending the virtues of the sentimental heroine with those of the adventure hero, she enacts, once again, an integration of opposites and rebalances, as it were, the gendered relations of the Southwest.

Although Winnemucca generally focuses on essential similarities between Native beliefs and customs and those of Euro-America, she also points to crucial divergences in regard to Indigenous conceptions of the divine (and natural) order. Her direct and approving treatment of them signals another notable departure from Occom and Apess, practicing ministers who remain committed in the bulk of their writing (notwithstanding the occasional exceptions mentioned in earlier chapters) to orthodox Christianity. Winnemucca recalls that, as a child, she was terrified by a Methodist minister's insistence that "the blessed ones in heaven looked down and saw their friends burning and could not help them" (55). Against this vision of human division and eternal torment, which made her wish she were "unborn" (55), she sets its inclusive Indigenous counterpart: "[My] mother and the others told me . . . that it was only here that people did wrong and were in the hell that it made, and that those that were in the Spirit-land saw us here and were sorry for us. But we should go to them when we died, where there was never any wrongdoing, and so no hell. That is our religion" (55). Winnemucca prefigures here Zitkala-Ša's even more pointed critique of fire-and-brimstone theology, along with extended examinations by Momaday, Erdrich, and Vizenor of Native alternatives to the punitive, binary emphases of Christian monotheism. The Paiutes have, Winnemucca asserts, a strong and vivifying connection to a themistic order understood to be in harmony with Christianity's commitment to fraternal love but nevertheless encompassing a range of sacred presences in the nonhuman environment. The editor of *Life among the Piutes*, Mary Tyler Peabody Mann, who with her sister helped organize Winnemucca's lectures in the East and advanced her activism in a variety of ways, includes a rare footnote which highlights, from her perspective, what seems distinctively valuable about the "education in heart and mind" given to Paiute children:

> They are taught a great deal about nature; how to observe the habits of plants and animals. It is not unlikely that when something like a human communication is established between the Indians and whites, it may prove a fair exchange, and the knowledge of nature which has accumulated, for we know not how long, may enrich our early education as much as reading and writing will enrich theirs. (n51–52)

The potentiality of that enrichment was suggested by Occom's list of therapeutic "Herbs & Roots" and by Apess's vision of the natural world "alive with its sons and daughters" (32–33). It will be realized much more fully, as we shall see, in the versions of eunomic autonomy articulated by the Native authors examined later in this study.

Winnemucca offers her own summary of the Paiute's eunomic worldview in noting that though her people may not have the "worldly knowledge" of whites, they remain superior to their oppressors because of their access to *themis* within the natural world: "[They] can see the Spirit-Father in everything . . . [and the] beautiful world talks to them of their Spirit-Father" (259). This avowal suggests a basic correspondence with what Catherine S. Fowler and Sven Liljeblad describe as the Northern Paiutes' traditional animism: "[They] believed that power (*puha*) could reside in any natural object, including animals, plants, stones, water, and geographic features, and that it habitually resided in natural phenomena such as the sun and moon, thunder, clouds, and wind" (451). Where Huck's encounters with such "natural phenomena" bring him, at times, to shuddering considerations of his own isolation and mortality, Winnemucca would affirm their life-giving potency. The self-rule she imagines for the Paiutes would, ideally, be subsumed within this nonhuman environment and thus set the terms of collective life according to a fusion of natural and social orders.

Winnemucca's description of a pronghorn antelope hunt provides a dramatic illustration of this eunomic autonomy and its collective enactment in Paiute life. As she explains, antelope are captured by being "charmed" according to complex, ritualized practices which take place over several days and involve all members of the community except the youngest children. Only those tribal members with shamanic powers have the ability to carry out such charming, which demands an understanding of, and intimate collaboration with, the themistic potencies animating the nonhuman. Communal solidarity and the transparency of any self to the group as a whole are, moreover, essential to the hunt's success. As Winnemucca notes of the preparation of sagebrush mounds which form part of the hunting "stage":

> The women and boys and old men who were in the camp, and who were working on the mounds, were told to be very careful not to drop anything and not to stumble over a sage-brush root, or a stone, or anything, and not to have any accident, but to do everything perfectly and to keep thinking about the antelopes all the time, and not to let their thoughts go away to anything else. It took five days to charm the antelopes, and if anybody had an accident he must tell of it. (56)

Circular formations—and every Paiute's participation in maintaining them—are vital to the ritual as the hunters submit themselves (and their prey) to a sacred conformity:

> On the fifth day the antelopes were charmed, and the whole herd followed the tracks of my people and entered the circle where the mounds were, coming in at the entrance, bowing and tossing their heads, and looking sleepy and under a powerful spell. They ran round and round inside the circle just as if there was a fence all around it and they could not get out, and they staid there until my people had killed every one. But if anybody had dropped anything, or had stumbled and had not told about it, then when the antelopes came to

the place where he had done that, they threw off the spell and rushed wildly out of the circle at that place. (57)

In such a context, the individual self is directly responsible to the communal whole and its themistic interactions, from which it cannot light out and still hope to be a self.

Life among the Piutes aims, as we have seen, to find a place for Indigenous peoples within Euro-America without finally sacrificing their distinctive cultural identity. Winnemucca's appeals display both an optimism that such a place might actually be found and a willingness to accept a significant amount of assimilation in the process of finding it. "Oh, dear friends," she writes in one of the narrative's direct appeals, "you are wrong when you say it will take two or three generations to civilize my people. No! I say it will not take that long if you will only take interest in teaching us" (89). Winnemucca's acceptance of the civilizing process extends to an endorsement of the military control of reservations and finally to a breaking up of reservation land into individual allotments. In a petition included in an appendix, she reinvokes her grandfather's originary trust in the potential of collaboration with the Paiutes' "white brothers" and argues for allotment as a way of preserving the culture:

> I, Sarah Winnemucca Hopkins, grand-daughter of Captain Truckee, who promised friendship for his tribe to General Fremont, whom he guided into California, and served through the Mexican war,— together with the undersigned friends who sympathize in the cause of my people,—do petition the Honorable Congress of the United States to restore to them said Malheur Reservation, which is well watered and timbered, and large enough to afford severalty without losing their tribal relations, so essential to their happiness and good character, and where their citizenship, implied in this distribution of land, will defend them from the encroachments of the white settlers, so detrimental to their interests and their virtues. (247)

Writing to a military commander in 1870, Winnemucca argued for the practical benefits of this move to privatization, however untraditional it might be:

> [If] the Indians have any guarantee that they can secure a permanent home on their own native soil, and that our white neighbours can be kept from encroaching on our rights, after having a reasonable share of ground allotted to us as our own, and giving us the required advantages of learning &eo [sic], and I warrant that the savage (as he is called to-day) will be a thrifty and Law abiding member of the community fifteen or twenty years hence. (Qtd. in Canfield 61)

Allotment, unlike the reservation system, whose abuses she knew and had fought against firsthand, might assist in the autonomy of Native peoples. Sally Zanjani notes that Winnemucca's attitude concerning a shift toward agriculture and assimilation sprang from her sense that the most compelling threat to Native life lay in "the tyranny of reservation agents" (125). In forging compromises with Euro-America, however, Winnemucca insisted on, and continued to believe in the plausibility of, retaining a distinctively Native identity: "On one point she clearly diverged from the reformers of her time: never would the English-speaking Paiute farmers of the future working their own parcels of land be assimilated to the point that they ceased to be Indian. Sarah prided herself on refusing to forsake the Indian world for the white one, as her sister Elma and others had done" (Zanjani 125).

Zitkala-Ša's writings reveal, as the next chapter illustrates, a decisive movement beyond Winnemucca's conciliatory attempts at preserving traditional lifeways, as Zitkala-Ša seeks bolder, more expansive efforts to reconstitute Indigenous autonomy. Those efforts will be carried further still by Momaday, Erdrich, and Vizenor, who also make fewer concessions to the demands of the Euro-American *nomos* and gradually mark out, in defining more sharply the terms of a benevolent themistic order harmonized with the human one, the terms of a distinctively Indigenous *eunomia*.

FOUR

The Tent and the *Thipi* I
Ernest Hemingway and Zitkala-Ša

THIS CHAPTER'S PAIRING of Hemingway and Zitkala-Ša brings us to the chiastic intersection of the imaginative trajectories I have been sketching in this study. Euro-American autonomy now evidences a marked decline in its positive potential, as obvious pathologies become manifest in nomistic detachment, whereas its Native American counterpart reveals surging possibilities for the dynamic *re-creation,* rather than merely the tenuous defense, of versions of eunomic autonomy.

In a selection of Nick Adams stories from Hemingway's *In Our Time* (1925), we encounter a self-pasture much more limited in its access to a vital themistic order, and more vulnerable and troubled in its isolation, than that represented by Twain. Though he remains drawn to solitude, Huck Finn nevertheless maintains robust social relations through much of the novel and even forms, if temporarily, a successful alternate society with his companion Jim. The themistic order Huck confronts is, if ambiguous in its ultimate benevolence, nevertheless potent and accessible, a resource as tangible and insistent as the Mississippi itself. Nick's estrangement from other selves is, however, starkly definitive, his escape from the nomistic world a more desperate proposition. The vacant territory he lights out for offers some pastoral relief, but not without insistent reminders of the taint of human corruption. Prominent here, too, is the emergence of a specific pathology in relation to self-consciousness, as the autonomous self begins, in its uneasy isolation, to feed *on* itself. Hemingway nevertheless affirms the remaining positive potential of an autonomy dependent on self-constructed rituals and whatever access to a nourishing, salvific *themis* can be claimed through them—a potential that, diminished as it is from what Jefferson, Emerson, and even Twain had imagined, gradually vanishes altogether as we move on to Heller and DeLillo's explorations of a tortured inwardness.

In *Old Indian Legends* (1901) and *American Indian Stories* (1921), Zitkala-Ša parallels Hemingway in her thematic concern for traumatized selves and ways they might be healed. She inverts her counterpart's basic assumptions, though, as she champions a Native autonomy that might yet be founded on the self's integration with its *nomos*, and specifically with a set of traditional practices and beliefs that emphasize communal responsibilities and a eunomic blending with the natural order. Like Winnemucca, she insists on the fundamental role to be played by women in the reclamation of self-rule. Zitkala-Ša exceeds each of the precursors examined in this study, however, in offering a much less conciliatory version of adaptation to the dominant culture and in creatively reconstituting Native selfhood in her contemporary moment. Rather than, as was the case for Occom, Apess, and Winnemucca, carrying out a largely preservative enterprise—dedicated to keeping alive the flame of traditional lifeways, as it were, amid the storms of historical oppression—she offers bold, imaginative *re*kindlings of that flame, using Indigenous fuel. Her writings speak to increasing possibilities for the assertion, within the broader Euro-American *nomos*, of vital new Indigenous identities, possibilities that will only increase, both in force and richness, in the works of Momaday, Erdrich, and Vizenor.

The Nick Adams stories from *In Our Time* chart their protagonist's movement from experiences of trauma and death through heuristic efforts at recovery complicated by a now overtly dysnomic environment. Jefferson's and Emerson's optimism about a eunomic blending of natural and human orders, and the powers of the rational self to order its experience with confidence, seems woefully belated here, as does the naive optimism of Huck's final declaration of withdrawal.

"Indian Camp" presents Nick as a young boy, traveling with his uncle George and his father, a doctor, to treat a Native American woman undergoing a prolonged, life-threatening delivery. The bare medical facts of the case, the father insists to his son, are all that is relevant, not the human suffering involved:

"This lady is going to have a baby, Nick," he said.

"I know," said Nick.

"You don't know," said his father. "Listen to me. What she is going through is called being in labour. The baby wants to be born and she wants it to be born. All her muscles are trying to get the baby born. That is what is happening when she screams."

"Oh, Daddy, can't you give her something to make her stop screaming?" asked Nick.

"No. I haven't any anaesthetic," his father said. "But her screams are not important. I don't hear them because they are not important."
(Hemingway *Complete* 68)

Having completed the operation, Nick's father feels "exalted and talkative as football players are in the dressing room after a game" (69). He has, seemingly, intended to showcase for his son his technical (and racial) mastery against an abject backdrop, the squalid conditions of the camp and the assumed inferiority of its Native inhabitants (they have been unable to assist the pregnant woman, and her husband is himself bedridden after having injured himself cutting wood).

Nick's actual education, however, climaxes with the suicide of the husband, who is unable to bear the screams of his wife. The grim lessons imparted concern the reality of unbearable anguish, the inefficacy and destructiveness of pretensions to rational control, and above all, the insensate cruelty of the white Euro-American autonomist. Familial and nomistic authority are undermined here, as Nick's father can only offer, it would seem, specious accounts of human vulnerability:

"Why did he kill himself, Daddy?"

"I don't know, Nick. He couldn't stand things, I guess."

"Do many men kill themselves, Daddy?"

"Not very many, Nick."

"Do many women?"

"Hardly ever."

"Don't they ever?"

"Oh, yes. They do sometimes."

"Daddy?"

"Yes."

> "Where did Uncle George go?"
> "He'll turn up all right."
> "Is dying hard, Daddy?"
> "No, I think it's pretty easy, Nick. It all depends." (69–70)

What is not easy, Nick comes to know, is the negotiation of two horrifically polarized responses to trauma: an opening of the self to others in total, self-destructive capitulation to their suffering (as in the husband's suicide) or a cool objectification of all that stands beyond the isolate self (as in his father's efforts at medical mastery). His stunned response involves a compensatory denial as he insulates himself—in, characteristically, a natural setting—from personal vulnerability: "In the early morning on the lake sitting in the stern of the boat with his father rowing, he felt quite sure that he would never die" (70). This fantasy of immortality cannot, of course, be sustained. In the remaining stories, Nick must navigate the forbidding space between untenable alternatives without the assistance of traditional guides. Liberation from nomistic authorities—what, for Emerson, one *achieves* after a dedicated and finally exhilarating process of estrangement—is itself part of the trauma to which he is exposed.

"The Three-Day Blow" gives us a teenaged Nick commiserating with a friend after a failed romance. A retreat to the natural world promises him relief, however provisional, from personal torment:

> "There's no use getting drunk."
> "No. We ought to get outdoors."
> They stepped out the door. The wind was blowing a gale.
> "The birds will lie right down in the grass with this," Nick said.
> They struck down toward the orchard.
> "I saw a woodcock this morning," Bill said.
> "Maybe we'll jump him," Nick said.
> "You can't shoot in this wind," Bill said.
> Outside now the Marge business was no longer so tragic. It was not even very important. The wind blew everything like that away." (92)

Human ties—especially romantic ones, it would seem—betray an unbearable frailty and transience, and hint of an entrapment in the feminine and familial even more punitive than that perceived by Huck. An ominous gulf lies, apparently, between the complicated nomistic world and the redemptive *themis* available outdoors.

The depth of that gulf is further established in a brief "inter-chapter" which brings Nick to adulthood in World War I. We find him here physically wounded in battle, surrounded by dead combatants and at imminent risk of dying himself. His exchange with a fellow soldier reflects a now well-developed yearning for detachment from the human order: "*Nick turned his head and looked down at Rinaldi. 'Senta Rinaldi. Senta. You and me we've made a separate peace.' Rinaldi lay still in the sun, breathing with difficulty. 'We're not patriots.' Nick turned his head away, smiling sweatily. Rinaldi was a disappointing audience*" (105; italics in original). Huck's boyish resilience is replaced by a new emphasis on the self's vulnerability and yearning for some mode of insulation. Wherever Nick withdraws to find his "separate peace," he will bring profound scars with him, along with a fundamental assumption developed in the earlier stories: that he must, given the uncertainty and ineluctable brutality of the nomistic order, finally navigate its troubled pasture alone, finding relief through communion, however temporary and attenuated, with the natural world's themistic order.

Home from war in "Big Two-Hearted River," Nick journeys to the woods on a solitary fishing trip.[1] In contrast to Jefferson and Emerson, whose sylvan withdrawals make possible grand self-affirmations, he does not presume to command the entirety of his environment but to secure, like a much older and chastened Huck, a therapeutic refuge within it. To get there he passes through "burned-over country" (163) and an abandoned town, evocative markers of a ruinous nomistic world threatening to extend its reach everywhere.[2] Against such desolation Nick turns to the reassuring presence of the river itself, whose teeming life, in the form of trout which "[keep] themselves steady in the current with wavering fins" (163), heralds a regenerative potential in the natural order. That potential is, however, decidedly fragile. The fish, we learn, might themselves be thrown out of balance by corrupting human contact:

> If a trout was touched with a dry hand, a white fungus attacked the unprotected spot. Years before when he had fished crowded streams,

with fly fisherman ahead of him and behind him, Nick had again and again come on dead trout, furry with white fungus, drifted against a rock, or floating belly up in some pool. Nick did not like to fish with other men on the river. Unless they were of your party, they spoiled it. (176)

Other selves represent a threat to whatever redemptive possibilities this solo fishing trip offers, and nothing else in the story suggests that the social order Nick has escaped might finally be redeemed by the natural one he encounters in his retreat.

Nick helps preserve his own steadiness through a series of ritualized actions, all carefully inventoried in the narrative to imply their significance. In clearing a campsite, setting up a tent, preparing coffee, catching and baiting grasshoppers, gutting fish, he submits himself to prescribed behavior, putting things in their proper place as he communes with *themis* (the name of the goddess Themis derives from the Greek verb *tithenai* and might be translated literally as "she who puts law/custom/convention in place"). These rituals are, of course, conspicuously private not just in their performance but in their a-nomistic implications: though Nick may have been taught them by others, they do not firmly bind him to any group beyond himself and in fact seem to serve, above all, a restorative sense of distance from other selves. Walking in the woods, he is able to feel that he has "left everything behind, the need for thinking, the need to write, other needs. It was all back of him" (164).

Intriguingly, an Indigenous context may have informed this account of nomistic evasion.[3] Several decades after writing "Big Two-Hearted River," Hemingway claimed, in an essay discussing his theory of omission, that Native Americans were in fact one of the work's elided presences and that the story's title itself indicated that elision: "The river was the Fox River, by Seney, Michigan, not the Big Two-Hearted. The change of name was made purposely, not from ignorance nor carelessness but because Big Two-Hearted River is poetry, and because there were many Indians in the story, just as the war was in the story, and none of the Indians nor the war appeared" ("Art" 3). Philip Melling, setting forth the work's "hidden history" as it relates to Native peoples, provocatively contends that "Nick's journey is an encounter with Indianness in which insects, fish, trees, and water are part of an ancient ecosystem that preserves and regenerates indigenous life" (49). At least imaginatively, Nick may perceive, in communing with a range of nonhuman presences, what a vital eunomic blending of the natural and social might be like (or might *have* been like before Euro-America's corruptive presence in the region).

Whatever his understanding of an Indigenous *eunomia*, Nick's own traumatized response suggests the impossibility of restoring any fertile blending of the social and natural. The self-defensive, isolate terms of his autonomy are perfectly epitomized by his tent, "his home where he had made it," where "[n]othing could touch him" (*Complete* 167). Beyond the reach of noxious influences, the self may cultivate its private access to divine nourishment, however limited:

> Across the river in the swamp, in the almost dark, he saw a mist rising. He looked at the tent once more. All right. He took a full spoonful from the plate.
> "Chrise," Nick said. "Geezus Chrise," he said happily. (168)

This moment does not, finally, seem ironic, for much of the *allure* of the story surely has to do with its suggestion that Nick's communion with the divine, if meagre and precarious, might indeed be enough to sustain the self. For our later Euro-American protagonists, who extend the centripetal movement we have been tracking from Emerson's expansive "transparent eye-ball" to Huck's nearly solitary raft to Nick's private tent, these self-pastured pleasures will no longer suffice. Heller's Slocum will pitch his own claustrophobic tent in a bureaucratic office, from which he will worry endlessly over the status of other tented selves. DeLillo's Packer constructs his in a private limousine, where he will, with the assistance of new technological aids enabling a nearly total dominion over his experience, effectively disappear as a self.

In leaving all behind him in the woods, Nick may, like Emerson, "find something more dear and connate than in streets and villages" but without the promise of encountering "[something] as beautiful as his own nature" (*Nature* 6). No matter the efficacy of its rituals, the self which aspires to an atomic self-rule here cannot presume mastery over its environment, and its "own nature" remains forbiddingly ambiguous. One may still find the means to heal and augment the self's powers in the natural world, that is, but on strictly qualified terms. Inward journeying has become perilous, and rationality itself potentially self-destructive. The optimism of Jefferson's endorsement of "[r]eason and free inquiry . . . [as] the only effectual agents against error" (*Notes* 165), Emerson's assurance that "[u]ndoubtedly we have no questions to ask which are unanswerable" (*Nature* 3), or even Huck's sylvan resolutions—"I went out in the woods and turned it over in my mind a long time, but I couldn't see no advantage about it—except for the other people; so at last I reckoned I wouldn't worry about it any more, but just let it go" (Twain 19)—seem travestied in Nick's pained efforts to avoid or at least defer thinking. Within his privacy, his goal becomes the containment of self-torturing thought: "His mind was starting to work. He knew he could choke it because he was tired enough" (*Complete* 169). One must be alone to heal, we are to understand, but solitude presents its own self-torturous dangers.

Nick's solitary communion with *themis*—while essential to healing whatever trauma we assume he has suffered—cannot confidently transform all the self would gaze upon. Where, for Emerson, the "eye is the best composer" and "[there exists] no object so foul that intense light will not make beautiful" (*Nature* 9), Hemingway's protagonist, an extremely careful, even obsessive observer, encounters both the limits of individual perception and its profound risks. As he discovers, one's own positioning *as* a self, far from empowering one's gaze, can occlude it. Gazing over sylvan territory, Nick's vision falters in proportion to the effort he commits to it: "If he looked too steadily [the distant hills] were gone. But if he only half-looked they were there, the far-off hills of the height of land" (*Complete* 164). What one sees can, in fact, become incapacitating: "When the sun was down [the biggest trout] all moved out into the current. Just when the sun made the water blinding in the glare before it went down, you were liable to strike a big trout anywhere in the current. It was almost impossible to fish then, the surface of the water was blinding as a mirror in the sun" (178). Even in this solitary idyll, a hostile, immobilizing (inner) territory remains, allied to the haunted space Huck discerns in solitude, though now further complicated by a menacing ineffability. The swamp near Nick's campsite—a figuration, perhaps, of whatever "blinding" memories he brings with him from the nomistic world—cannot be ignored nor fully engaged: to journey there would be "a tragic adventure" (180). How he might finally engage such exploration, if at all, is not revealed, but his ultimate isolation is made clear: leaving the woods with a renewed reverence for private communion with the nonhuman, and of the human threats he must insulate himself *from,* Nick will carry his tent with him.

This version of sylvan detachment assumes some enduring potency in Euro-American autonomy, though reduced and rather uncertain in its possibilities. Self-inhabitance must now negotiate a self-consumptive isolation. As we shall see, Hemingway's representation of this corrosive inwardness anticipates the more extreme pathologies examined in this study's next chapters. The de facto tents occupied by Heller's Slocum and DeLillo's Packer become plainly unnourishing sites of self-pasture, the self's separation from both human and natural orders ruinously intensified.

Writing in 1922 to her "California Kinsmen" on the subject of Native American political activism, Zitkala-Ša begins by citing the greeting of "a famous Kiowa Indian chief": "My heart is filled with joy when I see you as the brooks fill with water when the snow melts in the spring" (261). In linking human sociality with natural processes, this poetic simile suggests the broad eunomic terms of her Native vision and a stark departure from the atomistic assumptions of Hemingway's Nick. "[Born] on the Dakota Plains," Zitkala-Ša tells us, she "had the privilege of living in the great out-of-doors: and of knowing that an Indian tribe is really a big family circle" (262). As Occom, Apess, and Winnemucca before her noted, this communal emphasis models an ideal Christianity—"the very essence of the Sermon on the Mount of which our white brothers talk in their modern churches" (262)—while incorporating a reverence for the animate presences of the natural world: "Our Indian ancestors cultivated this wonderful spirit when they worshipped in the living temples, those ancient forests Nature took so many centuries to build, and which unfortunately our white brothers destroyed" (262). Euro-America has, with fatal results, "built little tiny houses in which to worship the Great Spirit, and from which to preach brotherly love"; its churches are, much like Euro-Americans themselves, merely "'little boxes' of God" (262). From this perspective, Hemingway's Nick, in venturing to the woods, may have located his communion in the right place, but his atomistic assumptions only exacerbate his culture's central, reductive mistake, the pitching of little tents. He remains, at last, much more confined and malnourished in his sylvan retreat than he realizes. Native autonomy demands, Zitkala-Ša would insist, a much more expansive—and *compressed*—home for the self, one that might sustain bonds extending widely through the human and nonhuman. Like Winnemucca before her and Vizenor after, she will assume a sometimes explicitly shamanic role in sketching that home, guided by a vision of holistic healing.

Born in 1876, Zitkala-Ša—Lakota for "Red Bird," a name she gave herself—was raised as Gertrude Simmons on the Yankton Indian Reservation in what is now southeastern South Dakota, her mother a Dakota, her father a French American who abandoned his family. When she was eight, missionaries recruited her for White's Indian Manual Labor Institute, a school catering to impoverished white, Native American, and African American children. After three years there, she returned home for another three years, before reenrolling at White's to complete her diploma. Zitkala-Ša's descriptions of her formal education note her growing sense of estrangement from family and Indigenous traditions, along with her exhilaration at absorbing new cultural knowledge related to book learning and music. She went on to study at Earlham College in Indiana, where she won widespread acclaim after delivering a speech on Native rights at a statewide oratorical competition, and then to Boston's New England Conservatory of Music, where she studied violin. Zitkala-Ša began to teach music at Carlisle Indian Industrial School in 1899, and soon after published articles on her experiences as a Native American within the residential school system. After deep conflicts developed between her and Carlisle's administrators, intensified by her public critiques of assimilationist policies, Zitkala-Ša was dismissed from the school in 1901. Politically active throughout her adult life, she cofounded in 1926 the National Council of American Indians, an organization devoted to the rights of Indigenous peoples.

The year before Zitkala-Ša began teaching at Carlisle, its founder and superintendent, Richard Henry Pratt, penned a telling editorial in the school's newsletter, *The Indian Helper*. Responding to a reader who had asked for more stories that "would describe the Indian a little better by telling how he is tamed and brought up" (1), he frankly set forth the school's assimilationist ideals:

> The author of the letter evidently has the idea of Indians that Buffalo Bill and other showmen keep alive, by hiring the reservation wild man to dress in his most hideous costume of feathers, paint, moccasins, blanket, leggins, and scalp-lock, and to display his savagery, by hair lifting war-whoops make those who pay to see him, think he is a blood-thirsty creature ready to devour people alive.
>
> It is this nature in our red brother that is better dead than alive, and when we agree with the oft-repeated sentiment that the only good Indian is a dead one, we mean this characteristic of the Indian. Carlisle's mission is to kill THIS Indian, as we build up the better man.
>
> We give the rising Indian something nobler and higher to think about and do, and he comes out a young man with the ambitions and aspirations of his more favored white brother.
>
> We do not like to keep alive the stories of his past, hence deal more with his present and his future. (1)

For Pratt, who no doubt spoke for much of Euro-America, Indigenous traditions represented a barrier to genuine civilization and were best discarded as Native peoples realized their full human potential in transitioning to Western modernity. Zitkala-Ša's literary career, begun at the turn of the century, would directly challenge such assumptions in attempting not just to preserve traditional Native lifeways but to reconstitute them as part of an extraordinary reversal of the direction of cross-cultural education. Much more extensively and ambitiously than Winnemucca, she would, as a kind of missionary *for* the Dakotas, render the living, prophetic genius of Indigenous traditions in English so that a benighted Euro-America might yet learn from those it had long silenced.

With *Old Indian Legends* (1901) Zitkala-Ša revives a series of traditional Sioux narratives, ultimately enacting a stunning intervention into Euro-American culture itself. Writing to her fiancé, Carlos Montezuma, while researching the work, she explains that "while the old people last I want to get from them their treasured ideas of life" (qtd. in Fisher 229). Zitkala-Ša first transcribed the narratives she heard in the Dakota language and then translated them, often altering the content significantly, into English. As she explains in her preface, the re-creation of these legends inevitably varies to some extent with each oral performance, while nevertheless maintaining coherence and continuity as different storytellers "[restore] some lost link in the original character of the tale" (5). Breathing new life into this tradition of communal practice and narrative flexibility, she creates in her own retellings a series of cultural links. Zitkala-Ša's aims extend, however, even further. Her intent, she explains, has been "to transplant the native spirit of these tales—root and all—into the English language, since America in the last few centuries has acquired a second tongue" (5). We do well to pay close attention to Zitkala-Ša's language here. Her essential activity is not to translate but to "transplant"—moving essential elements of a "native spirit" into a new milieu where they might thrive. Moreover, she seeks a transplantation that would carry over that spirit "root and all," bringing the entirety of its life-giving force, and thereby not simply preserve what is carried over but radically impact the environment into which it is carried. With the success of this project, the English language, and the broader nomistic world in which Native peoples might find a revivified place, would be transformed.

Following Occom, Apess, and Winnemucca before her, Zitkala-Ša challenges Euro-American readers by first reminding them of their own belated status on the American continent, which produced not a primary but a "second tongue." She moves beyond these precursors, however, in setting forth a rich, alternative, potentially transfigurative mythopoeic system with its own distinctive assumptions about, for instance, the dimensions of communal obligations, the ontological status of the nonhuman, and the consequences of transgressing the natural order. Not incidentally, these legends were told to her, she reminds us, "Under an open sky, nestling close to the earth ... [by] the old Dakota storytellers" (5). In offering the narratives to Euro-America, Zitkala-Ša surmises that her audience may be "forcibly impressed with the possible earnestness of life as seen through the teepee door" (6). This frame is crucial for the transfigurative enterprise she undertakes. Where Euro-America has organized its experience into little boxes or solitary little tents, the teepee is a shared space. *Teepee* is, in fact, a Lakota word (*thipi*) derived from a plural verb meaning "they dwell."[4] According to this fundamental Native architecture, one cannot be at home *alone*. In foregrounding this structure and its conceptual implications, Zitkala-Ša thus emphasizes distinctive, profound characteristics of Native autonomy: *Legends* would, we might say, confer an imaginative dynamism and plurality to the imagination of American dwelling, a communal redemption of its self-pasture. Hemingway's Nick looks out from his own tent door defensively, in morbid anticipation of intrusion. Zitkala-Ša imagines, in contrast, a social portal from which she may survey a vital inheritance—not just the remnants of a past nomistic world but the imaginative basis for a present and future one, bound in collective dwelling.[5]

One part of this enterprise involves bringing traditional material into dialogue with contemporary political realities and thereby inviting interpretation of the retellings as allegorical critiques. Jeanne Smith explains that Zitkala-Ša's version of "Dance in a Buffalo Skull," for instance, converts a comic narrative into a chilling "ghost story" (50). In the conventional telling, the spider spirit and trickster Iktomi humiliates himself by peering into, and becoming trapped inside, a buffalo skull in which a group of mice are dancing. By shifting the narrative's focus to the mice themselves, who are complacent about their safety until faced with an overwhelming predator, Zitkala-Ša delivers a forceful warning about "the threat of devouring colonialism" (50). Other narratives in *Legends* offer similar commentaries on the exploitative dynamics of relations with Euro-Americans and the specific perils now faced by Indigenous peoples. Connecting past and present as she takes her place as a tribal storyteller, Zitkala-Ša demonstrates the relevance and usefulness of engaging traditions, and the value of ancestors themselves. Healing and the assumption of a nourishing self-rule, for individuals and communities alike, is understood to depend on the forging of such connections.

Iktomi is the most prominent among the various traditional figures who appear in *Legends*. Like other tricksters, he moves fluidly across a range of conceptual barriers, often prompts consideration of fundamental values through their negation, and heralds both a constructive and destructive cultural potential. His exploits here most often emphasize the centrality of communal life to the Sioux and the madness of an isolate autonomy of the kind sought by Hemingway's Nick. The first narrative, "Iktomi and the Ducks," provides our introduction to this "wily fellow," known for dramatically and amusingly violating eunomic ideals: "His hands are always kept in mischief. He prefers to spread a snare rather than to earn the smallest thing with honest hunting. Why! he laughs outright with wide open mouth when some simple folk are caught in a trap, sure and fast" (7). We are repeatedly informed of Iktomi's bleak solitude: he "lives alone in a cone-shaped wigwam upon the plain" (7), "cannot find a single friend" (7), and "[n]o one helps him when he is in trouble. No one really loves him" (7). Setting out in search of food one day, he encounters a group of ducks involved, tellingly, in the social activities of "dancing and feasting" and who, with "wings outspread, tip to tip . . . [move] up and down in a large circle" (8). Iktomi breaks up that circle as he promises to share his own songs with the ducks, first luring them into a hut, where he beguiles them into dancing with their eyes closed, and then slaughtering as many of them as he can. He takes this great bounty—which exceeds, we are to assume, what he needs for his own sustenance—back to his teepee, where he greedily proceeds to prepare, like Nick in his "little box" tent, a private banquet.[6] These plans are interrupted by an "old tree man" who bends in the wind and ends up temporarily trapping him, making it possible for a pack of wolves to discover and seize the ducks for themselves. At the narrative's end Iktomi's atomistic self-pasture is thus countered, with the help of natural "spirits," by the resumption of communal feasting.

The next narrative, "Iktomi's Blanket," begins with another reminder of the trickster's solitude within a little box: "Alone within his teepee sat Iktomi" (13). Ruing his loss of food to the wolves, he "[cuddles] the evil memory" (13)—a version of Nick's self-consumptive inwardness—before determining that he might seek some compensation by praying to Inyan, the primordial stone spirit. Zitkala-Ša offers here, as she contrasts Inyan's profound solidity with Iktomi's shallow mutability, an explicit description of part of the themistic order which frames this world:

> The all-powerful Great Spirit, who makes the trees and grass, can hear the voice of those who pray in many varied ways. The hearing of Inyan, the large hard stone, was the one most sought after. He was the great-grandfather, for he had sat upon the hillside many, many seasons. He had seen the prairie put on a snow-white blanket and then change it for a bright green robe more than a thousand times. (13)

Iktomi prays to Inyan, offers him the gift of his blanket, and is soon rewarded with food. After becoming cold at night, however, Iktomi violates the eunomic ideal of reciprocity: he withdraws his gift and is soon punished by seeing his food disappear. Struggling to comprehend the loss, he continues to misunderstand his error and is confirmed in his isolation: "[his] tears no longer moved the hand of the Generous Giver. They were selfish tears. The Great Spirit does not heed them ever" (15).

Other narratives continue to explore the trickster's telling breaches. In "Iktomi and the Muskrat" he suffers again for not having hospitably "shared [his] food like a real Dakota" (18). In "Shooting of the Red Eagle" he disgraces himself by pretending to be an "avenger" and is "chased away beyond the outer limits of the camp ground" (41). Each narrative reminds us of a *nomos* shaped and nourished, eunomically, by *themis*. Within that order the self has, we learn by implication, strict responsibilities to other selves and can only flourish in (liberating) subordination to them. The self-pasture aspired to by Hemingway's Nick, Iktomi-like in its seclusion, is by this standard the height of folly. There can be no solitary nourishment, that is, beyond the limits of communal engagement.

Zitkala-Ša explores other, related cultural values in "Manštin, the Rabbit." The titular protagonist, a "kind-hearted [and] adventurous brave" (56) who "knew all the peculiar contrivances of the people" (57), rescues a human baby from a giant named Double-Face and restores him to his parents. Manštin then miraculously transforms the baby into an adult in his own image, with whom he will share an appreciation of and intimate ties with the natural world itself:

With his feet placed gently yet firmly upon the tiny toes of the little child, he drew upward by each small hand the sleeping child till he was a full-grown man. With a forefinger he traced a slit in the upper lip; and when on the morrow the man and woman awoke they could not distinguish their own son from Manštin, so much alike were the braves.

"Henceforth we are friends, to help each other," said Manštin, shaking a right hand in farewell. "The earth is our common ear, to carry from its uttermost extremes one's slightest wish for the other!" (57)

The passage suggests an at least implicit rebuke to presumptions of human mastery over the natural world and its inhabitants. Human and animal forms blend here—Manštin and the new "full-grown man" have features of both—in another reminder of the interdependence of all living presences. A "common ear" connects them and the world they share.

The remainder of the narrative sees Manštin make a critical moral error, however, as he betrays this earthly commonality in succumbing to the temptation of technological prosthetics (a theme that, as we shall see, becomes central to the work of DeLillo and his diagnosis of Euro-American pathologies of the self in the twenty-first century). Walking through the forest, he happens upon an elderly blind man who lives alone in a hut, sustained by "magic bags of choicest foods" (58) which allow him endless sybaritic leisure. Envying this life, Manštin trades his eyes for the man's place in the hut but then finds that he is unable to orient and care for himself while blind. The man ultimately returns and gives Manštin back his vision, the lesson having been imparted: this retreat to an atomic self-pasture has meant a separation from both the earth itself, as its resources are effortlessly consumed without connection to their origin, and from any communal life or responsibilities. Manštin, "with his own bright eyes fitted into his head again, went on happily to hunt in the North country" (60), participating once more in the broader networks and interconnected struggles which properly define the relations of all living beings.

Hemingway's Nick Adams stories chart, as we have seen, the development of pathologies associated with the self's estrangement from its *nomos*. In *Legends* Zitkala-Ša subtly but resolutely explores a contrary movement—one which affirms the value of the self's nomistic engagement according to a eunomic blending of human and natural orders. Her overall narrative arrangement itself in fact establishes, as Jeffrey Myers has cogently demonstrated, a circular thematic pattern which argues for the vital potential of the self's social and environmental integration. The first set of narratives (which includes "Iktomi and the Ducks" and "Iktomi's Blanket") represents the trickster's violations of communal norms and, after his comeuppances, the resumption of the harmonious world he has disturbed. The second set, which more directly allegorize contemporary political realities and suggest the toxicity of Iktomi-like tricksterism when no longer subordinated to the proper fusion of social and natural orders, are composed of "ominous tales that threaten destruction, division, and permanent disruption . . . as the implied threat of Euroamerican imperialist destruction intrudes on the scene" (Myers 126–27). In the third and final set (which includes the penultimate narrative, "Manštin, the Rabbit"), "the tales circle back . . . to imagine a socially just reintegration of people and the natural world," while suggesting that "respect for the natural world and the human place within it might offer hope to everyone" (133, 134). Where Hemingway limns, with highly qualified optimism, a solitary refuge for the self in private communion with *themis,* Zitkala-Ša proffers warnings about the perils of solitude and affirms the present value—and the ongoing plausibility—of reestablishing the terms of eunomic life.

With *American Indian Stories* (1921), Zitkala-Ša extends her consideration of cultural survival as she brings together a collection of semi-autobiographical writings, fiction, and an essay on "America's Indian Problem."[7] She offers here a withering assessment of what the "civilizing" process has meant and, much more strongly and extensively than Winnemucca had done in *Life among the Piutes,* a pointed affirmation of Native religiosity, on and in its own terms, against its Christian counterpart. Her revisionary efforts target seminal Euro-American narratives and aim for a liberating conceptual disruption as she imagines a revitalized Indigenous autonomy based on eunomic principles—an extraordinary prefiguration of the later, full-blown conception of Vizenor's "continent of liberty."

Stories opens with three semiautobiographical writings.[8] The first, "Impressions of an Indian Childhood," frames its protagonist as a youthful Eve within an Edenic world: "I was a wild little girl of seven. Loosely clad in a slip of brown buckskin, and light-footed with a pair of soft moccasins on my feet, I was as free as the wind that blew my hair, and no less spirited than a bounding deer. These were my mother's pride,—my wild freedom and overflowing spirits. She taught me no fear save that of intruding myself upon others" (68). Though such descriptions may seem to replay a noble savage stereotype, Zitkala-Ša in fact presents here, as she assumes a version of the trickster's role, a subversive retelling of the myth of Genesis. In the young girl's world, her mother takes on the status of an at least quasi-divine authority, from whose guardianship she will fall after succumbing to the silver-tongued exhortations of missionaries, the Garden's serpents, who tempt her in ironically familiar terms:

> [My brother] had told me of the great tree where grew red, red apples; and how we could reach out our hands and pick all the red apples we could eat. I had never seen apple trees. I had never tasted more than a dozen red apples in my life; and when I heard of the orchards of the East, I was eager to roam among them. The missionaries smiled into my eyes and patted my head. I wondered how my mother could say such hard words against him. (84–85)

Catherine Kunce explains, in analyzing Zitkala-Ša's biblical revisionism, how this Indigenization of a seminal cultural narrative targets Euro-America's core prejudices as it affirms liberating alternatives: "By likening her mother to the Judaic-Christian God, Zitkala-Ša simultaneously unsettles the foundation of racism, patriarchy, and theological hierarchy" (76). The boldness of this conceptual restructuring recalls that of Apess in his *Eulogy on King Philip*, though with a new emphasis on routine, collective cultural operations: where Apess reimagines Philip not as a forbidding military opponent but rather as "the greatest man that ever lived upon the American shores" (290), Zitkala-Ša imaginatively relocates all Native Americans to the tragic (and heroic) center of the nation's history, and Native women's teaching to the center of *that* center.

Much of "Impressions" explores the significance of Dakotan traditions and the various ways in which they are successfully transferred to the young. Unlike Hemingway's Nick, who has lost faith in familial and nomistic authorities and must rely on private rituals to orient himself, Zitkala-Ša's young protagonist encounters, before her estrangement from it, a nomistic world she can trust and which productively shapes her emerging selfhood. Oral storytelling, in particular, brings her community together—typically within the social space of the teepee—to hear and reflect upon shared values. Describing her protagonist's passion for hearing such stories, Zitkala-Ša draws attention to their inherently communal and moral dimensions, as well as to the importance of elders and women in their transmission: "At the arrival of our guests I sat close to my mother, and did not leave her side without first asking her consent. I ate my supper in quiet, listening patiently to the talk of the old people, wishing all the time that they would begin the stories I loved best. At last, when I could not wait any longer, I whispered in my mother's ear, 'Ask them to tell an Iktomi story, mother'" (72). Elders' voices command respect and function as a vivifying resource on which the young girl can, so long as she recalls them, continue to rely—spinning out their significance, like Iktomi himself in his liberating mode, into new symbolic webs.

A vivid and compelling counterpoint to the failed lessons provided by Nick's father in "Indian Camp" can be found, moreover, in those offered by the young girl's mother:

Close beside my mother I sat on a rug, with a scrap of buckskin in one hand and an awl in the other. This was the beginning of my practical observation lessons in the art of beadwork. . . . It took many trials before I learned how to knot my sinew thread on the point of my fingers, as I saw her do. Then the next difficulty was in keeping my thread stiffly twisted, so that I could easily string my beads on it. My mother required of me original designs for my lessons in beading. At first I frequently ensnared many a sunny hour into working a long design. Soon I learned from self-inflicted punishment to refrain from drawing complex patterns, for I had to finish whatever I began. . . . The quietness of [my mother's] oversight made me feel strongly responsible and dependent on my own judgement. She treated me as a dignified little individual as long as I was on my good behavior; and how humiliated I was when some boldness of mine drew forth a rebuke from her! (74)

An invigorating mix of discipline and freedom is retained in this passing along of cultural knowledge. The autonomy the young girl develops as an artist—and, more generally, as a tribal member—involves her ranging within communal limits laid down by tradition. The more she practices her beadwork and develops, from it, her own style of creation, the more she confirms her links with her mother and other ancestral relations.

"The School Days of an Indian Girl" explores the deprivations and abuse encountered by the protagonist at a mission school. In place of the spontaneous life of the reservation and its access to the themistic energies of the natural world, she is compelled here into a mechanized existence, an "iron routine" imposed by "the civilizing machine" (96). The telegraph poles she gazes at on her journey to school suggest a technocratic distancing of selves, and with it a pathological reduction of genuine communication and communality: she recalls investigating a pole installed near her reservation, "hearing its low moaning . . . [and wondering] what the palefaces had done to hurt it" (88). When, as an adolescent, the protagonist returns home, her estrangement from the natural (and divine) world is confirmed: "Even nature seemed to have no place for me. I was neither a wee girl nor a tall one; neither a wild Indian nor a tame one. This deplorable situation was the effect of my brief course in the East, and the unsatisfactory 'teenth' in a girl's years" (97). The protagonist also faces an increasing spiritual distance from her mother—who, we may recall, has been symbolically associated with an Indigenous *themis*—but in her return to school she ultimately learns to command English, winning prizes at oratorical competitions and so providing herself with a further means of claiming agency and defining the terms of an Indigenous identity within the Euro-American world.

Zitkala-Ša also adds here a new element of independence to the religious critiques launched by Occom, Apess, and Winnemucca. In contrast to Indigenous conceptions of the divine, the Christian tradition, as she has known it, has fostered a crippling fear. "Evil spirits" were part of the oral tradition on which she was raised, but they did not command overwhelming attention or concern. She was, she explains, "taught to fear them no more than those who stalked about in material guise" (94). In contrast, the "white man's legend," which posits "an insolent chieftain among the bad spirits, who dared to array his forces against the Great Spirit" (94), enacts in her understanding a kind of spiritual terrorism. Agitated by hearing of the devil, the protagonist has a nightmare in which she is chased by him. Revealingly, she is rescued by her mother, a symbolic defender of the traditional Indigenous *themis* whose ignorance of English acts as a kind of spiritual shield: "Just as the devil stooped over me with outstretched claws my mother awoke from her quiet indifference, and lifted me on her lap. Whereupon the devil vanished, and I was awake" (95). Acting on this triumph over the Christian view of evil, the protagonist goes on to deface an image of its forbidding representative by sneaking into a library and, with a "broken slate pencil" (95), defacing the image of the devil, beginning with his eyes, in a children's book of biblical stories. English literacy is finally esteemed here as potentially emancipatory, but only on terms that preserve the protagonist's ability to discard and *dis*esteem its blinding spiritual implications. Her act of creative destruction aligns her again with Iktomi, whose trickster status is itself a rebuke to strict binary definitions of good and evil.

"An Indian Teacher among Indians" relates the protagonist's growing awareness of the value of the culture from which she has become estranged. It also provides a suggestive portrait of what Euro-American autonomy has been like—a kind of spiritual confinement ("'little boxes' of God," or Nick's private tent). Disillusioned as she contemplates the destruction of her own culture in the wake of settlers' encroachment upon her people's lands, she notes again her estrangement from the natural world, *themis,* and kin: "At this stage of my own evolution, I was ready to curse men of small capacity for being the dwarfs their God had made them. In the process of my education I had lost all consciousness of the nature world about me. Thus, when a hidden rage took me to the small white-walled prison which I then called my room, I unknowingly turned away from my one salvation" (111–12). Replaying Iktomi's isolate role—"[a]lone in my room"—she becomes "like the petrified Indian woman of whom my mother used to tell me," sentenced to a living death: "alive, in my tomb, I was destitute" (112). Ultimately committing herself to reclaiming the identity her mother had sought to cultivate in her, the protagonist notes her discovery of "a new way of solving the problem of my inner self" (112), which is to leave the school as a teacher and continue her education in the East. She finally casts a severe judgment on the whole enterprise of boarding schools, remarking that among those Euro-Americans who have viewed them, "few there are who have paused to question whether real life or long-lasting death lies beneath this semblance of civilization" (113). Thus departing from Winnemucca's essentially conciliatory stance, Zitkala-Ša indicts the processes of acculturation themselves, especially those instantiated in the missionary schools, as inherently false and destructive. Euro-America would, she affirms, deliver Natives to its own barren self-pasture. Crucially, and in a striking anticipation of Momaday, Erdrich, and Vizenor, Zitkala-Ša turns her back here on the agonistic framework that had so defined Native experience and lights out for new territory, which—unlike that of Huck and, even more so, Hemingway's Nick—is at once a return to her traditional nomistic world.

"The Great Spirit" (a personal essay originally titled "Why I Am a Pagan") explores some of the terms of this homecoming as Zitkala-Ša maps her recovery of a Native *themis*. Where Occom and Apess, as Christian missionaries, fought for a place for Native peoples within the dominant faith and Winnemucca implied her own delicate balancing of faiths, Zitkala-Ša speaks here prophetically on behalf of a "paganism" lying outside the boundaries of Christianity and operating on its own distinctive terms. She opens the work with a poetic description of her love for, and awe of, the natural world and its animate presences: "When the spirit swells my breast I love to roam leisurely among the green hills; or sometimes, sitting on the brink of the murmuring Missouri, I marvel at the great blue overhead" (114). These moments of aesthetic appreciation, which may seem merely to reproduce tropes common to Western Romanticism, in fact highlight a contrary, Indigenous response to the self-aggrandizement reflected, for instance, in Jefferson's or Emerson's interactions with the natural world. A vitalizing *subordination* of the self to what it gazes on follows from Zitkala-Ša's communion with benevolent themistic powers: "My heart and I lie small upon the earth like a grain of throbbing sand. Drifting clouds and tinkling waters, together with the warmth of a genial summer day, bespeak with eloquence the loving Mystery round about us. During the idle while I sat upon the sunny river brink, I grew somewhat, though my response be not so clearly manifest as in the green grass fringing the edge of the high bluff back of me" (114). The self does not function here, as in the Emersonian fantasy, as a masterful container of its environment, but grows modestly *along with* nonhuman presences. The self-pasture claimed is thus nourished by, but does not abrogate for itself, the themistic authority coursing through the world.

Zitkala-Ša's retreat now turns explicitly to an Indigenous context for her experiences. She comes upon a "rock embedded on the side of a foothill facing the low river bottom" and imagines encountering the mythic warrior Stone-Boy and the primordial spirit Inyan, "our great-great-grandfather, older than the hill he rested on, older than the race of men who love to tell of his wonderful career" (115). These invocations furnish a reminder of Native responses to the land and its themistic order which predate—in mythic time, infinitely—those of Euro-America. Zitkala-Ša goes on to emphasize the enduring relevance of Indigenous histories and her own expanding awareness of sacred networks of the human and nonhuman: "Interwoven with the thread of this Indian legend of the rock, I fain would trace a subtle knowledge of the native folk which enabled them to recognize a kinship to any and all parts of this vast universe" (115). The retreat is not, that is, solitary or anti-nomistic at all—instead it brings her, like Apess's eunomic vision at the Bay of Quinte, into contact with welcoming networks of human and nonhuman presences and *back* to communal engagement: "By the leading of an ancient trail I move toward the Indian village" (115).

D. M. Dooling's telling of Inyan's role in one version of the Lakota creation story underscores exactly this sense of augmented, plural, "social" selfhood, of linked identities grounded in the earth itself and subject to spontaneous, dynamic change:

Inyan desired that there be others so that he might exercise his powers. To do so he would have to give part of his spirit and part of his blood, and the powers that were in the blood. So he decided to create another but only as part of himself, so that he could keep control over the powers. He took part of himself and spread it over and around himself in the shape of a great disk. He named the disk Maka, the Earth, and he gave Maka a spirit, Maka-akan, Earth Spirit, and she is part of Inyan. But in creating her, he took so much from himself that his veins opened and all his blood flowed from him, and he shrank and became hard and powerless.

As Inyan's blood flowed, it became the blue waters which are on the earth. Because powers cannot live in water, they separated themselves and became a great blue dome whose edge is near the edge of Maka. This blue dome of the powers of the blood of Inyan is now the sky and is not material but is the spirit of Taku Skanskan, the Great Spirit. When these powers assumed one shape, they said a voice spoke, saying: "I am the source of energy, I am Skan." This was the beginning of the third of the Sacred Beings who is the highest of all because he is spirit. Inyan and Maka are material, and the world of matter has no powers except what are given by Skan. (3)

Importing this mythos into her pastoral retreat, Zitkala-Ša develops imaginative connections *with,* rather than against, her *nomos,* now understood as much larger and more vital than she had previously reckoned. Hemingway's Nick would therapeutically leave behind human ties and histories in his retreat, communing alone with what themistic potency he can. After rejoining his community he will, in effect, bring his tent with him, defensively preserving his self-pasture against nomistic threats. But for Zitkala-Ša, as the story of Inyan reminds her, the natural and social orders are properly bound together, and human healing involves a recuperation of ties to networks of other selves. A nourishing autonomy depends on this eunomic fusion.

The remainder of the essay sets an Indigenous *themis* against its Christian counterpart, the latter personified in a "solemn-faced 'native preacher'" who parrots the "jangling phrases of a bigoted creed" (Zitkala-Ša 116). Exceeding the critiques offered by Occom, Apess, and

Winnemucca concerning the limitations and hypocrisies of Christian *practice,* Zitkala-Ša suggests that the faith itself is inherently hostile to nonwhites and to her own Indigenous appreciation that "all are akin" (116). Though she does not develop the argument, she implicates Christian monotheism in positing, with a mix of ignorance and sublimated viciousness, a clean division between good and evil: "In the upper region the Christian dead are gathered in unceasing song and prayer," according to her "native preacher," and "In the deep pit below, the sinful ones dance in torturing flames" (116). Zitkala-Ša intriguingly foretells here thematic preoccupations in the work of Erdrich and Vizenor, who similarly associate Christianity with a dangerous urge to divide and dominate. The monotheistic derogation of the other has contributed, Zitkala-Ša hints, to the oppression of Native peoples, improperly threatened humanity with hellfire, and obscured the polytheistic universe humming around us. There is, she insists, something more fluid in the themistic order than Christians have assumed, something inherently playful and welcoming. The Great Spirit wears, we are told, a "fluttering robe," and "the phenomenal universe"—rightly understood—"is a royal mantle, vibrating with His divine breath" (117). Within that enveloping dynamism the self may find its eunomic home.

That home's terms are further elaborated in the prophetic short narrative "A Dream of Her Grandfather." The narrator discovers here that she has been gifted by her ancestor with "a large cedar chest" (141), which opens to reveal a stunning vision of resurgent Native life (and an imaginative inversion of the desolation Hemingway will limn in his own "Indian Camp"):

> A picture of an Indian camp, not painted on canvas nor yet written. It was dream-stuff, suspended in the thin air, filling the inclosure of the cedar wood container. As she looked upon it, the picture grew more and more real, exceeding the proportions of the chest. It was all so illusive a breath might have blown it away; yet there it was, real as life,—a circular camp of white cone-shaped tepees, astir with Indian people. The village crier, with flowing head-dress of eagle plumes, mounted on a prancing white pony, rode within the arena. Indian men, women and children stopped in groups and clusters,

> while bright painted faces peered out of tepee doors, to listen to the chieftain's crier.
>
> At this point, she, too, heard the full melodious voice. She heard distinctly the Dakota words he proclaimed to the people. "Be glad! Rejoice! Look up, and see the new day dawning! Help is near! Hear me, every one."
>
> She caught the glad tidings and was thrilled with new hope for her people. (142)

Help is to come, seemingly, from the imaginative transfiguration of an ancestral heritage—its "circular camp" of communal dwellings—into a new reality. Zitkala-Ša thus prophesies the third, reintegrative stage of cultural evolution laid out in *Legends* and anticipates the work of Momaday, Erdrich, and Vizenor, whose own visions of Indigenous *eunomia* suggest its increasing, tantalizing proximity.

FIVE

The Tent and the *Thipi* II
Joseph Heller and N. Scott Momaday

JOSEPH HELLER'S *Something Happened* (1974) introduces us to Bob Slocum, a white, middle-aged, superficially successful corporate executive who detests, but can imagine no credible alternative to, the barrenness of his nomistic world. Paranoia radiates from the competitive ethos of Slocum's workplace, which he thoroughly absorbs and radiates back into all his interpersonal relationships. Both human and non-human tutors of the self are, it would seem, utterly unavailable here: miserably distanced from kin or any wider community and unable to connect with a benevolent divinity on solitary terms (as Twain's Huck Finn and Hemingway's Nick Adams sometimes can), Slocum languishes in sterile isolation.

With Slocum's intensified centripetal turn Heller charts, I suggest, a further nullification of Euro-American autonomy's seminal potencies and anticipates the ultimate collapse of autonomy explored, in this book's final chapter, through DeLillo's Eric Packer and his self-annihilating merger with technological prosthetics. Jefferson's rationalist commitments and Emerson's visionary nomistic detachment become in Slocum an essentially solipsistic and nihilistic enterprise, a means of evading self-understanding and of denying rather than deepening his relations with other selves. Such scrutiny borrows the basic method of its predecessors—a seemingly vigorous effort to command the self by understanding its fundamental truths—but only produces an insulated welter of self-loathing and self-pleasure, not the wisdom necessary for a vital autonomy. Lacking any meaningful connection to the natural world, Slocum confronts a hostile *themis* that resembles little more than a projection of his stricken *nomos*, a terrible and unfathomable something that has happened and keeps happening to him.

He will interrogate it endlessly—but fruitlessly. There is, according to the dysnomic terms of this dark and stagnant inwardness, no other territory one might light out for.

N. Scott Momaday's *House Made of Dawn* (1968) forms a dramatic contrast to Heller's pessimistic vision. Here, a troubled World War II veteran named Abel discovers the potential for a resurgent autonomy in encounters with kin and a nourishing *themis* still accessible within the natural world. Where Heller explores an inert, self-consumptive version of Euro-American self-rule against a spiritually barren and often strangely abstract backdrop, Momaday suggests a model for the ascendance of a vibrant Native counterpart informed by communal relationships and framed by the divine law governing specific geographies. A curious paradox, which began to emerge in the last chapter's exploration of Nick's privacy and Zitkala-Ša's communality, becomes starkly visible here: in freeing himself of meaningful ties beyond himself, Slocum is left perfectly enslaved, while Abel, in beginning to subordinate himself to versions of ancestral traditions and the themistic presences in nature, finds the ground of eunomic liberation.

Like Winnemucca and Zitkala-Ša, Momaday ultimately pursues, though now in even more expansive and ambitious forms than his precursors, a kind of shamanic healing and reverse missionary work. In his reimagination of Euro-American and Native narratives he brings to the dominant culture, in its own language and most esteemed literary genre, distinctive re-creations of an Indigenous heritage which challenge that culture's morbidities. Momaday would, in Zitkala-Ša's terms, enact his own prophetic "transplantation" of "vital spirits," not just to preserve the various Native cultures from which they arose but to transfigure the broader nomistic world in which they find a new home.

Heller's Bob Slocum—whose name may ironically allude to the adventurer Joshua Slocum, the first sailor to circumnavigate the world alone—works for a nameless corporation, performing vaguely defined and spiritually deadening, if handsomely rewarded, labor. Though he may have accumulated a good deal of nomistic power, confirmed in his professional role and ability to consume a range of physical pleasures,

Slocum is haunted by a "sense of pathless isolation" (122). Shadowy, malevolent powers seemingly rule his life:

> I get the willies when I see closed doors. Even at work, where I am doing so well now, the sight of a closed door is sometimes enough to make me dread that something horrible is happening behind it, something that is going to affect me adversely; if I am tired and dejected from a night of lies or booze or sex or just plain nerves and insomnia, I can almost smell the disaster mounting invisibly and flooding out toward me through the frosted glass panes. My hands may perspire, and my voice may come out strange. I wonder why. (1)

Huck Finn's fear of "lonesome" places and Nick Adams's of a psychic "swamp" are remarkably augmented here. In the haunting indeterminacy of *some*—"Something must have happened to me sometime" (1), "Somebody must have set me off in this direction" (286)—Slocum identifies a vestigial, malevolent, finally inscrutable *themis*. He will probe his anxieties with an alleged candor, carrying out a solitary and ostensibly intrepid circumnavigation of his *nomos*, but he never arrives at a firm sense of what, in fact, might have led him to the oppressive region he now inhabits. "The world," he tells us, "just doesn't work. It's an idea whose time is gone" (11).

The deep etymology of *some* is, however, curiously and metaphysically redolent here of a quite determinate affliction. The word, along with *same*, ultimately comes to English from the Proto-Indo-European root **sem*—"one; as one, together with." Evocations of a punitive themistic presence, read with these various senses in mind, take on shades of pathological nondifferentiation: "*one*-thing happened," "*as-one*-body happened," "*same*-thing must have happened." The world does not work, that is, because it has been reduced to a bleak oneness or sameness. Compelled to pursue an endless self-interrogation, but shirking genuine confrontations with other selves and any cooperative interaction with them, Slocum languishes, self-consumptively, in isolate autonomy.

Slocum's workplace, which functions according to a ruthless dynamic common to all his interpersonal relationships, models this oneness, a pathological *somewhere*. He fears, and is feared by, his coworkers, for every member of his corporation is set against each other in a finally private struggle for survival. The capitalist imperatives here—which in DeLillo's *Cosmopolis* sponsor an even more extreme sense of sameness and destructive predation—subvert the cultivation of a reliable, meaningful identity. Ostensible victories for the self, such as a promotion or some other marker of professional achievement, are always precarious, suggesting merely the deferral of a painful comeuppance. The salesmen who work for his corporation, Slocum notes, in a description that applies to himself, are "cheerful, confident, and gregarious when they are not irritable, anxious, and depressed" (23). Domestic life, anything but a refuge from the workplace, only reproduces the paranoia of solitary agents who mistrust one another's motives: "In the family in which I live there are four people of whom I am afraid. Three of these four people are afraid of me, and each of these three is also afraid of the other two" (333). A terrible *onething* or *samething*, whispering of the sequestered and morbidly defensive conditions of all selfhood, lurks in every potential contact with other selves, blighting self-pasture.

Tellingly, Slocum imagines his liberty to range at will in terms of the absence of others' moral claims on him. Bureaucratic structures themselves, which are otherwise condemned for entrapping him and exacerbating his paranoia, seem to promise sanctuary from interpersonal encumbrances and moral reckoning. Slocum's preferred tent, an utter negation of Zitkala-Ša's communal teepee, is even more interpersonally austere than that of Hemingway's Nick (who at least remembers certain others fondly): "Only in the army do I think I had more freedom of choice [than within corporate life], more room in which to move about. At least I *felt* I did. I did. I was outside my family, had no wife, job, parent, children, met no one I cared for. I had no ties. I had no one anywhere I cared for" (400). Slocum's family does indeed, he informs us, complicate his sense of atomic self-rule, his sameness and solitude, for his wife and children act as reminders of an obligation to care beyond himself: "(I feel more at home in my office now than I do at home, and I don't feel at home there. I get along better with the people there)" (459). Such declarations grimly ironize Emersonian detachment at the moment of revelation—"The name of the nearest friend sounds then foreign and accidental: to be brothers, to be acquaintances,—master or servant, is then a trifle and a disturbance" (*Nature* 6)—or the wistful yearning of Huck Finn to shed nagging social bonds—"All I wanted was to go somewhere; all I wanted was a change; I warn't particular" (Twain 10). What the self gets away *to* here is not some place outside the merely human order, where a revitalizing *themis* beckons, but rather a *sameplace* within it, offering shallow nomistic comforts in isolation as profound personal attachments are denied.

Slocum's feelings of homelessness, like every other aspect of his life, are subjected to what he would pass off as thoroughgoing analysis. He will, characteristically, identify some dimension of his misery, reflect on his own identification of it, condemn himself for prolonging it, wallow in that condemnation, but then, just as surely, neutralize the potential of the process to yield any ameliorative results by retreating into deflective, and ultimately self-flattering, mockery:

> Really, I ask myself every now and then, . . . is this *all* there is for me to do? Is this really the *most* I can get from the few years left in this one life of mine?
>
> And the answer I get, of course, is always . . . *Yes!*
>
> Because I have my job, draw my pay, get my laughs, and seem to be able to get one girl or another to go to bed with me just about every time I want; because I am envied and looked up to by neighbors and coworkers with smaller salaries, less personality, drab wives; and because I really do seem to have everything I want. (Heller 26)

The effect of these deliberations is, at last, only to mimic a genuine investigation.

Heller's protagonist ultimately models, as Andre Furlani has argued, the desolate endpoint of an ancient technique of wisdom-seeking. Rather than questioning himself and his *nomos* with unyielding honesty, in the manner of Socratic elenchus, Slocum in fact commits himself to "diversionary tactic[s]" (Furlani 251) meant to elude uncomfortable truths. Relishing the sense of mastery conferred by carrying out on others and himself an extended process of critical dissection, but nullifying disturbing discoveries through relentless irony (above all, in regard to his own ongoing complicity in his own and others' misery), he turns the effort to "know thyself" into a self-serving sham. Christopher Lasch's landmark *The Culture of Narcissism: American Life in an Age of Diminishing Expectations* (1979), which repeatedly turns to Heller's novel for illustrations of cultural pathologies, posits such insular enterprises as a definitive feature of contemporary American life. For Lasch, narcissism—a version of isolate autonomy—traps the self within itself, denying the potential for growth through genuine acknowledgment of the reality of other selves. As he notes in regard to Slocum's involuntary imitation of others' language and behavior:

> The narcissist cannot identify with someone else without seeing the other as an extension of himself, without obliterating the other's identity. Incapable of identification, in the first instance with parents and other authority figures, he is therefore incapable of hero worship or of the suspension of disbelief that makes it possible to enter imaginatively into the lives of others while acknowledging their independent existence. (86)

Though he does not specifically refer to Heller as he identifies an emergent literary mode of "anticonfession" and its ironic dynamics of pseudo-self-interrogation, Lasch aptly characterizes Slocum's emptying of elenctic potential:

> The voyage to the interior discloses nothing but a blank. The writer no longer sees life reflected in his own mind. Just the opposite: he sees the world, even in its emptiness, as a mirror of himself. In recording his 'inner' experiences, he seeks not to provide an objective account of a representative piece of reality but to seduce others into giving him their attention, acclaim, or sympathy and thus to shore up his faltering sense of self. (20–21)

Such voyages, propelled by a sense of the unreality, at last, of *both* self and other, can only map a shallow sameness.

Socrates and other elenctic inquisitors were able to engage benevolent divine presences through diligent effort and a willingness to make themselves vulnerable to unsettling encounters. Cut off from such engagement and convinced that whatever themistic potency exists in his world is set against (and for) him, Slocum feels untethered to anything beyond himself and thus able to dodge any responsibility he might feel to *change* because of what his self-scrutiny reveals. His elenctic efforts do not maintain the potential for a humble accumulation of wisdom nor a stimulus to intellectual and spiritual growth but amount instead to a cowardly refusal to pursue the examined life honestly. The novel at last illustrates for us, as Furlani contends, "the perversity of a representative modern soul, and in that perversity the elenchus becomes escapist: the elenctic confrontation itself becomes the essential means for avoidance of any genuine confrontation; the shaming becomes supportive; the doubt, reassuring; the undermining, constructive—of perfect moral *stasis*" (266). Too cowardly to devote himself to improving his actual relations with his family and others, and unable to discern a redemptive divinity in his all-too-human environment, Slocum concludes that his own predicament—the horrible *something* that happened and continues to happen to him—is finally inexplicable and beyond his control, a themistic order legislating his impotence: "I suppose it is just about impossible for someone like me to rebel anymore and produce any kind of lasting effect. I have lost the power to upset things that I had as a child; I can no longer change my environment or even disturb it seriously" (Heller 15). The forked quality of this confession is emblematic: Slocum diagnoses his own pathology with ostensible forthrightness, then affirms, self-pityingly and self-consolingly, that it relieves him of having to do anything. In a cynical simulation of analytic rigor, his lengthy inquiries intentionally circle round themselves and lead nowhere: he withdraws into a self-pasture that, though often as torturous as it is tortuous, at least offers a measure of complacent self-possession and self-inhabitance, an onanistic deferral punningly implied, perhaps, in his name itself. The role of gadfly, so important for Socrates and Emerson in their conceptions of vital selfhood, is utterly abandoned, as Slocum ensures, in his disavowal of otherness, that nothing happens to alter himself or his community.

Heller's pathological "modern soul" also empties, of course, the potential located in the versions of elenctic inquiry practiced by Jefferson and Emerson, whose celebrations of autonomy depend not just on moral resoluteness but on the self's access to a vivifying *themis* in the nonhuman environment. We might think again, for instance, of

Jefferson's orchestration in *Notes* of his responses to beautiful and sublime spectacles in the natural world, or Emerson's masterly considerations of what he takes to be Nature's inexhaustible resources. These moments depend upon a themistic stimulus which produces a sense of augmented power as the self identifies with and transmutes the potencies of the natural world. For Slocum, orchestration and a certain sense of mastery persist, but only in regard to the etiolated *themis* he knows through the nomistic world. Emerson's sense of innocent play—"Turn the eyes upside down, by looking at the landscape through your legs, and how agreeable is the picture, though you have seen it any time these twenty years!" (*Nature* 26)—yields here to a cynical toying with experience. Firmly and exclusively rooted in the human, all that the self beholds tends toward a self-referential abstractness: the offices Slocum describes lack distinguishing specificity and are essentially interchangeable, their most memorable feature being, typically, their ability to produce some manner of nagging anxiety or fleeting gratification related to the petty human dramas staged there. The closed doors that torment him might belong to any American corporation, in any American city. What environs the self becomes inconsequential next to that self's shielded, incessant analysis of its own terrors and satisfactions, its centripetal *somewhere*.

Descriptions of the natural world are, in fact, almost entirely absent from the novel, having been ingested and excreted, like everything else, by Slocum's malignant sameness. The seasons are human ones, a kind of themistic residua reflecting the pathologies of his *nomos,* which he nevertheless continues to probe, futilely, for deeper meanings. Cycles of firings or promotions and the annual company convention punctuate, but do not give any satisfying meaning to, the passage of time. On the rare occasions that we *do* hear about the nonhuman environment, its particulars simply shadow the human order and are marshaled with comic condemnation:

> All of us live now—we are very well off—in luxury . . . in a gorgeous two-story wood colonial house with white shutters on a choice country acre in Connecticut off a winding, picturesque asphalt road called Peapod Lane—and I hate it. There are rose bushes, zinnias,

and chrysanthemums rooted all about, and I hate them too. I have sycamores and chestnut trees in my glade and my glen.... Families with horses for pets do live nearby, and I hate them too, the families *and* the horses.... I hate my neighbor, and he hates me. (Heller 334)

The physical home Slocum shares with his family is, for him, merely a quantifiable, instrumental, fungible reflection of his prestige, and it encourages further anxieties about his status relative to others: "[A rival co-worker] lives not far away in a much better house in a much richer part of Connecticut than I do.... He has more land. (I own one acre, he owns four.) Most of the people around me seem to make more money than I do. Where I live now is perfectly adequate: and when I get my raise and move, it will again be among people who make more money than I do" (493). Distanced in this way, the self's physical ground can only yield such empty (and aggravating) hierarchies.

Within his defensive sameness Slocum also loses definition *as* a self. Having evaded honest confrontations with kin, as well as bracing interactions with what Emerson called the "natural history" that might "give us aid in supernatural history," the "outer creation" that might "give us language for the beings and changes of the inward creation" (*Nature* 13), he struggles to locate himself against an undifferentiated background. Whatever wretched autonomy he preserves through his version of the elenchus is haunted by the sense that he is himself little more than a symptom of a reduced, punitive *themis* and its expression through the nomistic world that environs him. Slocum in fact hyperbolizes Emerson's notions of bovine conformity in his compulsive brooding, morbidly choosing to "grope among the dry bones of the past, or put the living generation into masquerade out of its faded wardrobe" (*Nature* 3). Like a Huck Finn bereft of empathy and denied the themistic promise of raft or Territory, he moves within the nomistic world as a cynical and finally involuntary role-player, often unsure what self might exist beneath his various impostures. Rather than standing, with visionary boldness, outside of constrictive nomistic conventions, which he might revise and reinvigorate, he makes a bleak home within them, having developed a "subtle, sneaky, almost enslaving instinct to be like just about anyone I happen to find myself with" (Heller 64). Slocum's terminal mimicry is particularly evident in his failure to produce, as Emerson counseled, new and living speech: "It amuses me in a discouraging way to know I borrow adjectives, nouns, verbs, and short phrases from people I am with and frequently find myself trapped inside their smaller vocabularies like a hamster in a cage. Their language becomes my language" (66). A terrible *something* has happened, Slocum knows, to the vital self that might find expression in words, for he can only feed on and regurgitate the unnourishing human *nomos:* "(*I* may never speak. In dreams I often have trouble speaking. My tongue feels dead and dry and swollen enough to choke my mouth. Its coat is coarse. It will not move when I want it to, and I am in danger and feel terror because I cannot speak or scream)" (332).

Slocum recalls working as a youth for the "third largest automobile casualty insurance company in the whole world" (78–79). The industry is a fitting metaphor, since the death of fantasies of automobility and schemes for self-protection are this novel's presiding themes. What might, for Jefferson or Emerson, have been claimed robustly in direct engagement with the natural world—or, for Twain or Hemingway, delicately sustained in private retreats—has disappeared for Heller's protagonist. Only a malignant, inscrutable *themis* remains, and personal autonomy, a cursed one-and-the-sameness, finds no salvation within the communal whole. Isolate, antagonistic selves drift together down this sterile Mississippi: "I am a stick: I am a broken waterlogged branch floating with my own crowd in this one nation of ours, indivisible (unfortunately), under God, with liberty and justice for all who are speedy enough to seize them first and hog them away from the rest" (284). At the novel's end, having literally killed off, in his eldest son, the only self he seems capable of having loved (but who also threatened his sense of moral insulation), Slocum leaves us with an appropriately complacent summation of his vacuous self-rule and the vacuous *nomos* in which he practices it: "Everyone seems pleased with the way I've taken command" (530).

In his essay "An American Land Ethic" (1970), N. Scott Momaday affirms a fundamental, relational connection between human selves and the divine presences of the natural world. What Euro-America has long misunderstood and Native America might yet teach it, he avers, is how to subordinate—and liberate—the self within this themistic order. The "technological revolution" has "uproot[ed] us from the soil," and "we have suffered a kind of psychic dislocation of ourselves in time and space" ("American" 47–48). A proper reorientation would involve an acute, sustained attention to the interdependence of human and non-human presences:

> None of us lives apart from the land entirely; such an isolation is unimaginable. We have sooner or later to come to terms with the world around us—and I mean especially the physical world, not only as it is revealed to us immediately through our senses, but also as it is perceived more truly in the long turn of seasons and of years. And we must come to moral terms. There is no alternative, I believe, if we are to realize and maintain our humanity, for our humanity must consist in part in the ethical as well as in the practical ideal of preservation. And particularly here and now is that true. We Americans need now more than ever before—and indeed more than we know—to imagine who and what we are with respect to the earth and sky. (47)

Momaday's land ethic also demands a profound imaginative connection of the self to its ancestors. He frames his discussion of vital responses to the natural world with recollections and visionary conjurations of Ko-sahn, an elderly woman in whom rich tribal memories and a precious awareness of the conditions of eunomic autonomy are preserved. For Ko-sahn, a perfect foil to Heller's Slocum and the sameness of his atomic selfhood, "individual" and "racial" experience merge harmoniously, the personal and the collective "realized for her in the one memory, and that was of the land . . . the common denominator of everything that she knew and would ever know" (48). Such Native selfhood is thus located within, and remains radically responsible to and for, a network of the human and nonhuman.

House Made of Dawn is engaged in the moral and therapeutic enterprise Momaday sets out here, as he takes on in the novel, more ambitiously than Winnemucca or even Zitkala-Ša, the role of shaman and missionary *to* Euro-America. The novel follows the spiritual journey of Abel, a mixed-race member of the Jemez Pueblo whose traumatic experiences in World War II have intensified a lifelong sense of isolation. Failing to integrate with his culture after returning from service, he ends up murdering a man, is sent to prison and, after being paroled, to an urban relocation program in Los Angeles. Finally making his way back home, he begins, seemingly, to recover a vital, eunomic autonomy informed by the example of his grandfather Francisco. Momaday's adaptation in the novel of Pueblo, Navajo, and Kiowa traditions—set within a remarkably intricate text that employs modernist literary techniques and repeatedly echoes and alludes to canonical non-Native authors—aims to reorient Native selfhood and the conditions of its rule in time and space, preserving a traditional reverence for the natural world within the syncretic context of the contemporary age.

Where Heller presents a troubled protagonist who reduces his experience to a miserable oneness and sameness, Momaday gives us a Native counterpart who holds out the promise of opening himself to the potent, healing themistic order in the natural world. *Where* Abel is and has been will be critically important to that promise. The novel highlights the significance of place, and the myriad presences encountered there, as the essential wellspring of meaning and the necessary frame for understanding selfhood and self-rule. Unlike Slocum, whose spurious elenchizing only confirms his pained but all-too-comfortable isolation, ignorance, and nostalgia, Abel may ultimately reach beyond a barren self-pasture toward a nexus of human and nonhuman being. For him, as Vine Deloria Jr. claims of the spirituality of traditional Native peoples more generally, "revelation" is to be understood as "a continuous process of adjustment to the natural surroundings and not as a specific message valid for all times and places" (66). Revelatory things have been happening and continue to happen, that is, according to the locale where Abel and his ancestors have lived, and his selfhood depends utterly on how he will acknowledge his obligations to them.

Part of what has barred Abel from an integration with land and community is his insistence on acting—like Zitkala-Ša's Iktomi or Hemingway's Nick—as if he were an isolate self, without a responsibility to his *nomos* and the benevolent *themis* that informs it. In his recollection of leaving the pueblo as he headed off to war, he "had the sense of being all alone, as if he were already miles and months away, gone long ago from the town and the valley and the hills, from everything he knew and had always known ... centred upon himself in the onset of loneliness and fear" (Momaday *House* 21). Momaday further clarifies the terms of his protagonist's pathology in his killing of Juan Reyes, an albino tribal member associated in the novel with malevolent spirits. Humiliated by Reyes during a ceremonial performance in which his failure to perform tribal customs appropriately is publicly displayed, Abel attacks his rival outside a bar. The whiteness of the victim and the eroticized manner in which he seems to invite his own death suggest, among other implications, a critique of the toxic legacy of Euro-American culture on the Jemez (and other Indigenous peoples): "The white man raised his arms, as if to embrace him, and came forward. But Abel had already taken hold of the knife, and he drew it. He leaned inside the white man's arms and drove the blade under the bones of the breast and across. The white man's hands lay on Abel's shoulders, and for a moment the white man stood very still" (73). Abel is lured here into self-defeating violence against a symbolic antagonist, and in his paranoid aggression he will take on the role of solitary vengeance-seeker. Significantly, he loses agency the more he seeks to claim it: "The white hands laid hold of Abel and drew him close, and the terrible strength of the hands was brought to bear only in proportion as Abel resisted them. In his terror he knew only to wield the knife" (74). Though he will characterize himself as acting on behalf of some higher law—"It was the most natural thing in the world ... [knowing] what the white man was .... A man kills such an enemy if he can" (90–91)—he has, contrary to the tribal *nomos* which demands a communal sanction for violence, laid solitary claim to *themis*, a perverse and destructive autonomy.[1]

Francisco's own encounter with Reyes (who seems to approach him, in the form of a snake, while he tends a plot of corn) ends with a recognition of the other's presence and a humble withdrawal from it. The elderly man, possessing a wisdom his grandson has not yet inherited, departs from this representative of inimical obscurity—what lurks, for Slocum, behind every closed door—without fearing it or seeking its obliteration: "He was too old to be afraid. His acknowledgment of the unknown was nothing more than a dull, intrinsic sadness, a vague desire to weep, for evil had long since found him out and knew who he was" (59–60). Such a reaction, as Louis Owens (Choctaw-Cherokee) explains, highlights the folly of thinking that any self, or any community of selves, might finally triumph over evil:

> Particularly in the Navajo worldview, the universe from the time of creation has been a dangerous place balanced precariously between good and evil. Both Pueblo and Navajo healing ceremonies—such as the Night Chant in *House Made of Dawn*—are focused upon restoring harmony or balance within the individual and among natural, human, and supernatural elements that make up the world. In this vein, the rattlesnake is respected and feared by the Pueblo peoples and is considered a powerful, dangerous presence, but it is to be acknowledged and avoided, never killed. The identification of ... the albino with the serpent suggests that Francisco's is the only acceptable response. (104–5)

Like Zitkala-Ša in her essay "The Great Spirit"—and in anticipation of thematic concerns which become prominent in the novels of Erdrich and Vizenor—Momaday hints here at the wrongness of strict binary divisions between good and evil, associating them with ruinous efforts to dominate the nonhuman. Abel has responded unacceptably not merely by violating human laws, whose Euro-American representatives must prosecute him for his crime, but by ignoring overarching themistic imperatives. Though they may deny it, humans are embedded in and responsible to a balanced natural world, Momaday implies, and a distinctive ethic emerges from acknowledging this. That ethic would eschew the masterful aspirations of Emerson's effectively deified self and its efforts to "[b]uild, therefore, [its] own world" and finally "draw beautiful faces, warm hearts, wise discourse, and heroic acts, around its way, until evil is no more seen" (*Nature* 39). It would also reject Slocum's insulated self-pasture as another highly destructive, self-delusive evasion of relationality. Native autonomy would, instead, place the self where it properly belongs, within a liberating themistic subordination.

Relocated to Los Angeles [Greek *angelos:* "messenger"] after his prison sentence, Abel will further confirm his distance from that liberation. Though he has, from childhood, felt like an outsider at Jemez Pueblo, in an urban milieu he loses all hope of orientation. Abel has, in effect, become like the biblical *Cain,* exiled from the fecundity of the earth itself, "a fugitive and a vagabond" who "builded a city" (Gen. 4:14, 17). His cursed wandering emblematizes the folly of human presumptions to autonomy: "Now, here, the world was open at his back. He had lost his place. He had been long ago at the center, had known where he was, had lost his way, had wandered to the end of the earth, was even now reeling on the edge of the void" (Momaday *House* 92). Intriguingly, Momaday echoes here Jefferson's own biblical wordplay in a passage from *Notes on the State of Virginia* condemning the "mark set on those" who, distanced from "their own soil and industry," become prey to "tools for the designs of ambition" (*Notes* 170–71). Cain, we may recall, begat the toolmaker Tubalcain, "an instructer of every artificer in brass and iron" (Gen. 4:20 *KJV*). The city's murderous artificiality now carries the mark of Cain not just for his protagonist but for all Americans, we are to understand, for it exiles the self from nourishing self-pasture.

Like thousands of Native Americans who were moved to cities by federal agencies in the early 1950s, Abel is offered access to employment, housing, and social support services intended to accelerate his cultural assimilation. Euro-American methods of healing and nomistic integration fail him, however, for they emphasize a narrow, atomistic definition of selfhood while trusting the efficacy of impersonal bureaucratic structures. The job Abel takes on—as a stapler in a factory—does not offer a means of securing a meaningful identity, for such work itself, Momaday suggests, cannot bind the self to anything that would sustain it. Abel is supervised in his urban life by a series of state representatives who seek to guide his assimilation but only manage, in technocratic fashion, to be coolly intrusive. This mode of impersonal care is received, as his friend Ben Benally explains, as a kind of nagging distortion of genuine kin relations: "The parole officer, and welfare, and the Relocation people kept coming around . . . and they were always after him about something. They wanted to know how he was doing, had he been staying out of trouble and all" (139). Each bureaucratic figure in this trio is loaded with ironic significance. Euro-American parole officers [French *parole:* "speech"] police Abel's linguistic and spiritual alienation: "They have a lot of *words,*" Ben tells us, "and you know they mean something, but you don't know what, and your own words are no good because they're not the same; they're different, and they're the only words you've got" (139; italics in original). Welfare and relocation people, relying on abstract definitions of self and place, offer untherapeutic definitions of what wellness might mean. In the midst of such conceptual disharmony, Abel's solitude is only intensified by contact with others.

Through the Rev. J. B. B. Tosamah, a Los Angeles preacher (or angelic messenger) who mixes Christian and Kiowa spiritual traditions, the novel deepens its critique of the disorientation brought on by a hubristic disconnection from the land and its redemptive *themis*. In one of his sermons Tosamah declares that language, traditionally capable of preserving themistic truths, has been deadened by the artifices of Euro-American parole officers, in part because of the technological ease with which it can be produced and disseminated there: "'On every side of him there are words by the millions, an unending succession of pamphlets and papers, letters and books, bills and bulletins, commentaries and conversations. . . . He is sated and insensitive; his regard for language—for the Word itself—as an instrument of creation has diminished nearly to the point of no return'" (84). Older, preliterate generations were, Tosamah contends, able to vitalize their speech through a connection to the earth: "[For my grandmother] words were medicine; they were magic and invisible. They came from nothing into sound and meaning. They were beyond price; they could neither be bought nor sold. And she never threw words away" (85). Like the land itself, language is properly understood, in Tosamah's understanding, according to a benevolent *themis* that informs but cannot be reduced to the human order. Commercial, technocratic environments—the cities of Cain, like the one Slocum inhabits—endlessly rationalize experience but, cut off from the natural world's themistic wellspring, produce only deadened speech. Slocum's elenchic burlesque is one manifestation of that morbidity, an artificial, onanistic enterprise precluding communication (or any profound communion) with other selves. For Momaday's Abel, what must somehow be reclaimed is the curative potency associated with traditions of oral storytelling, a "magic and invisible" language animated by the nonhuman and passed on, communally, by genuine kin.[2]

To claim a eunomic self-rule, Abel will, Momaday suggests, have to place his human self in humble (but ultimately empowering) relation to both the human and nonhuman presences that environ it. William Bevis's explication of homing plots in twentieth-century Native American novels aptly describes this potential dwelling for Abel: "Nature is 'house.' . . . What gives this system divinity is the same authority, distant past, and brotherhood which unites the tribe; 'sacred reciprocity' does not derive its sacredness only from a transaction with the awesomely distant or alien 'other.' One's meaningful identity includes society, past, place, and all the natural inhabitants of that place" (602). Francisco's recollection of his efforts to educate Abel during his childhood outlines the conditions of such communal embeddedness. The version of Indigenous *eunomia* we encounter here is worth considering at length:

> He made them [Abel and his brother Vidal] stand just there, above the point of the low white rock, facing east. They could see the black mesa looming on the first light, and he told them there was the house of the sun. They must learn the whole contour of the black mesa. They must know it as they knew the shape of their hands, always and by heart. The sun rose up on the black mesa at a different place each day. It began there, at a point on the central slope, standing still for the solstice, and ranged all the days southward across the rise and fall of the long plateau, drawing closer by the measure of mornings and moons to the lee, and back again. They must know the long journey of the sun on the black mesa, how it rode in the seasons and the years, and they must live according to the sun appearing, for only then could they reckon where they were, where all things were, in time. There, at the rounder knoll, it was time to plant corn; and there, where the highest plane fell away, that was the day of the rooster race, six days ahead of the black bull running and the little horse dancing, seven ahead of the Pecos immigration; and there, and there, and there, the secret dances, every four days of fasting in the kiva, the moon good for hoeing and the time for harvest, the rabbit and witch hunts, all the proper days of the clans and societies; and just there at the saddle, where the sky was lower and brighter than elsewhere on the high black land, the clearing of the

ditches in advance of the spring rains and the long race of the black men at dawn. (Momaday *House* 173; italics in original)

By this reckoning, the self is bound, and freed, within the rule of a divine order, eunomic autonomy achieved through subordination to nonhuman determinants of how one must live. One encounters and comes to know those determinants not, of course, so that one might subordinate them—in the manner of Jefferson's environmental inventories or Emerson's definition of the natural world as mere medium—but to subordinate the self in a relational, balanced cosmos. In Pueblo culture, as Paula Gunn Allen explains, the "House of the Sun [. . .] is the calendar which allows the people to locate their own equilibrium in the continuous interplay of the forces of the universe" (575). Abel's imagination of other tribal members' participation in a ceremonial run implies exactly this kind of bonded emancipation within the natural order: the runners move "as water runs, deep in the channel, in the way of least resistance, no resistance" (Momaday *House* 91). Communal self-rule thus proceeds, naturally and productively, along the paths laid down by the nonhuman world; personal self-rule proceeds, similarly, according to a community's long-standing responses to that world. Private retreat, of the kind practiced by Hemingway's Nick in his private tent, or Slocum in the sameness of his "pathless isolation" (Heller 122), is anathema, effectively a form of self-annihilation.

An enlightening example of how one must live and what one owes to the nonhuman world comes near the end of the novel with Francisco's story of a bear hunt. In order to kill the animal appropriately, his description makes clear, the hunter must recognize the selfhood of the hunted and ritualize his sacrifice of it: *"He brought the rifle up, and the bear raised and turned its head and made no sign of fear. . . . The bullet slammed into the flesh and jarred the whole black body once, but the head remained motionless and the eyes level upon him. . . . He took out his pouch of pollen and made yellow streaks above the bear's eyes"* (Momaday *House* 177; italics in original). Though Slocum's self-scrutiny pretends to entertain such moments of vulnerable confrontation with the consequences of his interactions with other selves and with himself, it finally closes off any possibilities for genuine responsiveness in favor of endless deferral. He cannot tolerate any other presence looking back at him, since that gaze might disrupt his complacency, the perverse internal balance of insulated pain and pleasure he has so carefully cultivated. In contrast, Francisco's encounter with the bear affirms a relational responsibility to active, demanding presences rather than (as even family members become for Slocum) de facto commodities: what he consumes *sees* him, and he must make moral terms with his own visibility. The broader self-rule he claims in the world operates on similar terms, tying him to dynamic interactions with both human and nonhuman selves.

The descriptions we are given of Francisco's teaching further underscore the communal dynamics of eunomic autonomy: the wisdom he imparts to his grandsons could not, it is clear, be fully transmitted as solitary revelation but necessarily demands ongoing, perpetually renewed interaction with others through storytelling and ritual performances. Returning home from war, Abel finds himself estranged from such interactions but retains, crucially, the potential to reclaim them. As he struggles to "say the things he wanted" (53), he discerns redemptive possibilities in a language spoken and respoken by kin: "[He] had tried to pray, to sing, to enter into the old rhythm of the tongue, but he was no longer attuned to it. And yet it was still there, like memory, in the reach of his hearing, as if Francisco or his mother or [brother] Vidal had spoken out of the past and the words had taken hold of the moment and made it eternal" (53). Amplifying those voices and his understanding of them, Abel has the opportunity to orient and reintegrate himself within a vibrant, geographically rooted nexus of being. The placeless, kin-stripped Slocum, who can identify no worthwhile alternatives to his isolate selfhood, simply wallows, with a characteristic mix of shame and self-pleasure, in his most significant memory, his mother's scathing deathbed judgment of him. The moral force of her words—"You're just no good" (510)—is glibly deflected by him, at last, and nothing changes in his relation to her. Conversely, Abel can finally respond to his grandfather's own deathbed appeals and their themistic ground, which convey to him, in effect, "You're just no good *now*, but could be." Opening himself to this wisdom, he promises to recover links between human and natural worlds, a sense of how he, and his kin, must live:

"[Francisco's] voice had failed each day, only to rise up again in the dawn. The old man had spoken six times in the dawn, and the voice of his memory was whole and clear and growing like the dawn" (172).[3]

The potential of this restorative process, key to the assumption of eunomic autonomy, is suggested again in Abel's relationship with Ben, a Navajo who is himself partly alienated from both Native and Euro-American worlds but nevertheless takes on the role of shamanic healer. Adapting the traditional Nightway chant, using the partial knowledge he possesses of it, Ben prays for his friend on a Los Angeles mountaintop, seemingly setting in motion a reorientation toward the divine and communal. Susan Scarberry-Garcia, detailing the mythic patterns that frame Abel's spiritual journey, explains the traditional Navajo understanding of inner forms and their relationship to the therapeutic treatment of wounded selves:

> During Chantway performances, the sources of healing are the inner forms of the Holy People who are the inner forms of the elements of nature and natural phenomena. . . . When a singer (medicine man) identifies one-sung-over (patient) through a sandpainting with the Holy Person whom he or she had offended, the strength of that Holy Person is internalized. At such epiphanal moments the Holy Person's ill will is transformed into benevolence and healing takes place. Inner form of the Holy Person merges with inner form of the ill person, as the one-sung-over is brought toward a whole reintegration with the land, through association with specific places and phenomena. . . . The rupture between inner and outer landscapes is closed and illness recedes. (9–10)

Though no such recession is immediately achieved by Ben's efforts in praying over Abel, its potential is established (and apparently has begun to be realized by the novel's close). The porousness of the self's borders—its sacrifice of individuality or Slocum-like sameness as it makes contact with a redemptive *themis*—is the means to liberation here. As the self becomes receptive and responsible to other presences grounded in a specific environment, it blurs the boundaries of what belongs to it alone, and in doing so does not lose definition (and power) but gains it. The assumption of such power stands, of course, in stark contrast to

Emerson's description of a natural world "made to serve": the self's rule is claimed, instead, within a relational system, in an always communal service to it.

Autonomy, on these terms, involves a paradoxical form of self-abandonment as the self is absorbed, positively, into something larger. Early in the novel we learn of Abel's potential for such absorption, a merging with a seemingly benevolent *themis* that might, if somehow developed, contribute to his healing. A woman named Angela St. John—herself an angel or messenger and the receiver of a sacred message—hires him as a laborer and, watching him cutting wood, is moved by the way he seems to disappear into his work and assume a visionary "attitude of non being" (33). Though her perspective is complicated by her inability, at this stage of the narrative, to imagine her own vital participation in a redemptive themistic realm, she seems to apprehend its possibilities through Abel: "To see beyond the landscape, beyond every shape and shadow and color, *that* was to see nothing. That was to be free and finished, complete, spiritual. To see nothing slowly and by degrees, at last. . . . Somewhere, if only she could see it, there was neither nothing nor anything. And there, just there, *that* was the last reality" (33). In contrast to Slocum's narcissistic samewhere, which reduces the world to endless self-reflections, this somewhere would seemingly dissolve an isolate self-consciousness. The mystical rhetoric Momaday assigns to Angela evokes Rilke's famous description of a transcendent state, available to angels, animals, and children, beyond the self's quotidian rule: a "Nowhere without the No: that pure / unseparated element which one breathes / without desire and endlessly *knows*" (49; italics in original). Such selfless awareness would see "all time / and itself within all time, forever healed" (51). Entering that state, Abel becomes, we might say, the literal meaning of his name in Hebrew: "breath."

The extraordinary promise of such transcendence, a dissolution of the quotidian self into an empowering themistic order, is elaborated at the novel's end. Momaday apparently draws here on D. H. Lawrence's reflections on Pueblo tribal culture's receptivity to "the elemental life of the cosmos" in such practices as ceremonial running: "This effort into sheer naked contact, *without an intermediary or mediator,* is the root meaning of religion, and at the sacred races the runners hurled themselves in a terrible cumulative effort, through the air, to come at last into naked contact with the very life of the air, which is the life of the clouds, and so of the rain" ("New Mexico" 147; italics in original). Recovering from physical and psychic injuries sustained in Los Angeles, Abel makes another return home and joins, after his grandfather's death, a tribal ceremony that promises themistic reintegration:

> He came among them, and they huddled in the cold together, waiting, and the pale light before the dawn rose up in the valley. A single cloud lay over the world, heavy and still. It lay out upon the black mesa, smudging out the margin and spilling over the lee. But at the saddle there was nothing. There was only the clear pool of eternity. They held their eyes upon it, waiting, and, too slow and various to see, the void began to deepen and to change: pumice, and pearl, and mother-of-pearl, and the pale and brilliant blush of orange and of rose. And then the deep hanging rim ran with fire and the sudden cold flare of the dawn struck upon the arc, and the runners sprang away. (Momaday *House* 185)

A specific geography, and a ritualized response to it by kin, are crucial to Abel's reorientation. Surrendering himself to the tribal ceremony, he loses (and gains) himself in place: "Pure exhaustion laid hold of his mind, and he could see at last without having to think" (185). He enters, in Rilke's formulation of self-transcendence, a "Nowhere without the No," "that pure space into which flowers / endlessly open" (Rilke 49). As Abel recalls the Navajo Nightway sung over him by Ben, he begins to discover, it would seem, the means of realizing a eunomic autonomy. The novel's final word signals the formal end of a Jemez oral narrative and thus reinforces, again, the shared dimension of Abel's incipient claim to a self-rule informed by a mix of Native traditions: "He was running, and under his breath he began to sing. There was no sound, and he had no voice; he had only the words of a song. And he went running on the rise of the song. *House made of pollen, house made of dawn. Qtsedaba*" (Momaday *House* 185; italics in original).

Much remains uncertain in this narrative, of course, about Abel's future. He is left voiceless, and we do not see him actually integrated into his community. Nevertheless, the novel does seem to establish a compelling, optimistic framework for eunomic self-rule according to the coordinates of its protagonist's journey home. Whatever autonomy he *does* claim, Momaday implies, will involve the creative adaptation of traditional cultural practices—in ways, as we have seen, which often parallel those carried out by Occom, Apess, Winnemucca, and Zitkala-Ša.[4] Tosamah's tale of his grandmother emphasizes that adaptation over time and interaction with other cultures are natural processes and seemingly essential for communal growth. He points to the Kiowa's emancipating migration from the north centuries earlier: "[It was] a journey toward the dawn . . . [which] led to a golden age. Along the way the Kiowas were befriended by the Crows, who gave them the culture and religion of the plains. They acquired horses, and their ancient nomadic spirit was suddenly free of the ground" (113–14). The Jemez themselves are, moreover, striking illustrations of creative adaptation. The novel's narrator, in describing their long-standing resistance to colonization, underscores their ability to survive historical changes while preserving ancestral legacies:

> The people of the town have little need. They do not hanker after progress and have never changed their essential way of life. Their invaders were a long time in conquering them; and now, after four centuries of Christianity, they still pray in Tanoan to the old deities of the earth and sky and make their living from the things that are and have always been within their reach; while in the discrimination of pride they acquire from their conquerors only the luxury of example. They have assumed the names and gestures of their enemies, but have held on to their own, secret souls; and in this there is a resistance and an overcoming, a long outwaiting. (52–53)

Francisco himself is in fact a Catholic sacristan who maintains Jemez religious traditions, having Indigenized, like others in his community, the Christian *themis*.

If he is, indeed, to fulfil the promise that is held out for him at the novel's conclusion, Abel will not only have to accept his grandfather's vision of how one must live but *also,* it would seem, forge his own adaptation to modernity that will reject—or at least subordinate—part of that vision. Francisco's role as a farmer, or "tiller of the soil," might well suggest his status, from at least one perspective, as another ironic Cain, a brother who could slay Abel if the younger man does not find a way to adapt his ancestor's wisdom and make it flourish in the contemporary age. His eunomic self-rule must, that is, be critically informed by the gravity of place-bound memory and the force of established practices but remain flexible in its expression. What Abel and others will have to do, we are to understand, is find not just the right *old* forms and words, but the right *new* ones that will fit the evolving circumstances of the present day. Erdrich, and even more, Vizenor, as we shall see, furnish protagonists who undertake, with unprecedented assurance, exactly this sort of emancipatory blending of the traditional and modern.

SIX

Eunomia Lost and Regained
Don DeLillo, Louise Erdrich, and Gerald Vizenor

PREVIOUS CHAPTERS HAVE sketched the essentially chiastic trajectories of autonomy in two literary traditions, one suggesting morbid decline through an overdevelopment of the self's solitary rule, the other a gradual, hard-won ascendance rooted in traditional communalism. Among the ironies of this conceptual inversion is the dramatic reclamation in the Native American imaginary of what its Euro-American counterpart progressively lost: a version of *eunomia,* the vital blending of human and natural orders.

A juxtaposition of the work of Don DeLillo with that of Louise Erdrich and Gerald Vizenor illustrates the concluding stage of the story being told here. DeLillo's *Cosmopolis* (2003) charts, I contend, the culmination of pathologies first hinted at by Twain and explored in increasingly severe permutations by Hemingway and Heller. Here, a profoundly isolate self lacking and in fact contemptuous of significant ties to anything beyond itself aspires to an absolute rule over its environment. Augmented by contemporary technological prosthetics, that self would realize what was for Jefferson and (more extremely) Emerson an innocent fantasy—a comprehensive vision translated into masterful action. Instead of a fulfilling transcendence, however, such selfhood undergoes a paradoxical emptying out, losing definition and agency in its godlike rule, and finally seeking its own destruction.

Erdrich's *The Plague of Doves* (2008) also offers an indictment of the pathologies of Euro-American autonomy but sets against it a vibrant Native American alternative. In this sprawling, multigenerational tale of mass murder and its ramifying implications for a small community in North Dakota, Erdrich posits the fundamental linking of any self to a web of other selves, as well as to nonhuman presences within an animate, unpredictable, but not finally hostile or estranged natural order. The worldview she offers relies upon and elaborates crucial assumptions voiced from Occom through Momaday: that it is destructive folly to think of the self in isolation or as the locus of divine authority; that an embeddedness in place and an ultimate subordination to the various divine presences to be found there are essential for a flourishing selfhood; that self-rule is properly a collective ambition, not a personal one. Whereas DeLillo explores the end of the American Romantic faith in self-making—the final blindness of Emerson's "transparent eyeball" and the environmental command it seems to sanction—Erdrich insists on the potential of the self's vibrant response to and humble imbrication with all that would gaze back. The *themis* affirmed here is charged, in fact, with an extraordinary eroticism, at last uncontrollable in its operations but benevolent in its overall relationship to the human order. While acknowledging the tragic past and enduring afflictions that haunt Native America in the present, Erdrich finally outlines not merely a possible future for wounded "mixed-bloods" seeking integration with renovated traditions—as in Momaday's novel—but a firm, sustainable context for self-rule within a nourishing Indigenous *eunomia*.

Erdrich's representation of communal resilience exemplifies what Lawrence W. Gross calls the Anishinaabeg's "comic vision," narrative self-assertions that preserve and re-create links to an ancestral past with both mirth and resoluteness: "As long as we keep telling the old stories, we will persist as a people. And as long as we keep laughing at the old stories, not only will we survive, we will thrive once again" (458).[1] Vizenor's *Chair of Tears* (2012) shares this vision in its own exploration of eunomic autonomy as a vivifying dimension of contemporary Native life and an antidote to Euro-American pathologies. However, where Erdrich places her emphasis on the complex communal relations of her protagonists and on modest efforts to respect and practice Indigenous forms of self-rule in the wake of historical trauma and in resistance to an ongoing legacy of colonial abuse, Vizenor, while scrupulously giving voice to that trauma and legacy, also proffers a vatic assertion of how conceptually transformative Native self-rule can, and might yet, be. If DeLillo has sketched a tenebrous collapse, Vizenor limns, in this and other works, a luminous, ongoing resurgence. Providing what he calls a "stray vision" of Indigenous selfhood, he insists on the boundless creativity of its interaction with a capricious interplay of both divine and human presences. Autonomy involves here, in its radical opening of the self to chance and its erasure of strict divisions between self and other, a redemptive loss of individuality within an imaginatively dynamic "continent of liberty" (Vizenor *Chair* 112).

DeLillo's novel concerns a day in the life of one Eric [Old Norse *Eiríkr*: "lone ruler"] Packer, a billionaire financier who is, for much of the narrative, cocooned within an information-packed limousine as he tries to make his way across New York City in order to get a haircut with his favorite barber. Along the way he summons various guests into his moving office, makes brief trips outside it, seeks counsel from his security detail, is delayed in getting to his intended destination by traffic jams, and, at last, loses enormous amounts of money speculating badly in the foreign exchange markets.

A currency trader who covets "all the yen there [is]" (97), Packer would anticipate and exploit the yearning of market movements and thus collapse the future into the present. The penthouse triplex where he lives epitomizes that ambition, for it sits at the summit of an enormous tower, with a "rotating room at the top" (5), ostensibly presuming, like Emerson's transparent eyeball, to "see all" around it. Packer is, DeLillo implies, something like a (vestigially) human extension of this world-ordering panopticon: "The tower gave him strength and depth.... The one virtue of its surface was to skim and bend the river light and mime the tides of open sky. There was an aura of texture and reflection. He scanned its length and felt connected to it, sharing the surface and the environment that came into contact with the surface, from both sides" (9). Packer's limousine further suggests a vantage point of masterful containment and isolation (and a seer's effective disappearance into what is seen): the vehicle's characterization as a site of unidirectional observation is emphasized by its one-way glass windows, infrared cameras (which expand the range of the visible), and external nondescriptness: "Long white limousines had become the most unnoticed vehicles in the city" (11). Within this armored interior, DeLillo's ambitious speculator surveys streams of digitized information, commanding the world set before him, hardly separate from the technology he employs: "There were medleys of data on every screen, all the flowing symbols and alpine charts, the polychrome numbers pulsing.... The context was nearly touchless. He could talk most systems into operation or wave a hand at a screen and make it go blank" (13). Packer is himself a sort of personal cosmopolis, the point of convergence for an infinitely expanding "pack" or bundle of data. Ruthlessly predatory, he represents, too, a broader type or pack, the competitive capitalist hordes who share the atomistic proclivities of Heller's Slocum but now cultivate much more rationalized and etherealized retreats. This consumptive insulation involves, as Aaron Chandler explains in relation to the moral philosophy of Emmanuel Levinas, a reductive ordering (and exclusion) of other selves: "Packer's failure to see ethically is intimately connected with his compulsive systemization of the world. He cannot perceive others outside of the differential schematics of language.... [He] cannot sense the 'nudity' or 'ipseity' of others—their individuality—until he has filed them under a name and a genus to which they can be reduced" (251). Such selfhood, barred from knowledge of others and thus of itself, is finally isolated within its own presumptive rule, its centrifugal reach, and its centripetal pull.

Packer's mode of speculation thus modernizes and darkens Emerson's assumptions about the possibilities of transcendent vision. Though he is in fact being driven by someone else and is finally subject to the unknowable circumstances of the world outside his car (urban traffic, political protests, threats made by potential assassins, the indeterminacy of others' "yen")—external forces that shape his progress, as the Mississippi did Huck's—his limousine's interior space nurtures fantasies of a godlike automobility, the apogee of self-possession, self-regulation, self-rule. His currency speculation assumes, in fact, the possibility of establishing a comprehensive system of categorization and control, dramatically extending Jefferson's search in *Notes on the State of Virginia* for a supreme catalogue of empirical data:

> He looked past [his advisor] Chin toward streams of numbers running in opposite directions. He understood how much it meant to

him, the roll and flip of data on a screen. He studied the figural diagrams that brought organic patterns into play, birdwing and chambered shell. It was shallow thinking to maintain that numbers and charts were the cold compression of unruly human energies, every sort of yearning and midnight sweat reduced to lucid units in the financial markets. In fact data itself was soulful and glowing, a dynamic aspect of the life process. This was the eloquence of alphabets and numeric systems, now fully realized in electronic form, in the zero-oneness of the world, the digital imperative that defined every breath of the planet's living billions. Here was the heave of the biosphere. Our bodies and oceans were here, knowable and whole. (DeLillo 24)

For Packer, as Randy Laist observes, "information takes on the ontological character of the reality principle," and his efforts are directed toward "[living] authentically within his digital environment, just as sincerely as Thoreau sought to be true to his own vision of the natural" (262). Having largely blended with information technology and the ultimate reality it seems to reveal, Packer can seek to rule the natural much more thoroughly, of course, than the Transcendentalists. He dreams of the logical endpoint of such autonomy—the ascendance of a disembodied and all-but-selfless self—in pure disembodied code: "He'd always wanted to become quantum dust, transcending his body mass, the soft tissue over the bones, the muscle and fat. The idea was to live outside the given limits, in a chip, on a disk, as data, in whirl, in radiant spin, a consciousness saved from void" (DeLillo 206). Such desires correspond to what Katherine Hayles has famously explored as the posthuman fascination with disembodied seeing in virtualized environments:

> Cyberspace represents a quantum leap forward into the technological construction of vision. Instead of an embodied consciousness looking through the window at a scene, consciousness moves *through* the screen to become the pov [point of view], leaving behind the body as an unoccupied shell. In cyberspace, point of view does not emanate from the character; rather the pov literally *is* the character. (38)

This kind of transcendence would make permanent the bodiless vision of Emerson's transparent eyeball, while grounding it not in some natural scene—*Nature*'s woods or bare common—but in a human artifact, the chip or disk where a wraithlike, posthuman self endures. Wholly free of social entanglements, he would thus light out for a territory now perfectly abstract and private, perfectly *de*territorialized.

Cosmopolis explores the pathological terminus of such aspirations. An insomniac and hypochondriac, Packer is already, we are to understand, effectively "undead," ambiguously potent as a self even as he exercises tremendous worldly powers. Unlike Hemingway's Nick, who can claim a viable space for private pleasures, his social withdrawal is finally barren and unnatural: "Every act he performed was self-haunted and synthetic" (DeLillo 6). The expansive and affirmative logic of Emerson's "I am nothing; I see all" (*Nature* 6) is voided here, for Packer's seeing amounts, in amplifying a fantasy entertained by Heller's Slocum, to the solipsistic negation of everything the self would envision: "Nothing existed around him. . . . When he died he would not end. The world would end" (DeLillo 6). Where Jefferson imagined the fruitful blending of personal and corporate autonomy, DeLillo gives us its festering negation, an American anti-Arcadia marked by antisocial (and finally sterile) quests for private communion with the divine. For such a self, all that genuinely exists and might lay claim to moral attention is its own consumptive vision. A willful blindness enshadows Packer's efforts at visionary mastery, and he remains unmoved by the consequences of his actions for other selves or the nonhuman environment itself; they are, for him, abjectly made to serve. (We may recall here the voluntary blindness of Zitkala-Ša's Manštin, who trades his eyes for "magic bags of choicest foods" [Zitkala-Ša 58] and thus confines himself to an isolate and finally sterile self-pasture.) As one of Packer's advisors suggests about capitalism, in a judgment that seems to fall on Packer himself: "it pretends not to see the horror and death at the end of the schemes it builds" (DeLillo 91). Grand self-assertion becomes here, in the denaturalized settings in which these schemes are carried out, merely self-indulgent and destructive.

Packer is ultimately brought to acknowledge at least some of his own blindness as his limousine is stalled in traffic and his bet on the yen fails. Though he had dreamed of transcending his own body as the culmination of ordering (and blending with) networks of information, it is the hidden shape of an internal organ that suggests to him the intractability of the world as data, its resistance to final rationalization and control. After submitting to a prostate exam—a digital probing set in ironic contrast to the kind he has practiced himself—he is haunted by the news of his organ's asymmetry. His doctor's advice when he inquires about treating the condition is, fittingly, nonintervention:

> "What do we do about this?"
> "Let it express itself."
> "What. Do nothing."
> "Let it express itself." (45)

Packer's recalcitrant prostate [Greek *prostátēs:* "a person who stands before, a leader"] symbolically rebuffs his own efforts to stand before the world's ultimate flux as an *Eiríkr,* a lone ruler: "This was his method, to attain mastery over ideas and people. But there was something about the idea of asymmetry. It was intriguing in the world outside the body, a counterforce to balance and calm, the riddling little twist, subatomic, that made creation happen" (52–53). Though he has gone far in subduing the world, he will be reminded, catastrophically, that what "[makes] creation happen" exceeds the ambit of the mastering self and cannot finally be made to serve. An assassin calling himself Benno Levin has himself discovered the futility of efforts at radical self-rule—"But nothing is self-contained. Everything enters something else" (60)—and eventually lectures Packer on the folly of "[reducing] all things" to the "realized [human] will" (*Nature* 21):

> "You tried to predict movements in the yen by drawing on patterns from nature. Yes, of course. The mathematical properties of tree rings, sunflower seeds, the limbs of galactic spirals. . . . You made this form of analysis horribly and sadistically precise. But you forgot something along the way."
> "What?"
> "The importance of the lopsided, the thing that's skewed a little. You were looking for balance, beautiful balance, equal parts, equal

sides. I know this. I know you. But you should have been tracking the yen in its tics and quirks. The little quirk. The misshape."

"The misweave."

"That's where the answer was, in your body, in your prostate." (DeLillo 200)

According to this logic, Packer's error is that he has aspired to the condition of an atomic entity able to order and make neatly symmetrical everything outside himself. A hubristic expert in *currency*, he presumes to set down absolute prostatic termini, fixing the fluid future in an eternal present.

Packer's awareness of his failure ends in a quest for self-destruction, but not before his acknowledgment of the withering interpersonal toll exacted upon lone rulers. It is toward his father's old neighborhood that he has been heading for a haircut, as he seeks, with a kind of listless agitation, some connection to the past and kin: "There were times when [he] was compelled to come and let the street breathe on him. He wanted to feel it, every rueful nuance of longing. But it wasn't his longing or yearning or sense of the past. He was too young to feel such things, and anyway unsuited, and this had never been his home or street. He was feeling what his father would feel, standing in this place" (159). This feeling of being barred from a direct response to place, of having only ghostly relations with one's origin in a particular locale and the rituals established there, is another kind of prostate problem: Packer stands before an imagined ancestral home as an imposter, willing a vicarious sense of attachment to it. What he seeks in visiting his barber (and cannot ultimately find) is a topos to ground the self, some harmony of language and land, a set of commonplaces in a common place: "[The] man used the same words nearly every time [in telling a familiar story], with topical variations. This is what he wanted from [him]. The same words. The oil company calendar on the wall. The mirror that needed silvering" (161).

Near the end of *Cosmopolis,* Packer views his own coming demise through an apparently proleptic technology: "He is dead inside the crystal of his watch but still alive in original space, waiting for the shot to sound" (209). DeLillo sketches here the curious undeath of Euro-

American autonomy—a self-rule emptied of positive potential and conscious of its own passing but enduring anyway, isolated from and ruinously exploitative of the social and physical worlds around it.

The key events of Erdrich's *The Plague of Doves* are the killing, in 1911, of a white family in a North Dakota farming community and the subsequent lynching of three Native Americans falsely blamed for it. Multiple narrators recount seminal moments in the region's earlier history and describe the complex interrelations, unfolding throughout the twentieth century, of the various descendants of those involved in both sets of murders. The focal point of much of the action is the fictional town of Pluto—a settlement, built on reservation land, inadvertently named after the god of the underworld. Though the designation is an embarrassment to some, and an ironic reminder of the town's declining fortunes in the late twentieth century, it carries a positive intimation, too, for Pluto [Greek *Plouton:* "Wealthy One"] was the overseer of the earth's internal bounty in the form of agricultural and mineral wealth. The locale may host dead souls and myriad hauntings, that is, but also a latent, chthonic abundance, a prospective source of human flourishing.

Where DeLillo's *Cosmopolis* focuses on the terminal fantasies of a protagonist obsessed with the accumulation of power—a quest, finally, for abstraction from the world and the subordination of everything the self gazes upon—Erdrich's interest (in *Plague* and other works) falls on the role of land and community in determining selfhood. In "Where I Ought to Be: A Writer's Sense of Place," an essay appearing about a year after the publication of her breakout novel *Love Medicine* (1984), Erdrich affirms an essential affiliation with Momaday and other tribal storytellers in her emphasis on the significance of a people's thorough embeddedness within a particular setting. This sense of belonging marks, for her, a crucial difference between Native and Euro-American worldviews. Following Alfred Kazin and citing a lineage from "Hawthorne to Cather to Faulkner," she detects in canonical Euro-American writing a palpable estrangement from the land and an anxious commitment to mobility, out of which spring myriad pathologies. In contrast to the rootedness of traditional Indigenous life, "Western culture is based on progressive movement" ("Where" par. 3). A vital autonomy becomes plausible, Erdrich suggests, not through visionary mastery and restless progress but rather a humble recognition, consonant with that achieved at least tentatively by Momaday's Abel, of the interplay of animate presences which define any locale and the self's subordinate role within it.

In an eco-critical reading of *Plague*'s affirmation of Indigenous beliefs, Catherine Rainwater deftly anatomizes Erdrich's juxtaposition of the Euro-American emphasis on individuation and domination with Native Americans' (and specifically the Anishinaabeg's) fluid, relational, place-bound notions of selfhood. For Erdrich, Rainwater explains, a self cannot be properly understood apart from its interactions with, and radical exposure to, the other selves with whom it shares a particular place. Those selves need not, in fact, be human at all: a divine "single current of energy . . . runs through creation" and can, on occasion, occupy any material form: "[This] holy spirit is a trickster, a transformer, bearing blessings, wreaking havoc, or both. Spirit is borne by the most unlikely of 'emissaries,' who may even be non-human persons—drums or violins, doves or salamanders, horses, wolves or dogs" (Rainwater 161). Accordingly, the natural world cannot be reduced—as Euro-American vision has presumed—to an unchanging order ultimately open to human comprehension: "Where the Western mind sees fixed, impersonal 'laws of nature' governing the material world[,] . . . the indigenous mind sees the enfoldment of material and spiritual worlds. . . . No immutable laws dictate what can or cannot happen within the phenomenal world" (159). The laws that govern creation, though knowable in their general operations and tendencies, always elude a comprehensive gaze.

Pluto's nineteenth-century founders—"a bunch of greedy fools, or venture capitalists, who nearly starved dead but eventually became some of the first people to profit financially from this part of the world" (Erdrich *Plague* 94)—evoke the buffoonish dimension of Zitkala-Ša's Iktomi in their continual violation of eunomic principles. Though lacking the digital technology employed by DeLillo's Packer, they nevertheless share the basic terms of his consumptive vision. In a symbolically loaded scene, one of them, a white man named Joseph Coutts, encounters and impulsively shoots an otter, a representative in this context of the world's interdependent order. The incident leads him, however, to a revelatory (and distressing) apprehension of exactly what Euro-American rationality, and the blinkered efforts to rule the natural world it sponsors, have obscured: "[He] had the instant horror that he had committed a murder. And that conviction still filled him. The creature was an emissary of some sort. He'd known as they held that human stare. Joseph himself was part of all that was sustained and destroyed by a mysterious power. He had killed its messenger" (108–9). Rather than gazing so as to incorporate the world, the self is itself incorporated here as it peers into a broader network and is reminded of a divine potency which resists the claims of any lone ruler. A moral "ought" is, as it were, discovered in the otter's reciprocal gaze. Joseph's recognition of this presence aligns him with an Indigenous worldview and in fact prompts momentous changes: he will go on to marry a Chippewa woman, study law, and beget "a family of lawyers who were also tribal members" (115).[2]

The eponymous tale of the plague of doves exemplifies the animate and elusive network of being posited by Erdrich. One of the novel's narrators, Evelina Harp, relates the details of the event, which she has heard from her grandfather, Mooshum, a man whose colorful unreliability as a storyteller suggests his own role as a kind of trickster—one who reflects that figure's positive, creative potential along with its comic violation of conventions. In 1896, an enormous flock of birds is said to have visited the North Dakota community where Mooshum lived as a child, causing a widespread panic: "[One] could wring the necks of hundreds or thousands and effect no visible diminishment of their number. . . . [Each] morning when the people woke it was to the scraping and beating of wings, the murmurous susurration, the awful cooing babble, and the sight, to those who still possessed intact windows, of the curious and gentle faces of those creatures" (5–6). This fantastic visitation is disruptive both physically and conceptually: the birds represent a blessing and a curse, abundance and deprivation, comic spectacle and chilling horror. Their presence blurs, in particular, customary distinctions which separate human groups: "[The] Norwegians disregarded everyone but themselves and were quite clannish. But the doves ate their crops the same" (5). Mooshum's half-brother, "one of the first Catholic priests of aboriginal blood" (5), leads his parishioners in an unsuccessful attempt to "vanquish" (6) the birds by methodically marching through them with fervent prayers. The effort only confirms, however, the powerlessness of the community and its religious rituals against a taunting oppositional force: "[Mooshum] saw that the roof of the church was covered with birds who constantly, in play it seemed, flew up and knocked a bird off the holy cross that marked the cabin as a church, then took its place, only to be knocked off the crosspiece in turn" (7). With the arrival of these avian visitors, the orderly assumptions that underlie human demarcations, particularly in regard to the operations of the divine, are summarily exposed.

The birds also seem to deliver, as descending holy spirits, a message concerning a specific history of human abuses. John Gamber wryly proposes that they be seen as symbols of the blighting Euro-American presence on the continent itself: "[An] excessively large, migrating, white mass of life clamping down on the American landscape, overusing the land and starving out the indigenous population bears some slight similarities to Native history over the past few hundred years" (143–44). Erdrich's representation of the birds seems, however, more subtle and complex than this gloss on an imperialist legacy. Evelina identifies them as "surely the passenger pigeons of legend and truth" (19), a *multicolored* species, characterized by Mooshum as "brown doves" (8), which disappeared in the early twentieth century. In 1896, the birds should have been scarce, making their arrival all the more astonishing. The well-documented profusion of the species a century or more earlier has been attributed to Euro-American expansion on the continent, since the genocide of Native Americans, with whom they competed for tree fruit, initially removed one of the controls on their population; when the birds became a food source for the settler population in the nineteenth century, they were then hunted to extinction, with the last of the species dying in captivity in 1914 (Mann 364–66). If, therefore, the motley doves may in some ways parallel the consumptive rule of Euro-Americans—a collective autonomy illustrating the destructive shades of *nemo*—they also seem to accentuate, more broadly, the dangerous and unpredictable results of large-scale human interventions in a balanced natural order that, on occasion, affirms itself against those who disturb it. They symbolically parallel, in other words, the disorderly flights of data and materiality which ultimately plague DeLillo's Packer. Human presumption is targeted through these divine messengers, who act as reminders, in their trickster role, of a common human dependence on, and vulnerability to, a web of interconnected presences.

The pointed humor of Mooshum's version of the plague story seems crucial, moreover, to Erdrich's representation of how the human place within this web ought to be understood. Extending key elements of the religious critique offered by Zitkala-Ša in "The Great Spirit," the novel affirms a vision of the natural world's unpredictable powers as a liberating Indigenous alternative to the constrictive, sterile, humorless matrix of Catholic belief and practice (and Euro-American cultural hegemony generally). Though his half-brother intended him to be a priest in order to "[save him] from a life of excessive freedom" (6), Mooshum "fled [that] sanctified future" (12). His joking—which remains haunted by an acute awareness of personal and communal loss—targets lifeless abstractions and insists on the world's sometimes chaotic, always *erotic* vitality. For him, the parishioners' march against the doves becomes a farcical moment of sensual revelation:

> In delight, watching the women's naked, round, brown legs thrash forward, he lowered his candelabra, which held no candles but which his brother had given him to carry in order to protect his face. Instantly he was struck on the forehead by a bird hurtled from the sky with such force that it seemed to have been flung directly by God's hand, to smite and blind him before he carried his sin of appreciation any farther.
>
> At this point in the story, Mooshum became so agitated that he often acted out the smiting and to our pleasure threw himself upon the floor. He mimed his collapse, then opened his eyes and lifted his head and stared into space, clearly seeing even now the vision of the Holy Spirit, which appeared to him not in the form of a white bird among the brown doves, but in the earthly body of a girl. (8)

Mooshum's joyous storytelling sustains, in this comic assertion of the flesh, a sense of erotic possibility not opposed to the divine but intimately (if temporarily) aligned with it. The girl, his future wife Junesse Malaterre, tends to him in an ironic Pietà which blurs conventional boundaries in its mixing of the material and spiritual, the lowly and exalted: "she perhaps forced their fate in the world by kneeling in a patch of bird slime and then sealed it by using her sash to blot away the wash of blood from Mooshum's forehead" (11).[3] Late in the novel, we learn that Pluto's Euro-American founders almost chose to call the town Venus, before that name was vetoed "as conducive, perhaps, to future debauchery" (297). The goddess of love—or an Indigenized trickster version of her—is effectively reclaimed from the netherworld in Mooshum and Junesse's meeting and continues to make her definitive presence known in a series of other romantic affairs unfolding throughout the novel. These lovers' narratives may include the most harrowing sorts of tragedy but nevertheless reverberate with the lusty laughter of holy spirits.

Responding to these stories, Evelina creates a kind of anti-Edenic myth out of her grandparents' elopement after the doves' descent. Fleeing Euro-American restraints, the young couple achieve an idyllic, eunomic reintegration, however briefly, of the human and natural orders: "The two children in white clothes melted into the wall of birds. Their robes were soon to become as dark as the soil, and so they blended into the earth as they made their way along the edges of fields, through open country, to where the farmable land stopped and the ground split open and the beautifully abraded knobs and canyons of the badlands began" (13). This escape does not last long, of course, and Evelina's narrative quickly brings the pair back to their community, where they must negotiate an identity for themselves in relation to the region's complex human history. Part of the education Evelina undergoes as she absorbs her grandfather's stories and positions herself within that history involves a recognition of precisely what DeLillo's ahistorical Packer has long denied, the interdependence of all "individuals." As she learns of the darker elements of her own family's past, Evelina becomes "obsessed with lineage," acutely aware that to know herself, she must come to understand her community's underlying relations: "I wrote down as much of Mooshum's story as I could remember, and then the relatives of everyone I knew—parents, grandparents, way on back in time.

I traced the blood history in the murders through my classmates and friends until I could draw out elaborate spider webs of lines and intersecting circles" (86). As essential as this task is to self-knowledge and self-rule, it cannot, Erdrich implies, bequeath a sense of absolute certainty, permanence, or (above all) privacy: Evelina's diary has, tellingly, a broken clasp, its entries are recorded in pencil, and some of her erasures have "[worn] right through the paper" (86). The cosmopolis she inhabits is, in other words, not fundamentally centered on herself and her ruling powers but involves her subordination within a multitude of dispersed, porous, finally elusive presences.

Evelina's commentary on her adolescence extends Erdrich's representation of a potent eroticism linked to the divine. Unsatisfied with Catholic abstraction—conceived here as an insistence that only the "hunger of the spirit, alone, was real" (10)—she performs a trickster's transfiguration of religious dogma by "writing" the name of her beloved on her own flesh: "His name held for me the sacred resonance of those Old Testament words written in fire by an invisible hand. . . . As I wrote, I found places on myself that changed and warmed in response to the repetition of those letters, and without an idea in the world what I was doing, I gave myself successive alphabetical orgasms . . . shocking in their intensity and delicacy" (10). A "dead" scripture is provocatively resurrected here in a new, embodied script. Evelina's narrative will ultimately emphasize, however, that no self may *govern* that script with any sort of certainty: her romantic relationships, as well as those of other members of the community she describes, remain fundamentally unstable, a reflection of divine unpredictability. Her own name hints at the volatilities, both comic and tragic, associated with desire and their alignment against Euro-America's confining religious presumptions: "I was named for Louis Riel's first love, a girl he met soon after his release from Beauport Asylum, near Quebec, in 1878. He had been locked up there for treatment after suffering an attack of uncontrollable laughter during Holy Mass" (265). Human autonomy is, Erdrich implies, forever circumscribed by such losses of control.

Among the implications of Erdrich's relational model of the self and the flighty world in which it is embedded is the acknowledgment that all selves (including nonhuman ones) bear responsibility for one another through their interconnectedness and ought to assume a fundamental subordination to communal wholes. The novel furnishes a garish illustration of how such values might be compromised in the character of Billy Peace, a mixed-race spiritual leader who founds a cult informed by both Christian and Native American traditions. Billy's religious beliefs originally aimed at expanding the bounds of selfhood in ways that might seem consonant with traditional Anishinaabe beliefs. As his wife, Marne Wold, explains: "The task, as Billy saw it, was not to stretch the individual's barriers, as you might expect—not exactly that. Billy believed that a group of minds living together, thinking as one, had the potential to expand further than any individual. If we opened ourselves, all at once, in one place, we might possibly brush the outskirts, the edges of that vastness of spirit" (158–59). The unity sought here evokes the communal embeddedness Erdrich posits as fundamental to tribal identities, but Billy's faith eventually shifts from this orientation as he comes to understand himself as effectively deified, licensed to subordinate others in the service of his own divine vision. Exploiting his followers financially and sexually, he privatizes the world's "vastness of spirit" in his own atomic locus. As one of those abused by Billy describes his pathological form of self-aggrandizing, narcissistic vision, in a characterization suggestive of Slocum or Packer's self-referential gazing: "He put his hands on either side of my face, gazed into my eyes. He didn't really see me. He was looking at his own reflection. He was watching himself watch me and between him and his own regard of himself I was invisible" (169). Billy brings to mind, as Gina Valentino has observed, "a *windigo,* an Ojibwe figure of excessive consumption, predatory sexual appetites and greed" (131). The term itself, Basil Johnston (Anishinaabe) speculates, "may be derived from *ween dagoh,* which means 'solely for self,' or from *weenin n'd'igooh,* which means 'fat' or excess" (222). Blind to others in his pursuit of a radical form of personal autonomy—self-pasture as raging consumption or ulcerous spread—Billy spectacularly betrays Anishinaabe ideals.

Such monstrosity ironically reproduces, of course, several of the features Erdrich associates with Euro-American notions of autonomy: among them, a feeling of alienation from one's milieu and compensatory obsessions with mobility, domination, and atomic selfhood. Seeking to restore a primal connection to the divine, Billy leads his followers on a restless journey across the country, seeking "a religion based on what religion was before it was religion": "There was no God after Billings, no savior, for instance, by Minneapolis, where others told me Billy could have used it. By the time he and his followers backtracked across the border and then down, zigzagging home, there was only spirit" (Erdrich *Plague* 158–59). Seizing control of his wife's family farm after gaining "power of signature" from her father, Billy uncannily replays historical injustices as he declares his intention to reverse them: "This was reservation . . . and should be again. This was my family's land. Indian land. Will be again" (152). Unlike the eroticism at work in Mooshum's story of the plague of doves or Evelina's discovery of a fleshly scripture, Billy seeks to fix his command of others' desire: he inscribes the sign of eternity on Marne's inner thigh, for instance, apparently as confirmation of her limitless devotion to him. That presumption is paid back in the narrative by another set of spiritual emissaries, venomous snakes who have captivated his wife and, seemingly, lead her to murder him.[4]

The novel offers its most extended *positive* model of self-rule through another of its narrators, a mixed-blood tribal judge named Antone Bazil Coutts (the grandson of the repentant otter-killer, Joseph Coutts). Immersed personally and professionally in the lives of those living in Pluto and on the nearby reservation where he resides, he is well positioned to mediate conflicts in his community and to understand the complex interrelations that define its affairs; as he tells us, "Nothing that happens, *nothing*, is not connected here by blood" (115). Coutts's role, as he sees it, is to practice "Indian law" with a sort of humble devotion, respecting the often mercurial relations of a community tied to a specific place and history: "I do my work. I do my best to make the small decisions well, and I try not to hunger for the great things, for the deeper explanations. For I am sentenced to keep watch over this small patch of earth, to judge its miseries and tell its stories. That's who I am. Mii'sago iw ["That's all."]" (217). Coutts's "small decisions" are guided by a close observation of local circumstances, understood in relation to generations of common history. The "deeper explanations" he avoids have to do, we are to assume, with any sort of commanding vision of the world, a presumptive fixing of the laws of nature rather than an acknowledgment of their ultimate unpredictability.

Erdrich's exploration of these conceptual commitments forms the heart of her critique of Euro-American personal autonomy and its difference from its Indigenous counterpart. For Coutts, it is simple vanity to think that any human law, let alone the self-law of isolate individuals, could be the source of something stable and eternal. His ancestors who helped found Pluto, he reflects, were seduced by a familiar temptation, the possibility of fully securing the land and its various presences under human control: "As I look at the town now, dwindling without grace, I think how strange that lives were lost in its formation. It is the same with all desperate enterprises that involve boundaries we place upon the earth. By drawing a line and defending it, we seem to think we have mastered something. What? The earth swallows and absorbs even those who manage to form a country, a reservation" (115). Human social interactions are themselves unpredictable and reflect the flighty eroticism of the broader natural order; as Coutts says of his community, in a judgment that falls on all human affairs:

> But of course the entire reservation is rife with conflicting passions. We can't seem to keep our hands off one another, it is true, and every attempt to foil our lusts through laws and religious dictums seems bound instead to excite transgression.... [What] is the difference between the influence of instinct upon a wolf and history upon a man? In both cases, justice is prey to unknown dreams. (116–17)

Having learned one of the lessons DeLillo's Packer defers until the point of his own annihilation—that it is madness to seek a self-rule which denies the world's mercurial "yen in its tics and quirks" (DeLillo 200)—he unpretentiously negotiates his place within an interdependent nexus. Whatever humans seek to regulate is always open, Coutts suggests, to dynamic disruptions, a divine play, like that of the doves on the church roof, which cannot finally be contained theoretically or practically.

Coutts's response to a crime committed by a young man named Corwin Peace (the nephew of Billy) offers an illuminating model of how this understanding of law and community bears on notions of selfhood and self-rule. Corwin has stolen a violin from Mooshum's brother,

Shamengwa, who at this point in the narrative is an elderly man (when he commits the theft, Corwin does not know that the instrument once belonged to his own ancestors, who helped rescue Coutts's grandfather from starvation during the town's early history). In sentencing Corwin to a musical apprenticeship with the immediate victim of his crime, Coutts recognizes the profound if still mysterious ways in which their histories, and indeed their present lives, are bound together: "And perhaps as they had saved my grandfather, I was meant to rescue their descendant. These sorts of complications are simply part of tribal justice. I decided to take advantage of my prerogative to use tribally based traditions in sentencing and to set precedent" (Erdrich *Plague* 209). Coutts's verdict emphasizes the communal dimension of Corwin's misconduct and implies that the violin is not, ultimately, owned by anyone. At issue here in Coutts's legal reasoning is a critical divergence between what Eric Cheyfitz calls "Western oppositional logic" and the more flexible operations of "trickster logic": "In its agonistic structure, [Western] written law forms a zero-sum game founded in the exclusionary idea of property that is the antithesis of the communal ethos of Native oral narratives" (67). The purloined instrument is, the narrative implies, not property at all, having moved through a series of temporary custodians over several generations (and having displayed, in its appearance during pivotal moments in multiple characters' lives, a curious spiritual agency of its own). Corwin's theft has offended not merely an abstract law or an individual by this reasoning, but rather a web of interrelations that his participation in music lessons will, ideally, begin to restore. Justice is carried out here according to the ongoing interactions between Corwin and Shamengwa: the music the two produce forms an appropriate metaphor in these circumstances, since what is at stake is the harmonious relations of their community. The violin will, in fact, take on a larger role in the narrative as a literal instrument of justice, for Corwin goes on to play it for, and cause a spontaneous eruption of guilt in, the perpetrator of the original set of murders.

Late in the novel, we hear Coutts express sorrow for disturbing a large hive of bees during the demolition of a house: "The bees were everywhere, more than usual, and I felt a terrible guilt at having betrayed them. I apologized in a whisper as I looked around the back"

(288). This apprehension of the interconnectedness of sentient beings, who are always everywhere but sometimes make their presence known in ways more than usual, aptly summarizes the novel's vision of an Indigenous *eunomia,* a human order fused with the natural.

Gerald Vizenor's *Chair of Tears* explores the following outrageous scenario: the Department of Native American Indian Studies at the University of Minnesota [Dakota *Mni sota:* "sky-tinted water"] has been turned over to a trickster figure named Captain Shammer, who inaugurates a series of disruptive reforms linked to Anishinaabe traditions. Professors' private offices are replaced by large communal rooms, the library is converted to a casino, and, in the most surreal turn in the narrative, so-called irony dogs participate in all public lectures, barking madly (and with ultimate seriousness) at any utterance that does not suggest its own semantic multiplicity, thus reminding their auditors of the conceptual fluidity—the "sky-tinted water"—beyond the rigid, terminal structures of Euro-American rationality.

Like Erdrich, Vizenor implies that Euro-American versions of autonomy have been blind to the actual relations between humans and the rest of creation, while also targeting the historical and contemporary pathologies associated with lone rulers and their mastering presumptions. Against the notion of a commanding self capable of comprehensively seeing, identifying with, and finally exploiting a fixed divine order beyond the flux of Nature, he proffers an alternative that, once again, insists on the self's systemic exposure to mutability and chance, its subordination to an animate but finally unruly natural world, and its fundamental interconnection with a vivifying interplay of human and nonhuman presences. However, Erdrich's presiding concern for the social relations enveloping any self, and insistence on that self's humbly circumscribed (though undeniably potent) agency, give way in Vizenor to a distinctive exuberance about the conceptual possibilities of an Indigenous self-rule. *Chair of Tears,* like much of his other work, emphasizes the vast creative potential of a selfhood grounded in—but free to reinterpret—an ancestral heritage.[5]

Vizenor has explored similar territory before, in similarly challenging narratives, over roughly half a century.[6] *Chair of Tears* is exemplary, though, of his recurring concern with "native liberty" and "survivance," vibrant forms of self-rule that counter not just constrictive definitions of Indigenous identity but the very bedrock of Euro-American understandings of what constitutes a self and how it is related to other selves as well as to the natural (and indeed spiritual) world. The self in Vizenor's conception of self-rule is a fluid entity capable of endless, vitalizing transformations, yet it remains, in contrast to the Euro-American tradition, clearly subordinate to natural (and finally unpredictable) rule, through which it is linked to other entities just as fluid and potentially (self-)creative.

Set against this potential autonomy (in both its personal and corporate forms) are what Vizenor calls "terminal creeds." The phrase covers the presumptions, understood to be central to the Euro-American tradition, which suffocate the expression of Indigenous selfhood (especially according to racist or sentimental notions of "authentic" cultural values), as well as, more broadly, any ideologies that impose inelastic categories on experience and tend toward an ethic of domination. Interviewed in 1981, Vizenor locates a source of these terminal creeds in American Christianity, which he links with the impulse to "illuminate and annihilate evil" and contrasts with his own, tribal sense of "balance . . . which grows out of trickeries, of outwitting, or the modulation of experience" (Vizenor qtd. in Bowers *et al.* 44). (This judgment may remind us of Momaday's implicit critique of domineering spiritual impulses and his exploration of an Indigenous alternative to them in his descriptions of Abel's killing of Juan Reyes and Francisco's humble response to a confrontation with evil.) Vizenor's writing has continually explored variations on this essential commitment to continually modulated openness over limiting termination, to balanced coexistence over one-sided authority and control. As he explains of the playful, positive, liberating bent of his artistic ambitions in his haiku poems: "My poetic images create a sense of survivance not victimry, a signature of natural reason. I write to creation not closure, to the treat of trickster stories over monotheism, linear causality, and victimry" (Vizenor *Native Liberty* 6).

Chair of Tears opens with two intriguing epigraphs that bear directly on Vizenor's guiding assumptions. The first, from William Warren's

History of the Ojibway People, links the flight of a totemic bird with the stories told by obliging Native Americans to their white interlocutors:

> This bird [the crane] loves to soar among the clouds, and its cry can be heard when flying above, beyond the orbit of human vision. . . .
>
> Their innate curiosity and politeness often carry them so far that they seldom, if ever, refuse to tell a story when asked by a white man, respecting their ideas of the creation and the origin of mankind.
>
> These tales, though made up for the occasion by the Indian sage, are taken by his white hearers as their *bona fide* belief, and, as such, many have been made public and accepted by the civilized world.

Vizenor's construction of this quotation brings together passages from different chapters of Warren's text (on either side of the ellipses) and in fact reverses their order. This apposition encourages an identification of the distant bird with the storyteller, who is himself carried far in his creativity and whose narratives suggest, like the bird's cry, a telling indeterminacy of origins.[7] The epigraph thus underscores some of the major themes of Vizenor's work: the spontaneous, dynamic, oral quality of Native American storytelling (as opposed to the visual fixity of written language, located *within* the limiting "orbit of human vision"), the misinterpretation of those stories by white audiences (who attach their own static and hypostatized definitions to them), the blurring of boundaries between the human and nonhuman (in the linking of birds and storytellers), and indeed the productive potential in manipulating traditional materials (modeled in Vizenor's own reworking of Warren). These ideas and insinuations not only unsettle presumptions of hermeneutic mastery among readers—who must wonder, in advancing through the text that follows, about their own positioning as "white hearers"—but also affirm the inventiveness and liberatory potential of the "Indian sage."

The novel's second epigraph—"Nature is made to conspire with spirit to emancipate."—also sets up a critical departure from Euro-American notions of the self, its powers, and its place within a community of other selves. Vizenor draws the quotation from Emerson's *Nature,* though—significantly—he drops the sentence's final word, *us,* from the original text. This statement's placement here might, on first appraisal, appear less complex and less interesting than what precedes it. Emerson's affirmation of the natural world as a liberating reservoir of the divine is well known, and one may be tempted to assume a rough correspondence between the authors' ideas. That assumption would, however, miss some striking and profound divergences, toward which Vizenor's use of the (modified) quotation seems, slyly, to be gesturing. Emerson posits in *Nature* the legibility of a divine order fixed in place beyond the flux of appearances, through which the self may effectively claim its own deification, and insists that "God never jests with us" (*Nature* 25). In contrast, Vizenor's work assails presumptions of human control as he limns animate environments that are, in fact, *always* jesting. Those who would eschew the natural world's playful fluidity and aspire to visionary rule are, in fact, the greatest villains and dupes in the author's imaginative worlds—as in the Euro-American "wordies" from his novel *Dead Voices*, who "have overtaxed the cities with too much eye and not enough ears" (131). Trickster figures such as Captain Shammer adopt their own emancipatory jesting in targeting efforts to rule both physical and conceptual entities; as Vizenor puts it, "The native trickster teases the ownership of ideas and history, that long history of territorial dominance, and the reduction of imagination to serve the causes of cultural discovery and possession" (Vizenor and Lee 127).[8] Such causes, Vizenor insists, overlook a critical truth not just about the dynamic identities of Native Americans but about the phenomenal world as a whole: it does not, as Emerson implies (and as DeLillo's Packer, in his very late-stage, pathological Transcendentalism, wants to believe), simply lie between the self and a hypostatized divine order obligingly available for whatever uses we might make of it, but rather it *is* that divinity, in all its recalcitrant flux.

It makes sense to read the novel's second epigraph, therefore, as another cautionary commentary on misinterpretation (and another divergence, too, from the endgame of Euro-American autonomy): if Vizenor would seem to align himself with some of the possibilities articulated by Emerson in *Nature*—in particular, the notion that the divine potency of the natural world provides an infinite source of self-renewal—he just as surely would reject that alignment, ironizing the notion of a hypostatized order set beyond the natural world's appearances, along with any human conspiracy that would identify with it and exalt personal agency in the pursuit of totalizing control. Nature may be emancipatory, that is, but it will not, finally, be *made* to serve us. Human fantasies of mastery—including, one must presume, Emerson's "innocent" spectatorship, along with the more obviously predatory gazing of DeLillo's Packer in a hyper-technologized age—misunderstand a fundamental balance and amount to terminal creeds.

Beyond merely rejecting the visionary possessiveness articulated in Emerson's *Nature* and other formulations of Euro-American autonomy, however, *Chair of Tears* implies an opposing, Indigenous model of selfhood and the rule it might assume. Though Vizenor would affirm the divinity and liberating power of the natural world, the self he posits does not presume to comprehend a stable order beyond that world, nor does it seek individuation or domination in its relationship with it. Instead, such selfhood involves—in an efflorescent articulation of the eunomic ideals sketched out in some of Occom's writings and elaborated by each of the Native authors considered in this study—an embeddedness within and ultimate subordination to an interdependent community of human and nonhuman presences. This Indigenous self remains flexible in adapting to modern circumstances but always profoundly informed by ancestral traditions: "The Anishinaabe have endured," the novel's narrator tells us, "by traces of descent" (Vizenor *Chair* 3). Shammer's trickster role is in fact an extension of family tradition, represented in part by the figure of his grandfather, Captain Eighty—a man whose name puns on the atomic number for mercury and thus invokes the Roman god of, among other things, chance, trickery, and the crossing of boundaries.[9] Like the avian storyteller of Warren's epigraph, Eighty extemporaneously builds narratives which respond to the network of being environing any self. He lived "with a necessary sense of the seasons," for they "were the natural sources of his sense of presence, reason, and memory" (1–2). Formal surnames (which federal agents, we are told, seek to fix in an archive) are abjured by the family in favor of multiple, fluid nicknames animated through storytelling and the layered connections forged between teller and audience: "Clearly [Eighty] was more appreciated by a nickname, several nicknames, and each familiar moniker created a sense of his native presence, an epoch of memories because the actual native namers were never separated from the tease and stories of the nickname" (12–13). Captain Eighty's existence is thus, as Vizenor says in an essay on trickster hermeneutics, always "communal, an erotic shimmer in oral traditions" ("Trickster" 188); in speaking and being spoken of by kin, this representative figure simultaneously affirms its ties to other selves and defies static definition, emerging as a "comic *chance* in oral presentations" (188; italics in original). Where DeLillo's Packer stands detached from both ancestral and contemporary relations as he seeks a comprehensive inventory of the world as data, Vizenor's Anishinaabeg cultivate their autonomy in a relational, ever-evolving nominative process, an affirmative binding of selves and generations within an unpredictable, but vital and vitalizing, matrix.

As the novel's primary trickster figure, Shammer embraces what DeLillo's Packer neglected: the "asymmetry" or "riddling little twist" in creation. Raised on a houseboat and "educated by natural reason, by the tricky course of the wind and seasons, by stories of native epochs and remembrance," he is, according to the assumptions of Euro-American rationality, "uncounted, a reversal of civilization . . . buoyed in obscurity" (Vizenor *Chair* 11). Granted an imaginative and practical influence on others far exceeding that of Erdrich's Evelina, Mooshum, or Judge Coutts, Shammer rowdily deracinates terminal creeds as he inaugurates his own reversals. He does so not casually, as *mere* delight in disorder (though undeniably he finds pleasure in his efforts), but as part of an earnest religiosity that takes mutability as the vital "groundless ground" or "rule-less rule" of existence and assumes the insidious absurdity of any human aspiration to totalizing control. He enacts, we might say, the ultimate freedom from causality described in Warren's interpretation of the Anishinaabeg's autonym:

> Respecting their belief of their own first existence, I can give nothing more appropriate than a minute analysis of the name which they have given to their race—An-ish-in-aub-ag. This expressive word is derived from An-ish-aw, meaning without cause, or "spontaneous," and in-aub-a-we-se, meaning the "human body." The word An-ish-in-aub-ag, therefore, literally translated, signifies "spontaneous man." (27)

The Anishinaabeg are, their name-fate would imply, not simply uncaused in a temporal sense—as in having come from nowhere—but fundamentally and finally aleatory, elusive of human efforts to pin down causal chains. Being, by this reckoning, is always and importantly a matter of chance.

After assuming the Chair of Tears, Shammer opens a sort of portal to aleatory being, playing the role of a modern, Indigenous Mercury or Hermes. He enacts a new relocation of peoples and borders, voids the terms or boundaries that fix identities, and invites indiscriminate crossings—building, as it were, an uncontained continent of liberty. Shammer is, we are told, able to enjoy a stunning, transformative success in his academic appointment, becoming "the most original, inspired, admired, and productive chairman in the history of the department" (21). Previous chairs, it would seem, have simply reproduced Euro-American prejudices, perpetuating terminal creeds: "The six past chairmen had been honored and decorated as learned, rational, theory haughty academics, and yet they flunked as innovative native executives. They had deserted storiers, practices of natural reason, and survivance, and disregarded the very emotive sentiments of a native presence" (24). Many Native professors have themselves, it would seem, been guilty of terminal credence in their "cultural chauvinism" (79), cynical dependence on stereotypes, and failure to advance liberating new Indigenous identities. As Vizenor explains in his preface to a collection of narratives, *Earthdivers: Tribal Narratives on Mixed Descent* (1981), in which the character of Shammer is first introduced, he would restore, with his own (purposeful) jesting, a divine playfulness the academy—and in particular its bête noire, the anthropologist—has forsaken:

> Some anthropologists seem to have little appreciation for sacred games in tribal creations. Their secular seriousness separates the tribes from humor, from untimed metaphors, and the academic intensities of career bound anthropologists approach diarrhetic levels of terminal theoretical creeds. The creation myth that anthropologists never seem to tell is the one where *naanabozho*, the cultural trickster, made the first anthropologist from fecal matter. Once

made, more were cloned in graduate schools from the first fecal creation of an anthropologist. (xv)

The most egregious error identified here is, for Vizenor, an isolating and deadening attempt to reify all experience:

> Cultural *anthropologies* are monologues with science; moreover, social science subdues imagination and the wild trickster in comic narratives. These anthropologies are at last causal methodologies and expiries, not studies of anthropos, human beings or even natural phenomena; rather, anthropologies are remains, reductions of humans and imagination to models and comparable cultural patterns—social science is institutional power, a tragic monologue in isolation." ("Trickster" 187; italics in original)

Shammer, exerting a sensational agency and disruptive power that Erdrich's trickster figures could only dream of, uproots the claims of Vizenor's derided anthropologists as he becomes a "teaser of manners, missions, and conventions, and clearly more sensitive to chance and situational conscience than to customary academic practices" (*Chair* 34). If the university campus has fostered arrestive visions of Indigenous identity and in fact helped to ossify the imaginations of Natives themselves, Shammer's interventions would encourage, in the service of eunomic autonomy, the opening of new, provisional sight lines—always inclusive of and responsive to tradition but never terminally bound by it.

During Shammer's tenure he will dramatically dislodge Euro-America's hypostatizing commitments, stimulating new conceptual possibilities. One of his major innovations is the relocation of faculty to communal spaces: "[They] clearly had no tenure or treaty rights to private offices, an unnatural sentiment of absence and separation. Privacy was a denial of a native sense of presence. Private offices stimulated an elusive sense of nostalgia and melancholy" (40). Another signal act is the conversion of the "William Warren Memorial Library" (41) into a casino, which thus reanimates, if outlandishly, tribal traditions associated with gaming (along, of course, with debates about its economic and moral consequences in the contemporary era). Physical boundaries between selves are removed and the resulting collective submitted to aleatory entrepreneurship: "Straightaway over chance and a hand of cards the faculty renounced the sentiments of academic treaty rights of privacy, and instead celebrated survivance. The faculty embraced poker games, the traditional communal practices of moccasin games, songs, shams, teases, feigns, ironic stories, and the entrepreneurial adventures of higher education" (49). Shammer also upends departmental decorum (and the very idea of strict *departments*) by wearing "masks, bright hats, samurai surcoats, and academic robes at faculty meetings":

> The first masks were wooden images, shamanic visions, and some with twisted faces. Flush, my father, carved the masks from living trees near the headwaters. Shammer wore other synthetic masks that resembled famous authors, native leaders, and politicians. His favorite masks were White Cloud, the eminent native mediator of the Anishinaabe, Chief Joseph, the spiritual diplomat, the white hair, nasty gaze, and heavy frowns of Elizabeth Cook Lynn, the tender mercies of Simon Ortiz, the lovely countenance of LaDonna Harris, Jesus Christ in a turkey feather bonnet, three presidents, Theodore Roosevelt, Harry Truman, and Richard Nixon, and the mask of the movie actor, John Wayne. (30)

Dramatically elaborating Occom's ironizing of stereotypes in his letter to Wheelock, Shammer thus enacts an extraordinary revisionism, a playful (and, as ever, deadly serious) manipulation and attempted emancipation of Native and Euro-American identities. In wearing "the masks of his enemies," he would practice "a clever and imagic manner of resistance, and, of course, ironic survivance" (32). Pointing here to a vibrant, aleatory *sur-vie*, Shammer affirms a eunomic life beyond (mere human rule), an interminable sur-continent of liberty.

The irony dogs Shammer releases on campus, "mongrels of liberty" (69) trained by a woman named Chance "to bay over deadly sincerity" (17), are specific reminders of the contingency of language, the slipperiness even of semantic possession. One of them is named Derrida, in a nod to the poststructuralism that Vizenor often invokes as roughly analogous to the polysemous bent of Indigenous thought.[10] More profoundly, however, the irony dogs seem like the symbolic instruments of Anishinaabe religious ritual, voicing an effectively pre-ontological conviction about the inevitable indeterminacy of all creation, as well as its universal interconnectedness. Whereas Euro-Americans in the novel have used such dogs for scientific experiments—severing their vocal chords in order to silence their "irony"—Shammer would encourage their barking and its affirmation of the linking and leveling of the human self with what is never quite distinct from it, and what it can never presume to master: "The [Christian] monotheists forever separated animals as lowly creatures, as an unconnected creation, absent a soul or salvation, and with no godly significance as healers. Even so the trusty mongrels persisted to bark and warn the world that the absence of irony is terminal and the treacherous end of civilization" (67). The *presence* of irony cultivated by the dogs does not simply lead, moreover, to an endless, onanistic hermeneutics—as in, for some, the practices of deconstruction—but rather to a sacred imbrication of individual selves into communal wholes. As the narrator says of Shammer's own playfully serious narrations: "My cousin encouraged ironic stories about native houseboat captains, the songs and teases of moccasin games, visions, dreams, and thunderstorms late at night. Shammer coaxed and teased the students to run with the irony dogs and discover a continent of liberty" (109). For Vizenor, that continent was always there—flowing, like "sky-tinted water," and possessing all the abundant vitality implied by Occom in his own vision of a "Boundless Continent" (Occom 151)—and it *sur*vives beyond the continental matrix of Euro-American rationality and possession that has presumed to banish it from view.

Many of Vizenor's signature ideas—"imagic," "terminal creeds," "survivance," "native liberty," "victimry," and so on—are notoriously (and fittingly) resistant to static definition and can take on a shifting array of meanings depending on the context in which they are deployed. Such fluidity results from the practice of what Vizenor calls "natural reason," a dialectical mode of thought resistant to absolute conceptual divisions. Such thought, as David J. Carlson explains,

> involves a rejection of the premises of formal logic, especially the presumption that things or concepts must be *either* identical *or* different from one another, in absolute terms, but never both. Formal logic begins with an attempt to set and fix definitions of terms or concepts, while dialectical, natural reason seeks to emphasize how a single term may mean differently depending upon the set of "relations" in which it is placed. (18)

According to Vizenor's long-standing claims, a resistance to formal logic and a receptivity to natural reason can galvanize astonishing transformations—what he terms "the imagic scenes of nature" (*Native Liberty* 6)—which defy conventional (terminal) categories. His neologism *imagic* suggests, as Kathryn Hume has proposed, a combination of "*image, magic,* and *imagination*": "Through forming images and projecting oneself into those images, one achieves other selves and liberty of the spirit. One escapes the dead voices and creeds imposed by others, and some of the results—experiencing the world as a crow, for instance—can be called magical" (601).

Beyond this shedding of external figurations and the (at least temporary) assumption of new ones, however, Vizenor's imagic scenes posit a thorough openness to the aleatory that undermines any sense of a masterful self fully in charge of its own definition: where Euro-America would see through the world and discern its fixed order, Shammer would *un*see and spontaneously commingle past fixities. In affirming the potent and liberating—but effectively sel*fless*—selfhood achieved in his trickster's imagic enterprises, Vizenor reanimates, in fact, the deepest root sense of *magic* in the Proto-Indo-European **magh-* ("to be able, to have power") while adding to it the sense conveyed in that root's English descendent *may*.[11] Shammer's imagic scenes illustrate, that is, radical capability and ceaseless possibility, a formidable Indigenous autonomy.

Significantly, the imagic self-rule Vizenor envisions for contemporary Native America does not involve the utter rejection of advanced technology (especially in some manner of idealized reversion to a fixed conception of "traditional" life, a fantasy his work relentlessly impugns) but rather a selective incorporation of it that preserves the integral self

DeLillo's Packer (or for that matter Zitkala-Ša's Manštin the Rabbit) ultimately loses through various technological prosthetics. For Vizenor, transformation—grounded in the continent of liberty preserved by ancestral traditions—is the only means to life. A model of how such innovations might look can be found in the "laser holograms" (*Chair* 89–90) produced by Almost Browne (a recurring character in Vizenor's work, whom Shammer hires here as a professor), which project into the night sky ironic revisions of Euro-American and Native American authorities ("Christopher Columbus rising slowly over the white pine," "the distorted faces of reservation politicians," "hidebound tribal judge[s]" [90]). Students take up the holographic craft under Browne's tutelage, animating scenes of galloping horses from "native ledger art" (96): "The horses were in sublime motion with no vanishing point, and were not mere representations of realism or naturalism" (97). In a judicial hearing investigating the legality of Browne's holograms, a judge rules, at last, that "the laser is a native pen, a light brush in the wild night, and the laser warriors are new creations, an instance of native communal rights, continental liberty" (92). The laser performances imply, indeed, the primary characteristics of a thriving Indigenous selfhood: dynamically ironic in expression, relational in its ties to other selves and nonhuman presences, informed by tradition but uninhibited in its creative use of it (extending, of course, to the appropriation of nontraditional practices).

Vizenor suggests another productive blending of old and new in his description of so-called panic holes (a concept introduced by him in earlier narratives), through which humans contest affronts to eunomic principles by reaffirming both the interdependence of the human and nonhuman and the healing powers of the earth itself. In describing this playful transformation of the Anishinaabeg's traditional reverence for an animate—and suggestively *pan*theistic—environment, Vizenor also gestures toward ancient mythoi: as something akin to a pastoral deity, Shammer's grandfather Captain Eighty seems clearly aligned with the Greeks' Pan, even sharing with him a favorite instrument: "[He] carved several cedar or sumac flutes in the summer . . . The sound of a native flute restored the presence of nature" (43). D. H. Lawrence's lyrical description of Pan's powers (and indeed of that god's own decline and eventual "undeath" in the Christian tradition) forms a striking parallel to the story Vizenor tells here and is worth considering at length:

> In the woods and the remote places ran the children of Pan, all the nymphs and fauns of the forest and the spring and the river and the rocks.... [The] nymphs, running among the trees and curling to sleep under the bushes, made the myrtles blossom more gaily, and the spring bubble up with greater urge, and the birds splash with a strength of life. And the lithe flanks of the faun gave life to the oak-groves, the vast trees hummed with energy. And the wheat sprouted like green rain returning out of the ground, in the little fields, and the vine hung its black drops in abundance, urging a secret.
>
> Gradually men moved into cities. And they loved the display of people better than the display of a tree. They liked the glory they got of overpowering one another in war. And, above all, they loved the vainglory of their own words, the pomp of argument and the vanity of ideas.
>
> So Pan became old and grey-bearded and goat-legged, and his passion was degraded with the lust of senility. His power to blast and to brighten dwindled. His nymphs became coarse and vulgar.
>
> Till at last the old Pan died, and was turned into the devil of the Christians. The old god Pan became the Christian devil, with the cloven hoofs and the horns, the tail, and the laugh of derision. ("Pan" 22)

Pan's "power to blast and to brighten," suggests Vizenor, might yet be revived in Native America. Shouting into panic holes, we learn, reproduces an "ancient roar" and can make a "meadow [turn] blue with flowers" (*Chair* 58). Shammer's own shouting has made "the waves ... bluer on Lake Itasca near the headwaters of the Mississippi River," since the "hollers and roars of natives were natural" (58). Modernizing his ancestor's practices, he in fact arranges radio broadcasts of students' shouting, targeting here "the ironic narratives of treaties, selections from reports by missionaries on federal reservations, and other derogatory doctrines and documents of dominance" (61). The practice represents a modern form of eunomic autonomy, as Shammer's students—coursing through campus like Pan's sylvan nymphs—assert a collective agency sponsored by and vigorously reinforcing a redemptive natural order.

One of the assignments Shammer gives his students further illustrates the relational, "uncaused" selfhood involved in this mode of self-rule. So-called stray visions are to be collected in a single book constructed out of multiple, interdependent presences:

> Shammer warned that at the end of the semester every blank page in *Stray Visions* must be covered with notes, statements, literary perceptions, imagistic poems, original stories about natural reason and survivance, and the students must practice as storiers in the seminar. He meant that each student must contest historical representations of absence and create a sense of presence in a story, and other students would continue the same story with original scenes of natural reason and stray visions. (109)

Such vision counters any individual attempt at a mastering gaze with communal, cooperative acts of creation. Though Vizenor's narrator is (appropriately) resistant to defining what such an assignment finally aims to achieve, he affirms its essential affiliation with natural reason and resistance to terminal creeds: "Stray visions were always teachable by irony, by incongruity, and by the play of contradictions, but not by deadbolt structural interpretations, the definitions of culture by anthropology, or the representations of absence in history" (108). In running with the irony dogs, themselves dubbed "stray and vagrant mongrels" (65), Shammer's students would collectively claim some of the liberating potential inherent in the concept of a stray: a creature free to explore, to roam beyond limits (as in one theory of the word's origins in the Latin *extra vagare*), to see without attempting fixity (as in a historical sense of the word's verb form: "[To] cause (the eye) to wander (over something)."[12]

Chair of Tears thus affirms a stray vision of Indigenous self-rule and the continent of liberty it would reveal. Captain Shammer barks down, like one of the narrative's irony dogs, the hegemony of Euro-American rationality and its assertions of a fixed and wholly intelligible divine order, along with the mastering (and enslaving) selves sponsored by it. In its place Vizenor posits survivance: a eunomic "life beyond" which deracinates presumptuous termini within its aleatory flow.

Epilogue

AMONG MY GUIDING convictions in writing this book was that an awareness of the long-term evolutionary trajectories that define Native and Euro-American literary conceptions of autonomy, and the cultivation of more dialogue between them, would greatly help our understanding of both. In juxtaposition, many of these traditions' core assumptions—regarding, for instance, the proper relations of human and nonhuman presences or of any self and its kin—form dramatic and profound contrasts. Moreover, as I have argued, a remarkable irony can be discerned here, too, for the recovery in the Native literary tradition of a vision of *eunomia* is roughly and compellingly analogous to what its Euro-American counterpart gradually lost. In a sense, the chiastic narratives I have sketched may be summarized as charting a transition from the nourishing possibilities of Jefferson's "empire of liberty," to those, centuries later, of Vizenor's "continent of liberty."

There are, I suggest, a number of pressing reasons to reflect on this transition. It brings needed attention, of course, to the actual experiences and claims of peoples long denied self-rule, along with the extraordinary triumphs of their survivance. From Occom's accounts of the nearly obliterated Mohegans onward, a history of assault and resistance, dispossession and reclamation, is saved for reimagination. This study's evolutionary linking of early and contemporary Native writing—its delineation of a conceptual growth and continuity extending from the late eighteenth to the early twenty-first century—might also remind us that Native peoples are not simply archival subjects but continue to preserve and re-create their lifeways in the present. Their *search* for autonomy has not ended.

Contemporary social and environmental pathologies also speak to the broader relevance of the chiastic trajectories explored here. Recent developments in information technology have contributed, in at least some of their manifestations, to a disorienting erosion of traditional communal bonds and, for many, intensified a sterilely atomic sense of selfhood. The tented self now has many more ways to pasture in effective solitude and to keep itself insulated from the immediate reality of other selves than were available to Hemingway's Nick in the 1920s, Heller's Slocum in the 1970s, or even DeLillo's Packer in 2003. In his most recent novel, *Zero K* (2016), DeLillo has one of his characters use the word *autonomy* to describe what we sacrifice by entering a hyper-technologized, disincarnating mode of self-pasture:

> Haven't you felt it? The loss of autonomy. The sense of being virtualized. The devices you use, the ones you carry everywhere, room to room, minute to minute, inescapably. Do you ever feel unfleshed? All the coded impulses you depend on to guide you. All the sensors in the room that are watching you, listening to you, tracking your habits, measuring your capabilities. All the linked data designed to incorporate you into the megadata. Is there something that makes you uneasy? Do you think about the technovirus, all systems down, global implosion? Or is it more personal? Do you feel steeped in some horrific digital panic that's everywhere and nowhere? (239)

Zitkala-Ša's Iktomi, pathetically alone in his teepee, or Manštin the Rabbit, gifted with a magic bag of luxuries but confined to his own blind solitude, serve in this regard as stunningly proleptic admonitions. Vizenor's own panic holes, which affirm our need for the earth's healing potency and our proper humility in a nexus of interdependent being, suggest imaginative remediations in the face of "some horrific digital panic." The consumptive tendencies of Euro-American autonomy are also plainly implicated in ecological collapse, which now threatens the entire globe. A human self set sharply against the nonhuman and licensed to dominate it has proven catastrophic. The importance of re-evaluating one of Emerson's more naive formulations, that Nature is made to serve, has never been so obvious.

It seems clear, too, that Native authors' preservation and re-creation of a vision of eunomic autonomy addresses, and offers salutary alternatives to, precisely what has proven most destructive in Euro-American understandings of self-rule. Encouragingly, elements of these alternatives have been echoed, with mounting urgency, by a range of Euro-American authors over the last half century or so. Aldo Leopold's *A Sand County Almanac* (1949), to cite a seminal text, seeks a redemptive reconfiguration of androcentric and dangerously consumptive modes of autonomy. Leopold's invitation to decenter our view of the world and widen our moral consideration of living presences by, for instance, "thinking like a mountain"—"Only the mountain has lived long enough to listen objectively to the howl of a wolf" (137)—rephrases the message Zitkala-Ša had articulated in *Old Indian Legends* about Inyan, the primordial stone spirit of Sioux mythology:

> The all-powerful Great Spirit, who makes the trees and grass, can hear the voice of those who pray in many varied ways. The hearing of Inyan, the large hard stone, was the one most sought after. He was the great-grandfather, for he had sat upon the hillside many, many seasons. He had seen the prairie put on a snow-white blanket and then change it for a bright green robe more than a thousand times. (13)

Without such an apprehension of the animate profundity of the nonhuman environment, the human self is, both authors would agree, deluded and doomed.

Sarah Winnemucca's explanation of the Paiute's eunomic worldview—"[they] can see the Spirit-Father in everything ... [and the] beautiful world talks to them of their Spirit-Father" (259)—also forms an anticipatory analogue to Leopold's affirmation of a land ethic and its exhortation to "[enlarge] the boundaries of the community to include soils, waters, plants, and animals, or collectively: the land" (Leopold 239). Listening to "the flight-song of the upland plover" (37), Leopold connects to a potent themistic power, invigorating to encounter but not to be subsumed within merely human concerns:

> There he sits; his whole being says it's your next move to absent yourself from his domain. The county records may allege that you own this pasture, but the plover airily rules out such trivial legalities. He

has just flown 4000 miles to reassert the title he got from the Indians, and until the young plovers are a-wing, this pasture is his, and none may trespass without his protest. (37)

Such a conceptual flight finds Euro-America itself, we might say, sharing themistic titles with the Indians as it returns from eunomic alienation.

Gary Snyder's work, deeply informed by his study of the Haida and other tribes, represents another cogent effort to imagine a less anthropocentric self-rule. In the poem "For All" (1983), Snyder's speaker translates himself to an Indigenous worldview, substituting ecological for national loyalty as he endorses—two centuries after the parallel covenant sought by Occom at Brotherton—an ideal of eunomic relations:

> I pledge allegiance to the soil
>   of Turtle Island,
> and to the beings who thereon dwell
>   one ecosystem
>   in diversity
>   under the sun
> With joyful interpenetration for all. (504)

The self is, for Snyder, properly conceived of in such relational terms. Our fundamental challenge as humans, as he puts it in his essay "Ecology, Place, and the Awakening of Compassion," is in adequately answering a question arising from our interdependent being: "How do we encourage and develop an ethic that goes beyond intra-human obligations and includes non-human nature?" (239). Euro-American selves and their rule might begin to be redeemed, Snyder avers in much of his writing, by importing that conceptual transcendence from its Indigenous counterpart.

Significantly, literary works by Euro-American *women* have long evidenced a eunomic sensibility consonant, in some key respects, with that of Native writers. Susan Fenimore Cooper's nature diary *Rural Hours* (1850), for instance, offers in its careful attention to the range of living things occupying a particular locale and its sensitive appraisal of the interconnected relations between human and nonhuman orders (as well as the vulnerability of both) a moral argument for practicing a humble, self-limiting, familial mode of human autonomy. A contemporary literary descendent of Cooper can be found in Barbara Kingsolver, whose best-selling novel *Flight Behavior* (2012) elaborates on such biocentric ideas. The protagonist here, a restless young woman named Dellarobia, seeks to escape her claustrophobic small-town life. Her flight from family is linked with the disturbed migration of monarch butterflies, an anomaly prompted by the effects of climate change. The human and nonhuman are intimately related, the novel insists—an interdependence often ignored but now made increasingly obvious in the looming threat of worldwide environmental ruin. In the figure of Ovid Byron, a scientist who studies the misdirected butterflies, Kingsolver identifies an overemphasis on cool rationality as an essential flaw in Western (masculinist) attitudes toward the natural world. Though Byron mourns the looming extinction of the butterflies, he has trouble reconciling that emotional response with his role as a scientific observer. Dellarobia's own response, commensurate with Joseph Coutts's apprehension of kinship with an otter in Erdrich's *The Plague of Doves*, suggests a potential opening of the self to the nonhuman. Her scrutiny of an injured butterfly acknowledges both its otherness and sameness—"She held it close to her face. A female. And ladylike, with its slender velvet abdomen, its black eyes huge and dolorous" (Kingsolver 271)—and finally leads her to ask, in a consideration of her own and others' moral obligations to other forms of life, "To whom did a species belong?"

Such reconsiderations of the legacy of Euro-American autonomy highlight what is, perhaps, the greatest of the many ironies hovering about the chiastic story told in this study. Euro-American culture (and especially the white male who long dominated it) is now being driven, against its will, as Indigenous peoples once were, by its own ulcerous autonomy and misrule, out of its traditional way of life and into another, very different one—out of the city of Cain and into the shamanic missionary schools of the Natives, out of the tent and into the *thipi*, to look from *that* door on the laws of Nature and Nature's god, Eunomia.

NOTES

Introduction

1. All translations mine unless otherwise indicated.

2. For the sake of simplicity, I have chosen to use Anishinaabe to designate Erdrich's tribal affiliation, rather than Chippewa or Ojibwe, the terms she, and some critics, often use interchangeably. Deborah L. Madsen sums up the relevant differences: "Erdrich is . . . a member of the Chippewa tribe. Chippewa is the legal US term that describes the 'Ojibwe' (alternatively spelled 'Ojibway' or 'Ojibwa') people, who form a large part of the Anishinaabe tribal group. 'Anishinaabe' is the term used by members of the group to identify themselves" (*Louise* 2).

3. I should also note here that I do not wish to suggest that there is a plain uniformity within Native American conceptions of selfhood or self-rule. In speaking of these conceptions en masse, I merely intend to draw attention to some of their compelling similarities.

4. All definitions adapted from Liddell and Scott's *English/Greek Lexicon*.

5. A compelling literary illustration of this endpoint can be found in the central antagonist of Cormac McCarthy's novel *Blood Meridian, or The Evening Redness in the West* (1985). As I argue in *The Life and Death of Autonomy*, "[we] meet in the formidable and frightening Judge Holden the satanic zenith of American autonomy—a figure wandering the desert spaces of the Southwest in the mid-nineteenth century who is, ultimately, representative of autonomy's late-twentieth-century, urban pathologies. The Judge's pronouncements, at times suggestive of grandiose bluster but always profoundly resonant, articulate the bloody climax of a broader Western movement toward radical autonomy culminating in the American sublime and its valorization of the self-lawed person. The Judge's bellicose aim—to identify himself with the world, asserting dominion over all living things as 'suzerain of the earth' (McCarthy 198)—constitutes a gory *reductio ad absurdum* not only of the mythic frontiersman's aggression, but of some of Emerson's essential tropes and assumptions, and thus demonstrates

the horrific potential latent in the Transcendentalists' deification of personal autonomy" (98–99).

6. Winnemucca uses an alternative spelling of Paiute.

ONE. *Eunomia* Regained and Lost

1. The phrase was deployed by Jefferson, in the context of the Revolutionary War, in a letter to Brigadier-General George Rogers Clark on December 25, 1780: "Finally, our distance from the scene of action, the impossibility of foreseeing the many circumstances which may render proper a change of plan or dereliction of object, and above all our full confidence in your bravery, discretion, and abilities induce us to submit the whole of our instructions to your own Judgment, to be altered or abandoned whenever any event shall turn up which may appear to you to render such alteration or abandonment necessary: remembering that we confide to you the persons of our Troops and Citizens which we think it a duty to risque as long as and no longer than the object and prospect of attaining it may seem worthy of risque. If that Post be reduced we shall be quiet in future on our frontiers, and thereby immense Treasures of blood and Money be saved; we shall be at leizure to turn our whole force to the rescue of our eastern Country from subjugation, we shall divert through our own Country a branch of commerce which the European States have thought worthy of the most important struggles and sacrifices, and in the event of peace on terms which have been contemplated by some powers we shall form to the American union a barrier against the dangerous extension of the British Province of Canada and add to the Empire of liberty an extensive and fertile Country thereby converting dangerous Enemies into valuable friends" ("Brigadier" 103).

2. Joanna Brooks has provided "letter-faithful transcriptions of Occom's manuscripts" (J Brooks xvii) in which interlineations are included between two carets ("^ . . . ^").

3. Jefferson found his own model of agricultural life at his estate Monticello, where he was able, as a gentleman farmer, to "look down into the workhouse of nature, to see her clouds, hail, snow, rain, thunder, all fabricated at our feet!" ("Maria" 870). Startling contradictions nevertheless enshadow this vision; as Lucia Stanton explains: "Thomas Jefferson was not yet a farmer when he wrote the most potent and enduring expression of an American agrarian ideal. His vision of a republic of virtuous and independent farmers, from the 'Manufactures' chapter of his *Notes on the State of Virginia*, bore little relation to his own reality. Jefferson lived in a system that stifled virtue and independence and exploited both land and people. The men and women who labored in the earth of his property, state, and region cannot be described as the 'chosen people of

God.' The 'immensity of land' that was the foundation of his dream invited real farmers to flow westward, ignoring the preservation of their own acres. And the number of twirling spindles, if not distaffs, multiplied, in part because of his own political actions" (253).

4. As Albanese writes: "Yet, if Jefferson had conformed his memory to Burkean categories, he had also confused them, finding sublimity both in the view from below that gave him delight and in the (painful) view from above. Moreover, as Garry Wills has shown for Jefferson's delight, he had altered his evidence. Immediately following his account of the spectator's rapturous pleasure below, Jefferson described the scene as the mountains were cleft by the fissure. Significantly, he told of what could only be viewed from the high place. 'The fissure continuing narrow, deep, and straight, for a considerable distance above and below the bridge, opens a short but very pleasing view of the North mountain on one side and the Blue Ridge on the other, at the distance each of them of about five miles.' Jefferson had been caught in the act, so to speak" (69).

5. Jefferson's attitudes toward Native Americans are complex and shifting, but he generally assumes their (at least cultural if not racial) inferiority and the inevitability of their disappearance as autonomous peoples, along with the rightness of forcibly relocating them when they pose obstacles to American expansion. The Declaration infamously invokes "the merciless Indian savages, whose known rule of warfare is an undistinguished destruction of all ages, sexes, & conditions of existence" (21–22). In a letter to James Monroe in 1801, Jefferson muses on the presence of Indigenous peoples in continental land not yet claimed by America and expresses his desire for an exclusively white (and English-speaking) nation: "However our present interests may restrain us within our own limits, it is impossible not to look forward to distant times, when our rapid multiplication will expand itself beyond those limits, & cover the whole northern, if not the southern continent, with a people speaking the same language, governed in similar forms, & by similar laws; nor can we contemplate with satisfaction either blot or mixture on that surface" ("Governor" 316–17). Writing to Henry Dearborn in 1807, Jefferson makes clear his willingness to commit genocide if his nation feels provoked by Native America: "[As] we have learnt that some tribes are already expressing intentions hostile to the United States. we think it proper to apprise them of the ground on which they now stand, & that on which they will stand; for which purpose we make to them this solemn declaration of our unalterable determination; that we wish them to live in peace with all nations as well as with us, and we have no intention ever to strike them or to do them an injury of any sort, unless first attacked or threatened; but that learning that some of them meditate war on us, we too are preparing for war against those, & those only who shall seek it: and that if ever we are constrained to lift the hatchet against any

tribe, we will never lay it down till that tribe is exterminated, or driven beyond the Mississippi: adjuring them therefore, if they wish to remain on the land which covers the bones of their fathers, to keep the peace with a people who ask their friendship without needing it, who wish to avoid war without fearing it. In war they will kill some of us; we shall destroy all of them" ("Secretary" 487–88).

6. This document is a longer version of a draft composed in 1765.

7. Keely McCarthy sees Occom, for instance, as cannily invoking a passage from Paul's second letter to the Corinthians in order to set up a critique of the prejudicial constraints under which he is forced to explain himself: "What Occom finally '*must say*' is that he has been discriminated against, that the Christian world he has adopted is 'wicked'" (365). Drew Lopenzina, interpreting the narrative as "one of liberation rather than vindication, one of independence rather than indenture," argues that Occom ultimately "suggests the tautology by which even the assimilated preacher, whose actions have gained him an international reputation, is constrained to refer to himself as a 'poor Indian.' But he is also, in effect, defusing this discursive containment in the same instant that he deploys it, bringing into the open the racialized underpinnings of a term that was most often invoked out of a sense of altruistic pity" (*Red* 240, 245).

8. Joanna Brooks assigns a tentative date to the sermon of May 13, 1787 (199).

9. See, in particular, Reginald Dyck's "The Economic Education of Samson Occom"; Caroline Wigginton's "Extending Root and Branch: Community Regeneration in the Petitions of Samson Occom"; Drew Lopenzina's *Red Ink: Native Americans Taking up the Pen in the Colonial Period*; and Keely McCarthy's "Conversion, Identity, and the Indian missionary."

TWO. Prospective Domination, Retrospective Liberation

1. "The Experience of the Missionary" is included in Apess's *The Experiences of Five Christian Indians*. Although its publication date is later than that of *A Son of the Forest*, Barry O'Connell has persuasively argued for its prior composition (1).

2. Apess repeatedly invokes or alludes to the lost tribes theory in his writing, putting its implications to various rhetorical uses. For cogent discussions of the topic, see Sandra Gustafson's "Nations of Israelites: Prophecy and Cultural Autonomy in the Writings of William Apess" and Rochelle Raineri Zuck's "William Apess, the 'Lost Tribes,' and Indigenous Survivance." Gustafson contends that Apess's adoption of the theory sought a means both to incorporate Native Americans into Euro-America—"legitimat[ing] non-European, non-Christian societies in Judeo-Christian rather than autochthonous terms"—and to excavate a buried past—"acknowledg[ing] the suppressed history of King Philip and America's native peoples" (34). Zuck notes that the theory allowed Apess "to

present a vision of a unified 'past' so as to combat Anglo-American attempts to divide Indian peoples from one another" (3). Drew Lopenzina points out, however, an evolution in Apess's thought: "Later in life Apess apparently came to reject the lost tribes scenario as he staged a number of open debates with the newspaper editor and New York political operator Mordecai Noah, 'combatting' Noah's prominent public stances on lost tribes mythology" (*Through* 178).

3. See Introduction, note 5.

4. We may be reminded here, too, of one of Jefferson's warnings about urban life, which uses the same word, *canker* (a synonym for *cancer*), to describe a creeping nomistic pathology: "The mobs of great cities add just so much to the support of pure government, as sores do to the strength of the human body. It is the manners and spirit of a people which preserve a republic in vigour. A degeneracy in these is a canker which soon eats to the heart of its laws and constitution" (*Notes* 171).

5. Emerson's indulgence in "noble savage" rhetoric sometimes betrays a strong undercurrent of aggression, as in this passage from his most famous essay, "Self-Reliance": "What a contrast between the well-clad, reading, writing, thinking American, with a watch, a pencil, and a bill of exchange in his pocket, and the naked New Zealander, whose property is a club, a spear, a mat, and an undivided twentieth of a shed to sleep under! But compare the health of the two men, and you shall see that the white man has lost his aboriginal strength. If the traveller tell us truly, strike the savage with a broad axe, and in a day or two the flesh shall unite and heal as if you struck the blow into soft pitch, and the same blow shall send the white to his grave" (151).

THREE. Lighting Out, Circling In

1. Twain's literary representation of Native Americans often reflected a pronounced bigotry (see especially "The Noble Red Man" [1870] and *Roughing It* [1872], as well as the character Injun Joe in *The Adventures of Tom Sawyer* [1876]). Over the course of his career, however, his opinions did shift. As Lynn W. Denton summarizes: "A survey of references to the Indian in Twain's writings demonstrates that his attitudes can be grouped into two diametrically opposed categories. During his early years, especially while he lived in the West, Twain exhibited strong prejudice against the Indians; that prejudice eventually changed to toleration and then finally to idealism, as Twain grew older" (1). See Joseph L. Coulombe's "Mark Twain's Native Americans and the Repeated Racial Pattern in *Adventures of Huckleberry Finn*" for a consideration of parallels between Twain's representation of African Americans and Native Americans.

2. First Peter 5:8 seems at play here: "Be sober, be vigilant; because your

adversary the devil, as a roaring lion, walketh about, seeking whom he may devour" (*KJV*). Sarah Keyes, in a fascinating exploration of how Euro-American colonizers "wielded sound to establish territorial dominion and cultural control," speculates that Winnemucca's editor, Mary Peabody Mann, may have contributed the allusion in order "to evoke the sinfulness of the Euro-American invasion" (19).

3. As Sally Zanjani explains: "[It] seems likely that the Indian girls [Sarah and her sister, Elma] came primarily as servants, a condition that Sarah's pride would not allow her to admit in later years. Since Sarah relates that her family took her home after she had learned to 'talk very well,' it may well be that the Winnemuccas had made an arrangement with the Ormsbys [the white family that had taken her in]: Sarah and her sister would help with household tasks in exchange for learning English" (46).

4. Winnemucca renders his name as Reinhard.

FOUR. The Tent and the *Thipi* I

1. My consideration of this story combines "Big Two-Hearted River Part I" and "Big Two-Hearted River Part II."

2. Seney, the abandoned Michigan logging town described in the story, is in fact associated with large-scale industrial exploitation near the end of the nineteenth century. As Frederic J. Svoboda explains: "Seney was founded as the Alger, Smith Company began logging the white pine forest, huge trees five and six feet in diameter . . . [soon] six great companies and a number of smaller ones would join in raping the woods" (34).

3. See Eric Gary Anderson and Melanie Benson Taylor's "The Landscape of Disaster: Hemingway, Porter, and the Soundings of Indigenous Silence" for an astute consideration of Hemingway's representations of Native Americans. As Anderson and Taylor write: "Indians in Hemingway's Michigan stories bespeak an absence of speech, of articulation. That is, they are part of a larger silence—or, perhaps more accurately, they are part of a posttraumatic silence that seems larger, that has been enlarged because of trauma and that is not easily transformed into words, let alone into speech. Put another way, Hemingway is doing something vastly more complicated than stereotyping Indians; he understands them as part of Nick's silence, and Nick as part of theirs, and World War I and Indigenous history as bound up in each other's stories" (325).

4. As the *New World Encyclopedia* explains: "The word *thipi* consists of two elements: the verb *thí*, meaning 'to dwell,' and a pluralizing enclitic (a suffix-like ending that marks the subject of the verb as plural), *pi*, thus meaning, 'they dwell.'"

5. In *Lame Deer, Seeker of Visions* (1972), John (Fire) Lame Deer (Mineconju Lakota) and Richard Erdoes make a similar distinction between the circular,

communal, nature-based values of the Native teepee and the square, isolate, technocratic predilections of Euro-America:

> To our way of thinking the Indians' symbol is the circle, the hoop. Nature wants things to be round. The bodies of human beings and animals have no corners. With us the circle stands for the togetherness of people who sit with one another around the campfire, relatives and friends united in peace while the pipe passes from hand to hand. The camp in which every tipi had its place was also a ring. The tipi was a ring in which people sat in a circle and all the families in the village were in turn circles within a larger circle, part of the larger hoop which was the seven campfires of the Sioux, representing one nation. The nation was only part of the universe, in itself circular and made of the earth, which is round, of the sun, which is round, of the stars, which are round. The moon, the horizon, the rainbow—circles within circles within circles, with no beginning and no end.
>
> To us this is beautiful and fitting, symbol and reality at the same time, expressing the harmony of life and nature. Our circle is timeless, flowing; it is new life emerging from death—life winning out over death.
>
> The white man's symbol is the square. Square is his house, his office buildings with walls that separate people from one another. Square is the door which keeps strangers out, the dollar bill, the jail. Square are the white man's gadgets—boxes, boxes, boxes and more boxes—TV sets, radios, washing machines, computers, cars. (112)

6. Zitkala-Ša uses the words *teepee* and *wigwam* interchangeably in this text; Iktomi's private dwelling is described using both words.

7. As Davidson and Norris explain: "Most of the stories in *American Indian Stories*, Zitkala-Ša's most acclaimed literary work, were originally published between 1900 and 1902. Zitkala-Ša collected these published and a few unpublished stories together in one volume in 1921, including two new pieces, 'A Dream of Her Grandfather' and 'The Widespread Enigma Concerning Blue-Star Woman.' Zitkala-Ša concluded this edition with 'America's Indian Problem,' parts of which were culled from an article she wrote for *Edict Magazine*, with her own added commentary" (67).

8. It should be noted, again, that though these writings are largely autobiographical, Zitkala-Ša has changed some details of her own life.

FIVE. The Tent and the *Thipi* II

1. See Lawrence J. Evers's "Words and Place: A Reading of *House Made of Dawn*" for a revealing discussion of the murder's ceremonial context. As Evers

explains, "The very day then that Abel kills the albino the community from which he is estranged could have provided him with a way of ritually confronting the white man. Had his return not been a failure, he might have borne his agony.... Separated from [his] community, he acts individually against evil and kills the white man" (309).

2. Momaday's articulation of these ideas through Tosamah sometimes strongly echoes Emerson. The contention, for instance, that "[c]hildren have a greater sense of the power and beauty of words than have the rest of us in general" (Momaday *House* 84)—is, of course, emphatically made in *Nature*: "The sun illuminates only the eye of the man, but shines into the eye and the heart of the child" (Emerson *Nature* 6).

3. In the Jemez Pueblo's priest, Father Olguin, Momaday offers a contrasting response, a closure of the self to land and kin similar to that enacted by Slocum. Failing at ministering to anything but his own self-protective (and finally self-annihilating) insularity, Olguin has devoted himself to a "safe and sacred solitude" (170).

4. See Kenneth M. Roemer's "Making Do: Momaday's Survivance Ceremonies" for an incisive discussion of such adaptations in Momaday's work. As Roemer argues, improvisational refashionings of ceremonial traditions "are survival performances that embody resistance to exterior (social, economic, cultural, legal) and interior (physical, psychological) forces. They also represent the survival of tribal concepts, stories, rituals, and skills modified to meet changing circumstances and to reflect the particular presence or absence of traditional knowledge and skills of the performers" (80).

six. *Eunomia* Lost and Regained

1. Scholars use both *Anishinaabe* and *Anishinaabeg* to refer to the plural noun (and some, like Gerald Vizenor, switch between these spellings), but I have chosen to stick with the latter, employing *Anishinaabe* as an adjective.

2. Catherine Rainwater explains the significance to the novel of the name "Joseph" itself: "In *Plague*, identities and partial identities repeat from character to character in a manner suggestive of biblical typology, according to which, incidentally, Joseph is a 'type' for Jesus or the Paraclete. This same technique of character development achieves an even more significant, and profoundly non-Western end; it suggests how personhood resists containment within Western, individualist categories, for the 'Joseph' identity migrates throughout the human community in a manner reminiscent of the comings and goings of the Old Testament divine spirit of nature" (162).

3. Kenneth M. Roemer astutely notes the scatological wordplay apparently at

work in Mooshum's name itself: "In Mitchif *Mooshum,* a combination of Cree, Anishinaabe, and French, means 'grandfather.' He is indeed Evelina's biological grandfather. Mooshum's Christian name is Seraph Milk. A seraph is an angel of the highest order. The first syllable (*moo*) of his Mitchif name, by way of punning, is the source of his Christian last name Milk. According to Richard A. Rhodes' dictionary, in Eastern Ojibwe, *moo* can mean feces. Hence, one way to combine the meanings of his transnational Christian and Mitchif names would be to call this trickster-like figure Grandfather Holy Bullshitter, a name that certainly fits his character" ("Naming" 120). The possibility of other puns, one of them scatological, seems to lurk in the fate of the birds who have become trapped in an outhouse used by Mooshum; they are subjected to "the horror of . . . death by excrement" (Erdrich *Plague* 6), or pigeon-holed, in other words, by human architecture as they become literal stool pigeons.

4. A less sensational but nevertheless suggestive instance of the novel's commentary on presumptuous and destructive vision can be found in the character of Cordelia Lochren, a doctor who refuses to treat Native Americans yet takes, in an act of fetishistic predation, the teenaged Antone Bazil Coutts as her lover. He refers to her as "C," suggesting her consumptive misperception; their lovemaking is also connected to the notion of a pathological *mobility:* "It was like we were going somewhere every time we got in bed, cross-country or on a train trip, and we'd have trouble with hunger while making love" (Erdrich *Plague* 274).

5. *Chair of Tears* might well be thought of as a fictive complement to the definitions of tribal autonomy Vizenor helped articulate as the principal author of the *Constitution of the White Earth Nation* (*CWEN*), which he worked on while also composing *Chair of Tears* (both were published in 2012). As the preamble of the *CWEN* declares in its appeal to the liberating possibilities of an autonomy defined and invigorated by communal practices and a relational understanding of the self: "The Anishinaabeg of the White Earth Nation are the successors of a great tradition of continental liberty, a native constitution of families, totemic associations. The Anishinaabeg create stories of natural reason, of courage, loyalty, humor, spiritual inspiration, survivance, reciprocal altruism, and native cultural sovereignty" (Vizenor "Constitution" 63).

6. As Deborah Madsen remarks in reviewing the work, *Chair of Tears* is in part a "campus novel" and is perhaps closest in conception to *Chancers* (2001), though it redeploys a range of conceits and characters from such novels as *The Trickster of Liberty* (1988) and *The Heirs of Columbus* (1991). As she notes of the world inhabited by the trickster Captain Shammer: "Vizenor's satire does not work to propose a utopian alternative to present realities; as elsewhere in his writing, his effort is directed into creative processes of disruption and dismantling through a militant style of satire" (101).

7. As Vizenor notes in "Constitutional Consent: Native Traditions and Parchment Rights," "The crane was one of the original five traditional totems of the Anishinaabe" (37).

8. Shammer is, according to Vizenor's original definition of him in an early short story, a trickster and "earthdiver" (as in the land-flinging, world-creating hero of creation myths), who would defy fixed binaries and spontaneously negotiate liberating identities: "The trickster secures his earth, his urban places now, and then he dreams out of familiar time and space. Métis tricksters and earthdivers are the metaphors between new sources of opposition and colonial ideas about savagism and civilization" (*Earthdivers* xi).

9. Mercury is commonly associated with the Greek god Hermes.

10. As Lisa Brooks notes, one of the extraordinary features of the *CWEN* is its affirmation of irony as an inherent right of the Anishinaabeg: "While irony has often been invoked in Native stories, petitions, and essays, and humor has long been a powerful force in tribal communities for diffusing conflict and enabling everyday survival, the Constitution of the White Earth Nation is likely the first governing document to honor its citizens' right to irony, making it wholly unique within the genre" ("Constitution" 71).

11. A concept related to imagic in Vizenor's work is "transmotion," which he provisionally defines, in *Fugitive Poses: Native American Indian Scenes of Absence and Presence*, as follows: "The connotations of transmotion are creation stories, totemic visions, reincarnation, and sovenance; transmotion, that sense of native motion and an active presence, is *sui generis* sovereignty. Native transmotion is survivance, a reciprocal use of nature, not a monotheistic, territorial sovereignty. Native storiers of survivance are the creases of transmotion and sovereignty" (15). As Vizenor explains in a recent interview: "I really write about this everywhere: that Natives did have, should have, better have, must have this sense of continental liberty as transmotion. You can live anywhere and have a story of presence on this continent, have a connection to the stories that created this continent—this hemisphere, actually—not just the metes and bounds and treaty borders and territorial boundaries" (qtd. in Eils et al. 225).

12. See "stray" in the Online Etymology Dictionary: http://www.etymonline.com/index.php?term=stray; and "stray" in the *Oxford English Dictionary*.

WORKS CITED

Albanese, Catherine L. *Nature Religion in America: From the Algonkian Indians to the New Age.* U of Chicago P, 1990.

Allen, Paula Gunn. "Bringing Home the Fact: Tradition and Continuity in the Imagination." *Recovering the Word: Essays on Native American Literature,* edited by Brian Swann and Arnold Krupat, U of California P, 1987, pp. 563–79.

Anderson, Eric Gary, and Melanie Benson Taylor. "The Landscape of Disaster: Hemingway, Porter, and the Soundings of Indigenous Silence." *Texas Studies in Literature and Language,* vol. 59, no. 3, Fall 2017, pp. 319–52.

Apess, William. *On Our Own Ground: The Complete Writings of William Apess, a Pequot.* Edited by Barry O'Connell, U of Massachusetts P, 1992.

Bevis, William. "Native American Novels: Homing In." *Recovering the Word: Essays on Native American Literature,* edited by Brian Swann and Arnold Krupat, U of California P, 1987, pp. 580–620.

Bowers, Neal, et al. "An Interview with Gerald Vizenor." *MELUS,* vol. 8, no. 1, Spring, 1981, pp. 41–49.

Brooks, Joanna. *The Collected Writings of Samson Occom, Mohegan: Leadership and Literature in Eighteenth-Century Native America.* Oxford UP, 2006.

Brooks, Lisa. *The Common Pot: The Recovery of Native Space in the Northeast.* U of Minnesota P, 2008.

———. "The Constitution of the White Earth Nation: A New Innovation in a Longstanding Indigenous Literary Tradition." *Studies in American Indian Literatures,* vol. 23, no. 4, Winter 2011, pp. 48–76.

Cajete, Gregory. *Native Science: Natural Laws of Interdependence.* Clear Light Publishers, 2000.

Canfield, Gae Whitney. *Sarah Winnemucca of the Northern Paiutes.* U of Oklahoma P, 1983.

Carlson, David J. "Trickster Hermeneutics and the Postindian Reader: Gerald Vizenor's Constitutional Praxis." *Studies in American Indian Literatures,* vol. 23, no. 4, Winter 2011, pp. 13–47.

Chandler, Aaron. "'An Unsettling, Alternative Self': Benno Levin, Emmanual Levinas, and Don DeLillo's *Cosmopolis*." *Critique: Studies in Contemporary Fiction*, vol. 50, no. 3, April 2009, pp. 241–60.

Cheyfitz, Eric. "The (Post)Colonial Construction of Indian Country: US American Indian Literatures and Federal Indian Law." *The Columbia Guide to American Indian Literatures of the United States since 1945*. Columbia UP, 2006.

Cooper, Susan Fenimore. *Rural Hours*. Putnam, 1850.

Coulombe, Joseph L. "Mark Twain's Native Americans and the Repeated Racial Pattern in *Adventures of Huckleberry Finn*." *American Literary Realism*, vol. 33, no. 3, Spring, 2001, pp. 261–79.

Davidson, Cathy N., and Ada Norris, editors. *American Indian Stories, Legends, and Other Writings*. Penguin Books, 2003.

DeLillo, Don. *Cosmopolis*. Scribner, 2003.

———. *Zero K*. Simon and Schuster, 2016.

Deloria, Vine, Jr. *God Is Red: A Native View of Religion*. 30th anniversary ed., Fulcrum Publishing, 2003.

Denton, Lynn W. "Mark Twain and the American Indian." *Mark Twain Journal*, vol. 16, no. 1 (Winter 1971–72), pp. 1–3.

Dooling, D. M., editor. *The Sons of the Wind: The Sacred Stories of the Lakota*. From the James R. Walker Collection, U of Oklahoma P, 2000.

Dyck, Reginald. "The Economic Education of Samson Occom." *Studies in American Indian Literatures*, vol. 24, no. 3, Fall 2012, pp. 3–25.

Eils, Colleen, Emily Lederman, and Andrew Uzendoski. "'You're Always More Famous When You Are Banished': Gerald Vizenor on Citizenship, War, and Continental Liberty." *American Indian Quarterly*, vol. 39, no. 2 (Spring 2015), pp. 213–27.

Eliot, T. S. "An Introduction to *Huckleberry Finn*." *Huck Finn: Bloom's Major Literary Characters*, edited by Harold Bloom, Chelsea House, 2004, pp. 17–24.

Emerson, Ralph Waldo. "Letter to Martin Van Buren." *Emerson: Political Writings*, edited by Kenneth S. Sacks, Cambridge UP, 2008, pp. 49–52.

———. *Nature*. *The Essential Writings of Ralph Waldo Emerson*, Modern Library, 2000, pp. 1–39.

———. "Self-Reliance." *The Essential Writings of Ralph Waldo Emerson*, Modern Library, 2000, pp. 132–53.

Erdrich, Louise. *The Plague of Doves*. HarperCollins, 2008.

———. "Where I Ought to Be: A Writer's Sense of Place." *New York Times*, 28 July 1985, https://www.nytimes.com/1985/07/28/books/where-i-ought-to-be-a-writer-s-sense-of-place.html.

Evers, Lawrence J. "Words and Place: A Reading of *House Made of Dawn.*" *Western American Literature,* vol. 11, no. 4, Winter 1977, pp. 297–320.

Fisher, Dexter. "Zitkala Sa: The Evolution of a Writer." *American Indian Quarterly,* vol. 5, no. 3, August 1979, pp. 229–38.

Fowler, Catherine S., and Sven Liljeblad. "Northern Paiute." *Handbook of North American Indians,* edited by Warren L. D'Azevedo, vol. 11, Smithsonian Institution, 1986, pp. 435–65.

Furlani, Andre. "'Brisk Socratic Dialogues': Elenctic Rhetoric in Joseph Heller's *Something Happened.*" *Narrative,* vol. 3, no. 3 (October 1995): 252–70.

Gamber, John. "So, a Priest Walks into a Reservation Tragicomedy: Humor in *The Plague of Doves.*" *Louise Erdrich:* Tracks, The Last Report on the Miracles at Little No Horse, The Plague of Doves, edited by Deborah L. Madsen, Continuum, 2011, pp. 136–51.

Gross, Lawrence W. "The Comic Vision of Anishinaabe Culture and Religion." *American Indian Quarterly,* vol. 26, no. 3, Summer 2002, pp. 436–59.

Gura, Philip F. *The Life of William Apess, Pequot.* U of North Carolina P, 2015.

Gustafson, Sandra. "Nations of Israelites: Prophecy and Cultural Autonomy in the Writings of William Apess." *Religion and Literature,* vol. 26, no. 1, Spring 1994, pp. 31–53.

Hamilton, Geoff. *The Life and Undeath of Autonomy in American Literature.* U of Virginia P, 2014.

Hauptman, Laurence M. "The Pequot War and Its Legacies." *The Pequots in Southern New England: The Fall and Rise of an American Indian Nation,* edited by Laurence M. Hauptman and James D. Wherry, U of Oklahoma P, 1993, pp. 69–80.

Hayles, N. Katherine. *How We Became Posthuman: Virtual Bodies in Cybernetics, Literature, and Informatics.* U of Chicago P, 1999.

Heller, Joseph. *Something Happened.* Ballantine Books, 1979.

Hemingway, Ernest. "The Art of the Short Story." *New Critical Approaches to the Short Stories of Ernest Hemingway,* edited by Jackson J. Benson, Duke UP, 1990, pp. 1–13.

———. "Big Two-Hearted River Part 1" and "Big Two-Hearted River Part II." *The Complete Short Stories of Ernest Hemingway,* Collier Books, 1987, pp. 163–80.

Hinderaker, Eric. *Elusive Empires: Constructing Colonialism in the Ohio Valley, 1673–1800.* Cambridge UP, 1997.

Hume, Kathryn. "Gerald Vizenor's Metaphysics." *Contemporary Literature,* vol. 48, no. 4, Winter 2007, pp. 580–612.

Jefferson, Thomas. "To Brigadier-General George Rogers Clark, Richmond, December 25, 1780." *The Works of Thomas Jefferson in Twelve Volumes,*

Federal Edition, edited by Paul Leicester Ford, vol. 3, G. P. Putnam's Sons, 1904, pp. 96–103.

———. "Declaration of Independence." *Thomas Jefferson: Writings,* Library of America, 1984, pp. 19–24.

———. "To Maria Cosway. Paris, Oct. 12, 1786." *Thomas Jefferson: Writings,* Library of America, 1984, pp. 866–77.

———. "To the Governor of Virginia (James Monroe), Washington, Nov. 24, 1801." *The Works of Thomas Jefferson in Twelve Volumes, Federal Edition,* edited by Paul Leicester Ford, vol. 9, G. P. Putnam's Sons, 1904, pp. 315–17.

———. *Notes on the State of Virginia.* Edited by Frank Shuffleton, Penguin, 1999.

———. "The Ordinance of 1784, 23rd April 1784." *National Archives: Founders Online,* https://founders.archives.gov/documents/Jefferson/01-06-02-0420-0006.

———. "To the Secretary at War (Henry Dearborn), Monticello, August 28, 07." *The Works of Thomas Jefferson in Twelve Volumes, Federal Edition,* edited by Paul Leicester Ford, vol. 10, G. P. Putnam's Sons, 1905, pp. 485–88.

Johnston, Basil. *The Manitous: The Spiritual World of the Ojibway.* HarperCollins, 1995.

Keyes, Sarah. "'Like a Roaring Lion': The Overland Trail as a Sonic Conquest." *Journal of American History,* vol. 96, no. 1, June 2009, pp. 19–43.

Kingsolver, Barbara. *Flight Behavior.* Harper, 2012.

Krupat, Arnold. *Ethnocriticism: Ethnography, History, Literature.* U of California P, 1992.

Kunce, Catherine. "Fire of Eden: Zitkala-Ša's Bitter Apple." *Studies in American Indian Literatures,* vol. 18, no. 1, Spring 2006, pp. 73–82.

Laist, Randy. "The Concept of Disappearance in Don DeLillo's *Cosmopolis.*" *Critique,* vol. 51, no. 3, 2010, pp. 257–75.

Lame Deer, John (Fire), and Richard Erdoes. *Lame Deer, Seeker of Visions: The Life of a Sioux Medicine Man.* Simon and Schuster, 1972.

Lasch, Christopher. *The Culture of Narcissism: American Life in an Age of Diminishing Expectations.* W. W. Norton, 1979.

Lawrence, D. H. "New Mexico." *Phoenix: The Posthumous Papers, 1936,* edited by Edward D. McDonald, Penguin Books, 1978, pp. 141–47.

———. "Pan in America." *Phoenix: The Posthumous Papers, 1936,* edited by Edward D. McDonald, Penguin Books, 1978, pp. 22–31.

Leopold, Aldo. *A Sand County Almanac: With Essays on Conservation from Round River.* Ballantine Books, 1970.

Lopenzina, Drew. *Red Ink: Native Americans Picking Up the Pen in the Colonial Period.* SUNY P, 2012.

———. *Through an Indian's Looking-Glass: A Cultural Biography of William Apess, Pequot.* U of Massachusetts P, 2017.
Madsen, Deborah, editor. *Louise Erdrich: Tracks, The Last Report on the Miracles at Little No Horse, The Plague of Doves.* Continuum, 2011.
———. "Review of *Chair of Tears* by Gerald Vizenor." *Studies in American Indian Literatures,* vol. 26, no. 2, Summer 2014, pp. 101–4.
Magill, Frank N., editor. *The 17th and 18th Centuries: Dictionary of World Biography.* Vol. 4, Routledge, 2013.
Mann, Charles C. *1491: New Revelations of the Americas before Columbus.* 2nd ed., Vintage Books, 2011.
Marx, Leo. *The Machine in the Garden: Technology and the Pastoral Ideal in America.* Reprint ed., Oxford UP, 2000.
McCarthy, Cormac. *Blood Meridian, Or the Evening Redness in the West.* Vintage, 1992. McCarthy, Keely. "Conversion, Identity, and the Indian Missionary." *Early American Literature,* vol. 36, no. 3, Fall 2001, pp. 353–69.
McMillin, T. S. *The Meaning of Rivers: Flow and Reflection in American Literature.* U of Iowa P, 2011.
Melling, Philip. "'There Were Many Indians in the Story': Hidden History in Hemingway's 'Big Two-Hearted River.'" *The Hemingway Review,* vol. 28, no. 2, Spring 2009, pp. 45–65.
Miller, J. Hillis. "Three Problems of Fictional Form." *Victorian Subjects,* Duke UP, 1991, pp. 91–108.
Momaday, N. Scott. "An American Land Ethic." *The Man Made of Words: Essays, Stories, Passages,* St. Martin's Press, 1997, pp. 42–49.
———. *House Made of Dawn.* HarperCollins, 1999.
Moore, David L. *That Dream Shall Have a Name: Native Americans Rewriting America.* U of Nebraska P, 2013.
Myers, Jeffrey. *Converging Stories: Race, Ecology, and Environmental Justice in American Literature.* U of Georgia P, 2005.
Norton-Smith, Thomas M. *The Dance of Person and Place: One Interpretation of American Indian Philosophy.* SUNY P, 2010.
Occom, Samson. *The Collected Writings of Samson Occom, Mohegan: Leadership and Literature in Eighteenth-Century Native America.* Edited by Joanna Brooks, Oxford UP, 2006.
O'Connell, Barry. "Part 1: *A Son of the Forest: The Experience of William Apess, A Native of the Forest, Written by Himself.*" *On Our Own Ground: The Complete Writings of William Apess, a Pequot.* Edited by Barry O'Connell, U of Massachusetts P, 1992.
Olafson, Harold. "Northern Paiute Shamanism Revisited." *Anthropos,* vol. 74, nos. 1–2, 1979, pp. 11–24.

Owens, Louis. *Other Destinies: Understanding the American Indian Novel*. U of Oklahoma P, 1992.
Pearce, Roy Harvey. "'Yours Truly, Huck Finn.'" *Huck Finn: Bloom's Major Literary Characters*, edited by Harold Bloom, Chelsea House, 2004, pp. 83–98.
Poirier, Richard. *A World Elsewhere: The Place of Style in American Literature*. U of Wisconsin P, 1985.
Pratt, Richard Henry. "Wants Indian Stories." *The Indian Helper: A Weekly Letter*, vol. 13, no. 22, 18 March 1898, p. 1.
Rainwater, Catherine. "Haunted by Birds: An Eco-Critical View of Personhood in *The Plague of Doves*." *Louise Erdrich*: Tracks, The Last Report on the Miracles at Little No Horse, The Plague of Doves, edited by Deborah L. Madsen, Continuum, 2011, pp. 153–67.
Rilke, Rainer Maria. *The Duino Elegies: The Sonnets to Orpheus*. Edited and translated by Stephen Mitchell, Vintage, 2009.
Roemer, Kenneth M. "Making Do: Momaday's Survivance Ceremonies." *Studies in American Indian Literatures*, vol. 24, no. 4, Winter 2012, pp. 77–98.
———. "Naming Native (Living) Histories: Erdrich's Plague of Names." *Studies in American Fiction*, vol. 43, no. 1, Spring 2016, pp. 115–35.
Scarberry-Garcia, Susan. *Landmarks of Healing: A Study of* House Made of Dawn. U of New Mexico P, 1990.
Shattuck, Lemuel. *A History of the Town of Concord, Middlesex County, Massachusetts: From Its Earliest Settlement to 1832; and of the Adjoining Towns, Bedford, Acton, Lincoln, and Carlisle, Containing Various Notices of County and State History Not Before Published*. Russell, Odiorne, 1835.
Silko, Leslie Marmon. *Ceremony*. Penguin, 1986.
Smith, Jeanne. "'A Second Tongue': The Trickster's Voice in the Works of Zitkala-Ša." *Tricksterism in Turn-of-the-Century American Literature: A Multicultural Perspective*, edited by Elizabeth Ammons and Annette White-Parks, UP of New England, 1994, pp. 46–60.
Snyder, Gary. "Ecology, Place, and the Awakening of Compassion." *The Deep Ecology Movement: An Introductory Anthology*, edited by Alan Drengson and Yuichi Inoue, North Atlantic Books, 1995, pp. 237–41.
———. "For All." *The Gary Snyder Reader: Prose, Poetry and Translations*, North Point Press, 1983, p. 504.
Solon. "Fragment 4." Reprinted in Maria Noussia Fantuzzi, *Solon the Athenian: The Poetic Fragments*. Brill Academic Publishers, 2010.
Stanton, Lucia. "Thomas Jefferson: Planter and Farmer." *A Companion to Thomas Jefferson*, edited by Francis D. Cogliano, Blackwell, 2012, pp. 253–70.
Svoboda, Frederic J. "Landscapes Real and Imagined: 'Big Two-Hearted River.'" *The Hemingway Review*, vol. 16, no. 1, Fall 1996, pp. 33–42.

Twain, Mark. *The Adventures of Huckleberry Finn.* Penguin Books, 1985.
Valentino, Gina. "'It All Does Come to Nothing in the End': Nationalism and Gender in Louise Erdrich's *The Plague of Doves.*" *Louise Erdrich: Tracks, The Last Report on the Miracles at Little No Horse, The Plague of Doves,* edited by Deborah L. Madsen, Continuum, 2011, 103–14.
Vizenor, Gerald. *Chair of Tears: A Novel.* U of Nebraska P, 2012.
———. *Dead Voices: Natural Agonies in the New World.* U of Oklahoma P, 1994.
———. *Earthdivers: Tribal Narratives of Mixed Descent.* U of Minnesota P, 1981.
———. *Fugitive Poses: Native American Indian Scenes of Absence and Presence.* U of Nebraska P, 1998.
———. *Native Liberty: Natural Reason and Cultural Survivance.* U of Nebraska P, 2009.
———. "Trickster Discourse: Comic Holotropes and Language Games." *Narrative Chance: Postmodern Discourse on Native American Indian Literatures,* edited by Gerald Vizenor. U of Oklahoma P, 1993, pp. 187–211.
Vizenor, Gerald, and Jill Doerfler, editors. *The White Earth Nation: Ratification of a Native Democratic Constitution.* U of Nebraska P, 2012.
Vizenor, Gerald, and A. Robert Lee. *Postindian Conversations.* U of Nebraska P, 2003.
Walker, Cheryl. "Sarah Winnemucca's Mediations: *Gender, Race, and Nation.*" *Indian Nation: Native American Literature and Nineteenth-Century Nationalisms,* Duke UP, 1997, pp. 139–63.
Warren, William W. *History of the Ojibway People.* 2nd ed., edited and with an introduction by Theresa Schenck, Minnesota Historical Society, 2009.
Wigginton, Caroline. "Extending Root and Branch: Community Regeneration in the Petitions of Samson Occom." *Studies in American Indian Literatures,* vol. 20, no. 4, Winter 2008, pp. 24–55.
Winnemucca Hopkins, Sarah. *Life among the Piutes: Their Wrongs and Claims.* U of Nevada P, 1994.
Wisecup, Kelly. "Medicine, Communication, and Authority in Samson Occom's Herbal." *Early American Studies,* vol. 10, no. 3, Fall 2012, pp. 540–65.
Zanjani, Sally. *Sarah Winnemucca.* U of Nebraska P, 2001.
Zitkala-Ša. *American Indian Stories, Legends, and Other Writings.* Edited by Cathy N. Davidson and Ada Norris, Penguin Books, 2003.
Zuck, Rochelle Raineri. "William Apess, the 'Lost Tribes,' and Indigenous Survivance." *Studies in American Indian Literatures,* vol. 25, no. 2, Spring 2013, pp. 1–26.

INDEX

Albanese, Catherine L., 25, 187n4
Allen, Paula Gunn, 138
Anderson, Eric Gary, 190n3 (ch4)
Apess, William, 3, 10, 11–12, 13, 14, 33, 36, 43–44, 50–68, 69, 70, 80, 84, 90, 91, 96, 103, 106, 114, 116, 117, 118, 143, 188n2; and ancestors, 9, 12, 51, 52, 54, 56–57, 66; and communality, 12, 54–55, 59–61, 65–66, 68; *Eulogy on King Philip: As Pronounced at the Odeon, in Federal Street, Boston*, 51, 61–67, 82, 112; "The Experience of the Missionary," 50–51, 54–55, 188n1; "An Indian's Looking-Glass for the White Man," 51; *A Son of the Forest*, 51, 55–61, 188n1

Barbé-Marbois, François, 19
Bevis, William, 6–7, 40, 137
Bonnin, Gertrude Simmons. *See* Zitkala-Ša (Gertrude Simmons Bonnin)
Brooks, Joanna, 11, 28, 41, 186n2, 188n8
Brooks, Lisa, 7, 35–36, 61, 194n10
Brotherton (settlement), 11, 18, 28, 34, 41–42, 182
Burke, Edmund, 24–25, 187n4. *See also* sublime, the

Cain, 21, 135, 136, 144, 183
Cajete, Gregory, 1, 3, 41
capitalism, 38, 124, 148, 150, 154
Carlisle Indian Industrial School, 104–5
Carlson, David J., 173–74
Chandler, Aaron, 148
Cheyfitz, Eric, 163
Christianity: as best illustrated in Native lifeways, 36–37, 64, 82, 103; blending with tribal religion, 33, 36–38, 41–42, 44, 50, 54–55, 61–62, 82, 103, 136, 143–44, 160; contrasted with tribal religion, 8, 90–91, 111–12, 114–15, 116–19, 133–34, 157–59, 165, 173, 175–76; hypocrisy of practitioners, 30–33, 36–37, 51, 56, 64–65, 82, 119, 188n7
continent of liberty, 16, 32, 35, 111, 147, 170, 172, 173, 175, 177, 179, 193n5, 194n11
Cooper, Susan Fenimore, 182–83
Coulombe, Joseph L., 189n1

Davidson, Cathy N., 191n7
de Buffon, Comte. *See* Leclerc, Georges-Louis, Comte de Buffon
Declaration of Independence. *See under* Jefferson, Thomas

DeLillo, Don, 3, 10, 15, 27, 69, 74, 77, 78, 96, 101, 103, 110, 124, 145–53, 154, 157, 158, 162, 167, 168, 169, 175; as terminal Emersonianism, 15, 20, 22, 48, 50, 121, 145, 147–50; *Zero K*, 180
Deloria, Vine, Jr., 7, 132
Denton, Lynn W., 189n1
Dooling, D. M., 117–18
Dyck, Reginald, 42, 188n9
dysnomia, 3, 6, 20, 29, 49, 63, 69, 74, 80, 96, 122

elenchus, 125–27, 129, 132, 136
Emerson, Ralph Waldo, 10, 11–12, 20, 22, 43–50, 61, 62, 67–68, 69, 70, 71–75, 77, 78, 96, 99, 102, 116, 117, 127, 128, 129, 130, 134, 138, 141, 166, 167, 180, 185n5, 189n5, 192n2 (ch5); and antihistoricism, 9, 44, 51, 54, 56, 61; and nomistic detachment, 14, 24, 27, 43, 60, 69, 74, 95, 98, 101, 124; and vision, 15, 16, 45–47, 49, 52, 58, 59, 60, 71, 102, 121, 145, 146–48, 150, 168
Erdoes, Richard, 190n5
Erdrich, Louise, 3, 10, 15–16, 52, 65, 90, 94, 96, 116, 119, 120, 134, 144, 145–46, 153–64, 169, 171, 185n2; and divine eroticism, 146, 157–58, 159–60, 161, 162; and importance of place to identity, 146, 153–54, 193n4; and interdependence of all creation, 145–46, 155, 156–57, 158–59, 164, 183; *Love Medicine*, 153; and playful unpredictability of natural/divine order, 146, 154, 155, 157, 162, 193n3; "Where I Ought to Be: A Writer's Sense of Place," 153–54

Eunomia (goddess), 1–2, 18, 20, 183
Evers, Lawrence J., 191n1

Fielding, Stephanie, 41
Flinty Rock (Tawiskaron), 1, 7
Fowler, Catherine S., 91
Furlani, Andre, 125, 127

Gamber, John, 156
Great Spirit, the (deity), 65, 66, 104, 109, 115, 116–19, 181
"Great Spirit, The" (essay). *See under* Zitkala-Ša (Gertrude Simmons Bonnin)
Gross, Lawrence W., 146
Gura, Philip F., 52
Gustafson, Sandra, 188n2

Hamilton, Geoff, 2–3, 5, 185n5
Haudenosaunee, 1, 2, 7, 36
Hayles, Katherine, 149
Heller, Joseph, 10, 14–15, 20, 50, 74, 77, 78, 121–30, 145, 180; and isolate autonomy, 14, 69, 101, 103, 121, 130, 131, 132, 138, 139, 141, 148, 150; and tortured thought, 27, 96, 125–28
Hemingway, Ernest, 10, 13, 20, 74, 77, 95–103, 107, 108, 109, 113, 116, 124, 130, 132, 138, 150, 180, 190n3 (ch4); "Big Two-Hearted River," 13, 99–103, 190n1; and healing of natural world, 14, 96, 99–103, 118, 121; "Indian Camp," 96–98, 113, 119; inter-chapter (from *In Our Time*), 99; and isolate autonomy, 13, 14, 50, 69, 78, 95, 103, 104, 108, 109, 111, 118, 132, 138; "The Three-Day Blow," 98–99; and tortured thought, 15, 27, 95, 101–3, 110–11, 145

Hinderaker, Eric, 22
Horae, the, 1
Hume, Kathryn, 174

Iktomi, 14, 107, 108–9, 111, 113, 115, 132, 154, 180, 191n6
Inyan, 108–9, 117–18, 181
irony: irony dogs (Vizenor), 164, 172–73, 177; as rhetorical strategy in Euro-American texts, 124–27, 144, 151; as rhetorical strategy in Native texts, 30–33, 35, 37, 57, 112, 135, 153, 158, 160, 167–68, 172–73, 175–77, 188n7, 194n10

Jefferson, Thomas, 2, 3, 7, 9, 10, 11, 15, 17–27, 28, 29–30, 36, 38, 43, 44, 47, 48, 49, 64, 70, 73, 75, 77, 78, 95, 96, 116, 130, 135, 150, 186n1, 186n3, 189n4; and American destiny, 2, 7, 10, 17, 20, 179, 187n5; and Declaration of Independence, 2, 3, 187n5; and mastery of nature, 12, 19, 21–23, 25, 35, 37, 39–40, 41, 45, 46, 72, 99, 128, 138, 145, 148, 187n4; and nomistic detachment, 14, 17, 19, 24, 26–27, 69, 74, 102, 121, 127
Johnston, Basil, 160

Kazin, Alfred, 153
Keyes, Sarah, 190n2 (ch3)
Kingsolver, Barbara, 183
Krupat, Arnold, 81
Kunce, Catherine, 112

Laist, Randy, 149
Lame Deer, John (Fire), 190n5
Land Ordinance of 1784, 22
Lasch, Christopher, 126
Lawrence, D. H., 141–42, 175–76

laws of nature, 2, 18, 27, 154, 162, 183
Leclerc, Georges-Louis, Comte de Buffon, 19, 22, 39–40
Leopold, Aldo, 181–82
Levinas, Emmanuel, 148
Liljeblad, Sven, 91
Lopenzina, Drew, 37, 42, 61, 188n7, 188n9, 189n2 (ch2)

Madsen, Deborah L., 185n2, 193n6
Mann, Charles C., 156
Mann, Mary Tyler Peabody, 86, 91, 190n2 (ch3)
Massasoit, 5
McCarthy, Cormac, 185n5
McCarthy, Keely, 188n7, 188n9
McMillan, T. S., 53
Metacomet (King Philip), 11, 51, 61–62, 65–67, 82, 112, 188n2
Momaday, N. Scott, 3, 10, 14, 15, 16, 65, 90, 94, 96, 116, 121–22, 130–44, 146, 153, 154, 165, 192nn2–4 (ch5); "An American Land Ethic," 130–31; and ancestors, 52, 120, 122, 131, 132, 136, 139–40, 144; and healing, 83, 122, 131, 132, 135–36, 140, 141; and importance of place to identity, 15, 122, 130–32, 134–43
Moore, David L., 65
Myers, Jeffrey, 111

Nature's God, 2, 18, 27, 183
nemo, etymology and figural senses of, 5–6; in positive sense as "to feed upon or graze," 46; as "ulcerous spread" or "fiery consumption," 15, 58, 63, 83–84, 156
Neoplatonism, 47
Norris, Ada, 191n7
Norton-Smith, Thomas M., 8

Occom, Samson, 3, 10–11, 12, 14, 17–19, 27–42, 43, 44, 50, 56, 57, 64, 82, 84, 90, 96, 106, 114, 116, 118, 143, 146, 172, 173, 179, 182, 186n2, 188n7; and ancestors, 18, 33, 34–35; and communality, 9, 11, 18, 35–36, 38, 41–42, 103; and relational responsibilities to the nonhuman, 11, 15, 35–36, 39–41, 91, 168; "A Sermon Preached at the Execution of Moses Paul, an Indian," 32–33. *See also* Brotherton (settlement)
O'Connell, Barry, 188n1
Olafson, Harold, 82
Owens, Louis, 134

Philip, King. *See* Metacomet (King Philip)
Poirier, Richard, 58
Pratt, Richard Henry, 105

Rainwater, Catherine, 154, 192n2 (ch6)
Rilke, Rainer Maria, 141, 142
Roemer, Kenneth M., 192n4, 192n3 (ch6)

Scarberry-Garcia, Susan, 140
shamanism, 13, 82–83, 88, 92, 104, 122, 131, 140, 172, 183
Shattuck, Lemuel, 53
Silko, Leslie Marmon, 7–8
Simmons, Gertrude. *See* Zitkala-Ša (Gertrude Simmons Bonnin)
Skyholder (Teharonghyawago), 1, 2, 7
Sky Woman, 1, 36
Smith, Jeanne, 107
Snyder, Gary, 182
Solon, 2
sovereignty, 4–6, 194n11
Stanton, Lucia, 186n3

Stone Boy, 117
sublime, the, 20, 24–25, 47, 48, 128, 175, 185n5
survivance, 68, 165, 170, 172, 173, 177, 179, 193n5, 194n11
Svoboda, Frederic J., 190n2 (ch4)

Tawiskaron. *See* Flinty Rock (Tawiskaron)
Taylor, Melanie Benson, 190n3 (ch4)
teepee/tepee (as metaphor), 14, 107, 108, 113, 119, 120, 124, 180, 191nn5–6. *See also thipi*; wigwam (as metaphor)
Teharonghyawago. *See* Skyholder (Teharonghyawago)
Ten Lost Tribes of Israel, 57, 188–89n2
tent (as metaphor), 13, 14, 81, 84–85, 100, 101, 103, 104, 107, 108, 115, 118, 124, 138, 180, 183
Themis (goddess), 1, 18, 100
thipi, 107, 183, 190n4 (ch4). *See also* teepee/tepee (as metaphor)
tipi. *See* teepee/tepee (as metaphor)
Thoreau, Henry David, 149
Trail of Tears, 67
transparent eyeball, 45–46, 50, 52, 101, 146, 147, 150
trickster figure: and Erdrich's *Plague of Doves*, 155–59, 163; and Native American conceptions of the divine, 154; and Vizenor's *Chair of Tears*, 16, 164, 165, 167–71, 174, 193n3; Zitkala-Ša as, 112, 115; and Zitkala-Ša's Iktomi as, 14, 107–11, 115, 154
Tubalcain, 21, 22, 135
Twain, Mark, 10, 12–13, 15, 20, 27, 50, 69–78, 79, 81, 83, 85, 86–88, 95, 102, 121, 125, 130, 145, 189n1

Valentino, Gina, 160
Vizenor, Gerald, 3, 9, 10, 16, 35, 52, 57, 68, 94, 96, 111, 116, 120, 144, 145–47, 164–77, 179, 180, 192n1 (ch6), 193nn5–6, 194nn7–8, 194nn10–11; *Chancers*, 193n6; and Christianity, 32, 65, 90–91, 119, 134, 165, 173, 176; "Constitutional Consent: Native Traditions and Parchment Rights," 194n7; *Dead Voices*, 167; *Earthdivers: Tribal Narratives of Mixed Descent*, 170, 194n8; and Emerson's *Nature*, 166–68; *Fugitive Poses: Native American Indian Scenes of Absence and Presence*, 194n11; and healing, 104, 173, 175–76, 180; *The Heirs of Columbus*, 193n6; *Native Liberty*, 165, 174; "Trickster Discourse: Comic Holotropes and Language Games," 169, 171; *The Trickster of Liberty*, 193n6. *See also* continent of liberty; irony; shamanism; survivance

Warren, William, 165–66, 169, 171
Wheelock, Eleazar, 30, 31, 57, 172
Wigginton, Caroline, 188n9
wigwam (as metaphor), 108, 191n6. *See also* teepee/tepee (as metaphor)
Wills, Garry, 25, 187n4

Winnemucca, Sarah, 3, 10, 12–13, 14, 36, 43, 52, 69–70, 78–94, 96, 103–4, 105, 106, 111, 114, 116, 119, 143, 181, 186n6, 190nn2–4 (ch3); and allotment, 93–94; as shaman, 82–85, 104, 122, 131; and women's agency, 70, 84–86, 88–90, 96
Wisecup, Kelly, 40

Zanjani, Sally, 94, 190n3 (ch3)
Zitkala-Ša (Gertrude Simmons Bonnin), 3, 10, 13, 14, 70, 90, 94, 95–96, 103–20, 122, 124, 132, 143, 154, 180, 181, 191nn6–8; "America's Indian Problem," 111; and ancestors, 52, 107, 113, 119–20; "Dance in a Buffalo Skull," 107; "A Dream of Her Grandfather," 119–20, 191n7; "The Great Spirit," 65, 116–19, 134, 157; and healing, 14, 96, 104, 107, 111, 118, 120, 122, 131; "Heart to Heart Talk," 103; "Iktomi and the Ducks," 108, 111; "Iktomi and the Muskrat," 109; "Iktomi's Blanket," 108–9, 111; "Manštin, the Rabbit," 109–10, 111, 150, 175, 180; "Shooting of the Red Eagle," 109; and women's agency, 96, 112, 113
Zuck, Rochelle Raineri, 188n2

www.ingramcontent.com/pod-product-compliance
Lightning Source LLC
Chambersburg PA
CBHW031816220426
43662CB00007B/671